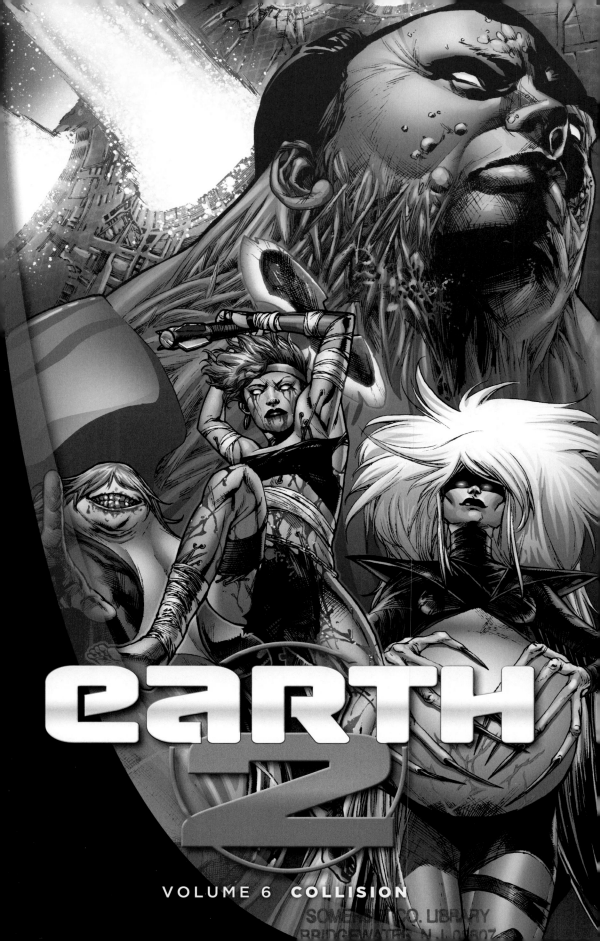

eaRTH 2

VOLUME 6 COLLISION

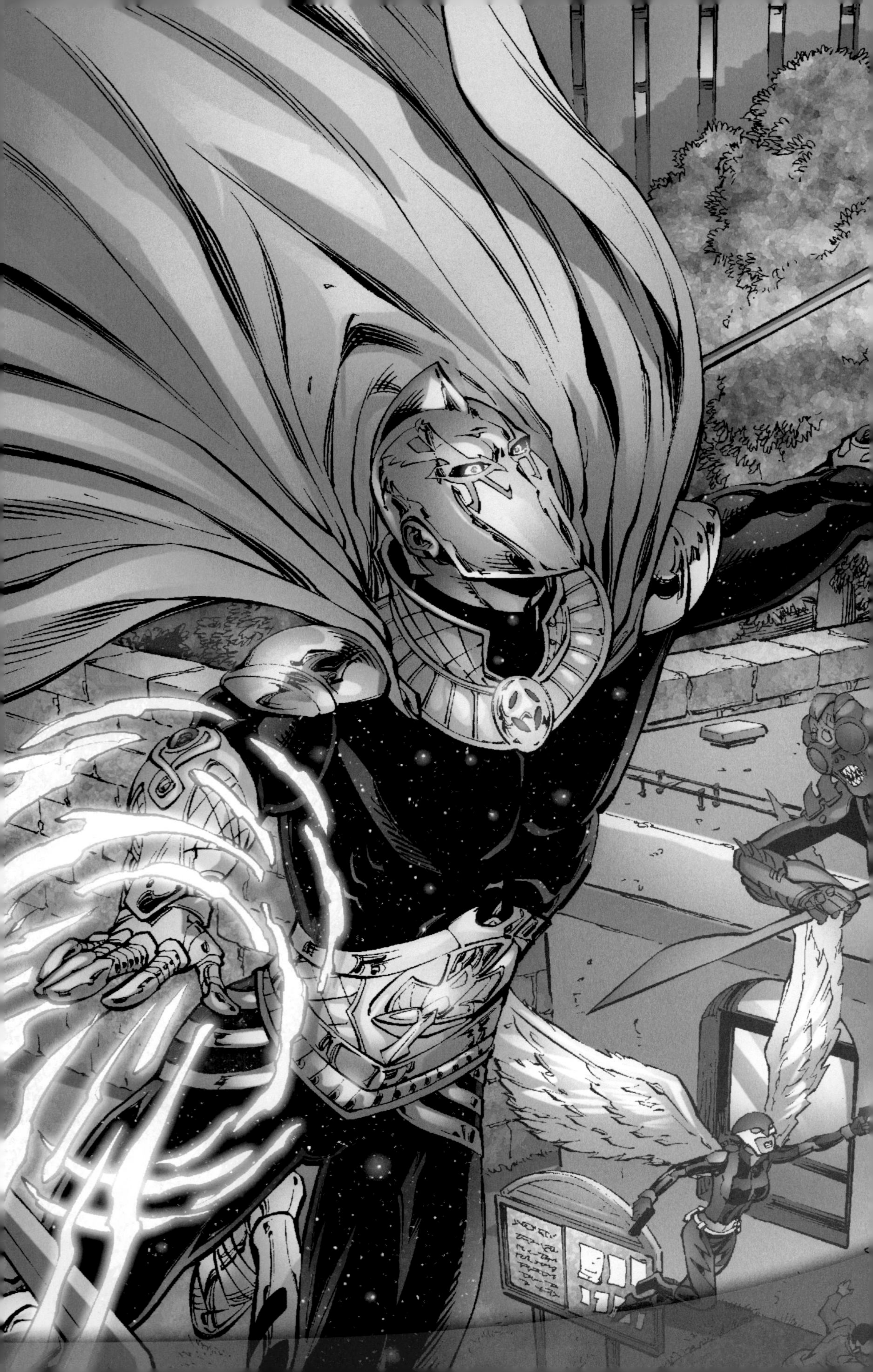

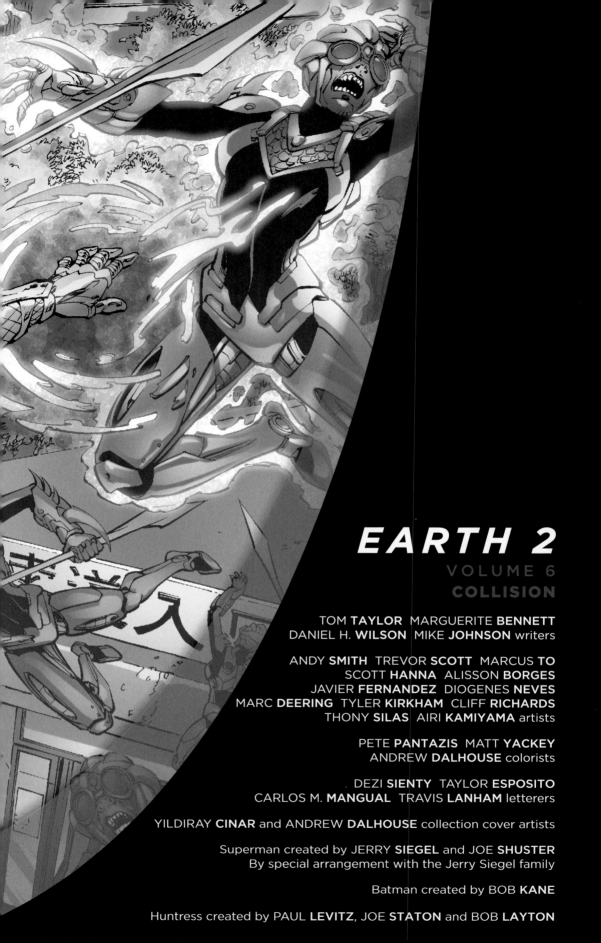

EARTH 2
VOLUME 6
COLLISION

TOM **TAYLOR** MARGUERITE **BENNETT**
DANIEL H. **WILSON** MIKE **JOHNSON** writers

ANDY **SMITH** TREVOR **SCOTT** MARCUS **TO**
SCOTT **HANNA** ALISSON **BORGES**
JAVIER **FERNANDEZ** DIOGENES **NEVES**
MARC **DEERING** TYLER **KIRKHAM** CLIFF **RICHARDS**
THONY **SILAS** AIRI **KAMIYAMA** artists

PETE **PANTAZIS** MATT **YACKEY**
ANDREW **DALHOUSE** colorists

DEZI **SIENTY** TAYLOR **ESPOSITO**
CARLOS M. **MANGUAL** TRAVIS **LANHAM** letterers

YILDIRAY **CINAR** and ANDREW **DALHOUSE** collection cover artists

Superman created by JERRY **SIEGEL** and JOE **SHUSTER**
By special arrangement with the Jerry Siegel family

Batman created by BOB **KANE**

Huntress created by PAUL **LEVITZ**, JOE **STATON** and BOB **LAYTON**

EDDIE BERGANZA MIKE COTTON Editors – Original Series RICKEY PURDIN Associate Editor – Original Series
JEREMY BENT Assistant Editor – Original Series JEB WOODARD Group Editor – Collected Editions
LIZ ERICKSON Editor – Collected Edition ROBBIE BIEDERMAN – Publication Design

BOB HARRAS Senior VP – Editor-in-Chief, DC Comics

DIANE NELSON President DAN DIDIO and JIM LEE Co-Publishers GEOFF JOHNS Chief Creative Officer
AMIT DESAI Senior VP – Marketing & Global Franchise Management NAIRI GARDINER Senior VP – Finance
SAM ADES VP – Digital Marketing BOBBIE CHASE VP – Talent Development
MARK CHIARELLO Senior VP – Art, Design & Collected Editions JOHN CUNNINGHAM VP – Content Strategy
ANNE DePIES VP – Strategy Planning & Reporting DON FALLETTI VP – Manufacturing Operations
LAWRENCE GANEM VP – Editorial Administration & Talent Relations ALISON GILL Senior VP – Manufacturing & Operations
HANK KANALZ Senior VP – Editorial Strategy & Administration JAY KOGAN VP – Legal Affairs
DEREK MADDALENA Senior VP – Sales & Business Development JACK MAHAN VP – Business Affairs
DAN MIRON VP – Sales Planning & Trade Development NICK NAPOLITANO VP – Manufacturing Administration
CAROL ROEDER VP – Marketing EDDIE SCANNELL VP - Mass Account & Digital Sales
COURTNEY SIMMONS Senior VP – Publicity & Communications JIM (SKI) SOKOLOWSKI VP – Comic Book Specialty & Newsstand Sales
SANDY YI Senior VP – Global Franchise Management

EARTH 2 VOLUME 6: COLLISION

DC Comics, 4000 Warner Blvd., Burbank, CA 91522
A Warner Bros. Entertainment Company.
Printed by RR Donnelley, Salem, VA, USA. 10/23/15. First Printing.
ISBN: 978-1-4012-5758-3

Library of Congress Cataloging-in-Publication Data is available.

PEFC Certified

Printed on paper from
sustainably managed
forests and controlled
sources

PEFC

PEFC/29-31-75   www.pefc.org

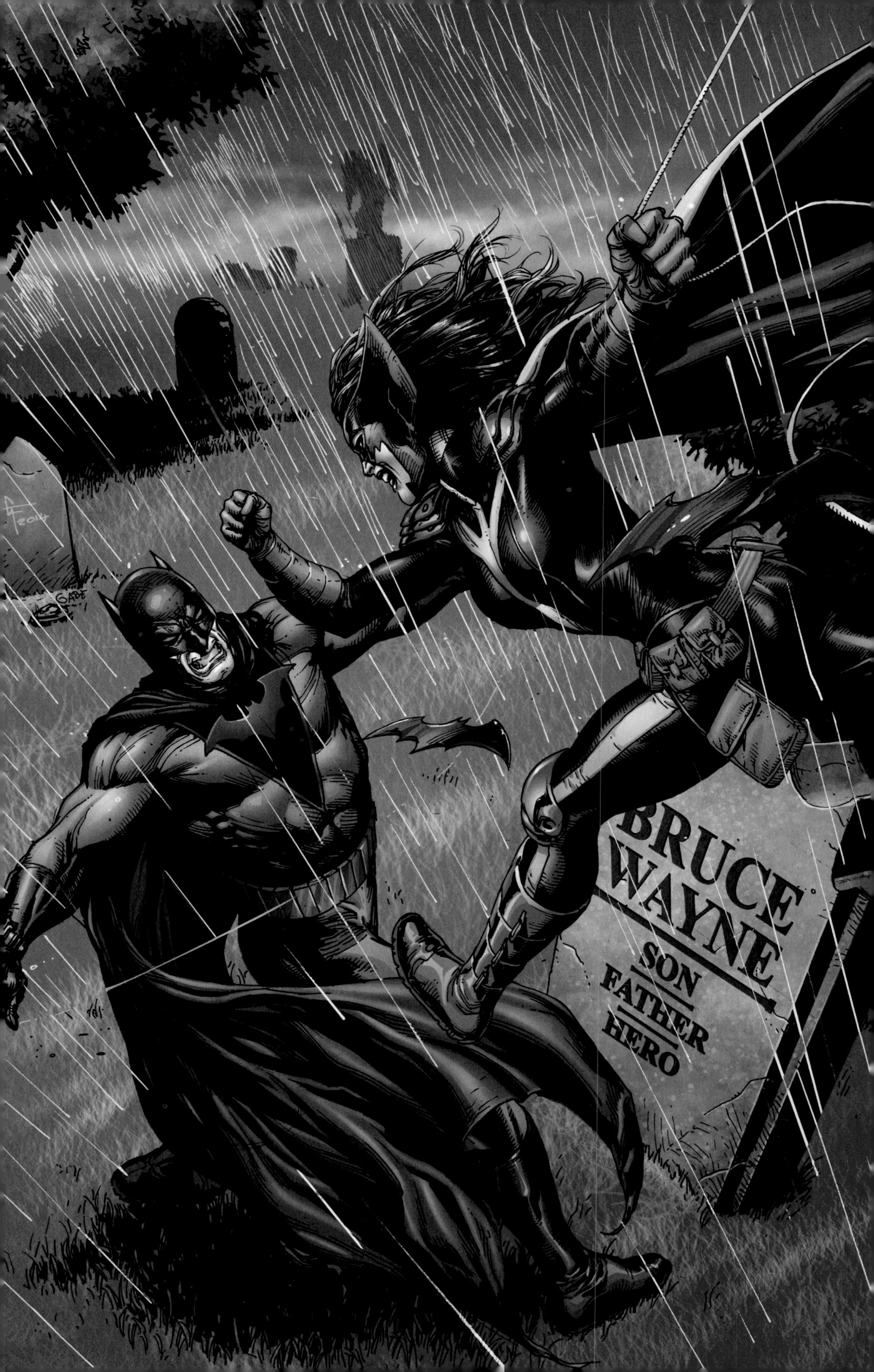
BRUCE WAYNE
SON
FATHER
HERO

COLLISION

MARGUERITE BENNETT, TOM TAYLOR writers **ANDY SMITH, TREVOR SCOTT, MARCUS TO, SCOTT HANNA** artists
PETE PANTAZIS colorist **DEZI SIENTY** letterer cover by **GARY FRANK** with **GABE ELTAEB**

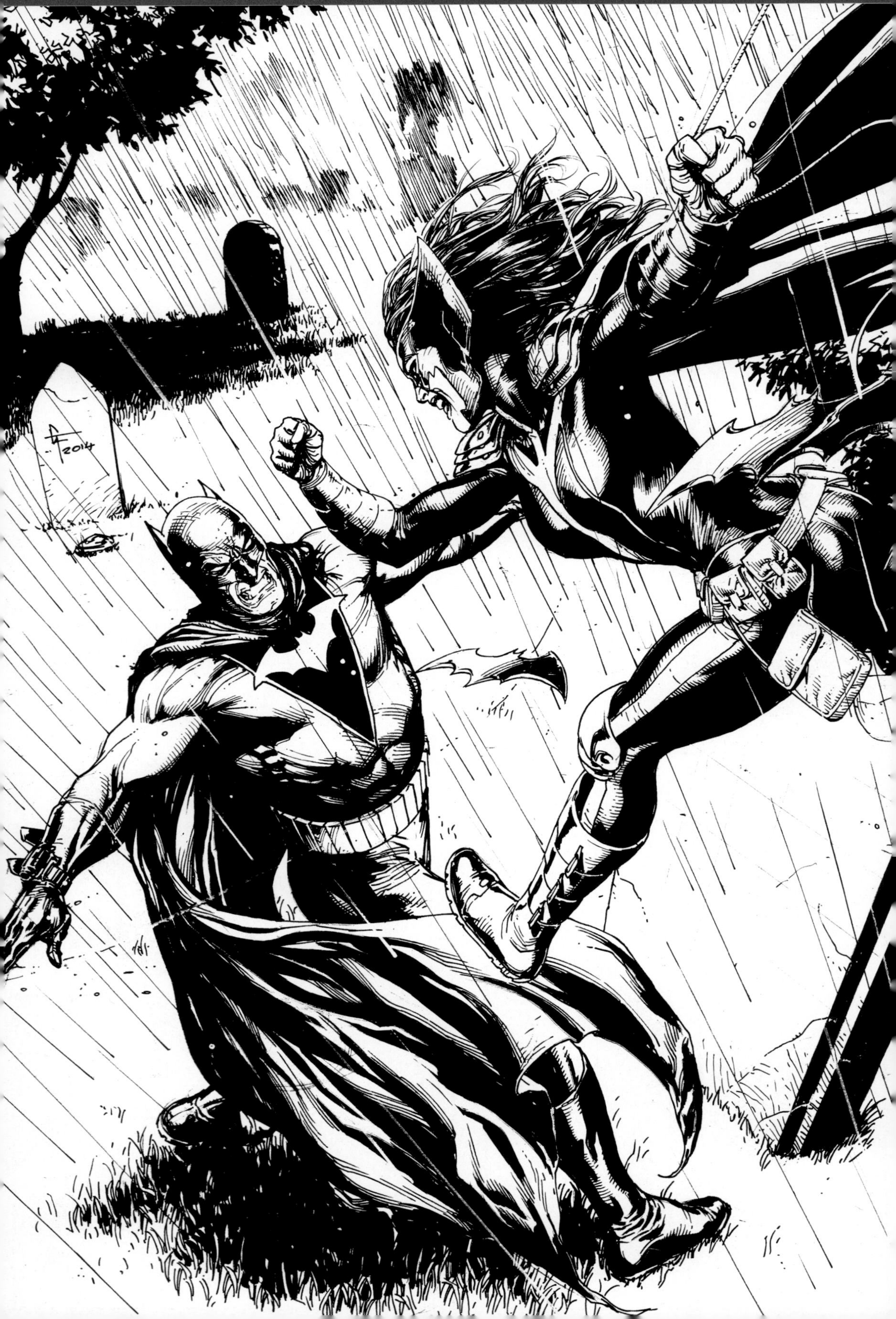

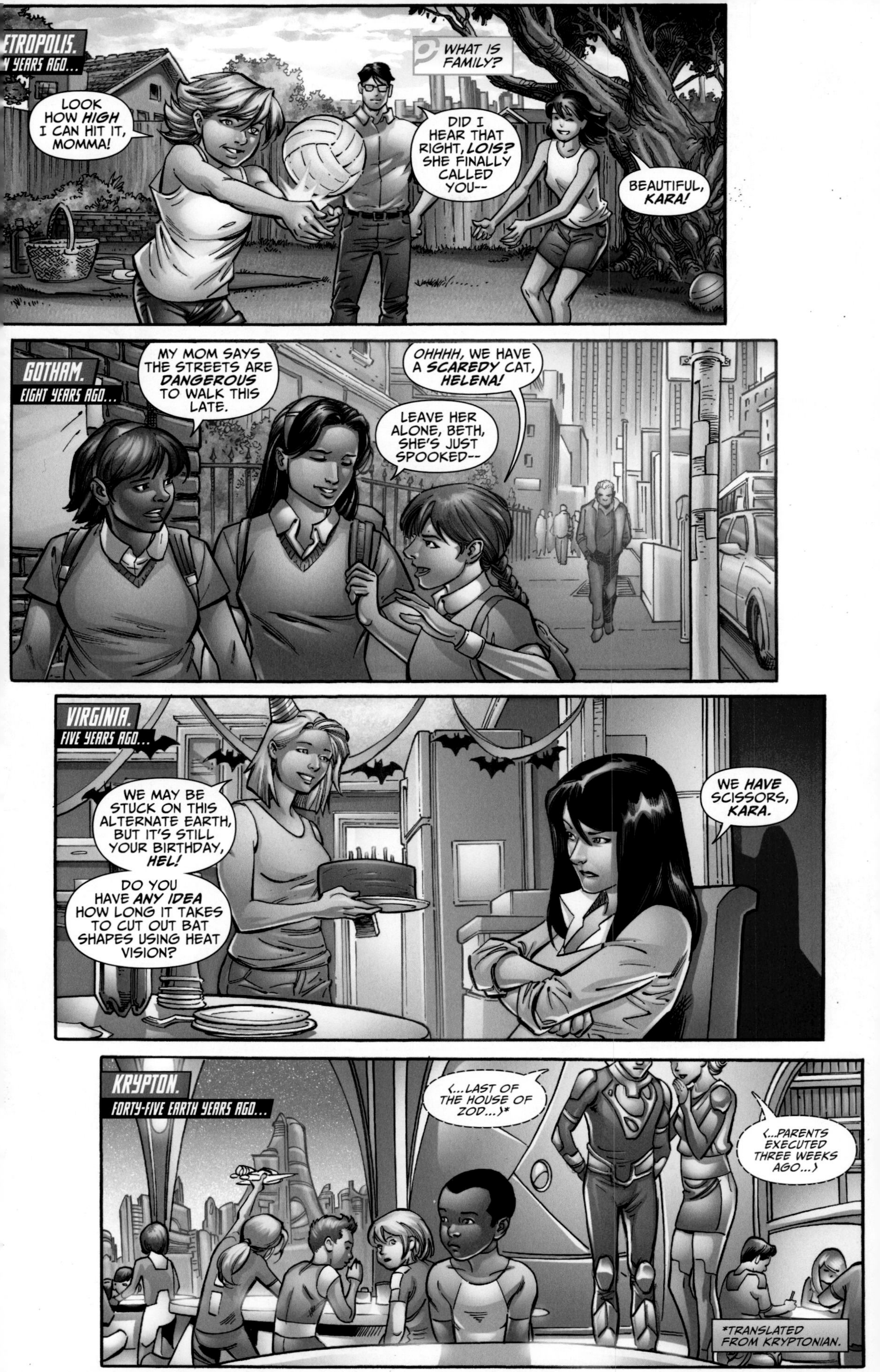

ETROPOLIS.
N YEARS AGO...
WHAT IS FAMILY?
LOOK HOW HIGH I CAN HIT IT, MOMMA!
DID I HEAR THAT RIGHT, LOIS? SHE FINALLY CALLED YOU--
BEAUTIFUL, KARA!
GOTHAM.
EIGHT YEARS AGO...
MY MOM SAYS THE STREETS ARE DANGEROUS TO WALK THIS LATE.
OHHHH, WE HAVE A SCAREDY CAT, HELENA!
LEAVE HER ALONE, BETH, SHE'S JUST SPOOKED--
VIRGINIA.
FIVE YEARS AGO...
WE MAY BE STUCK ON THIS ALTERNATE EARTH, BUT IT'S STILL YOUR BIRTHDAY, HEL!
DO YOU HAVE ANY IDEA HOW LONG IT TAKES TO CUT OUT BAT SHAPES USING HEAT VISION?
WE HAVE SCISSORS, KARA.
KRYPTON.
FORTY-FIVE EARTH YEARS AGO...
‹...LAST OF THE HOUSE OF ZOD...›*
‹...PARENTS EXECUTED THREE WEEKS AGO...›
*TRANSLATED FROM KRYPTONIAN.

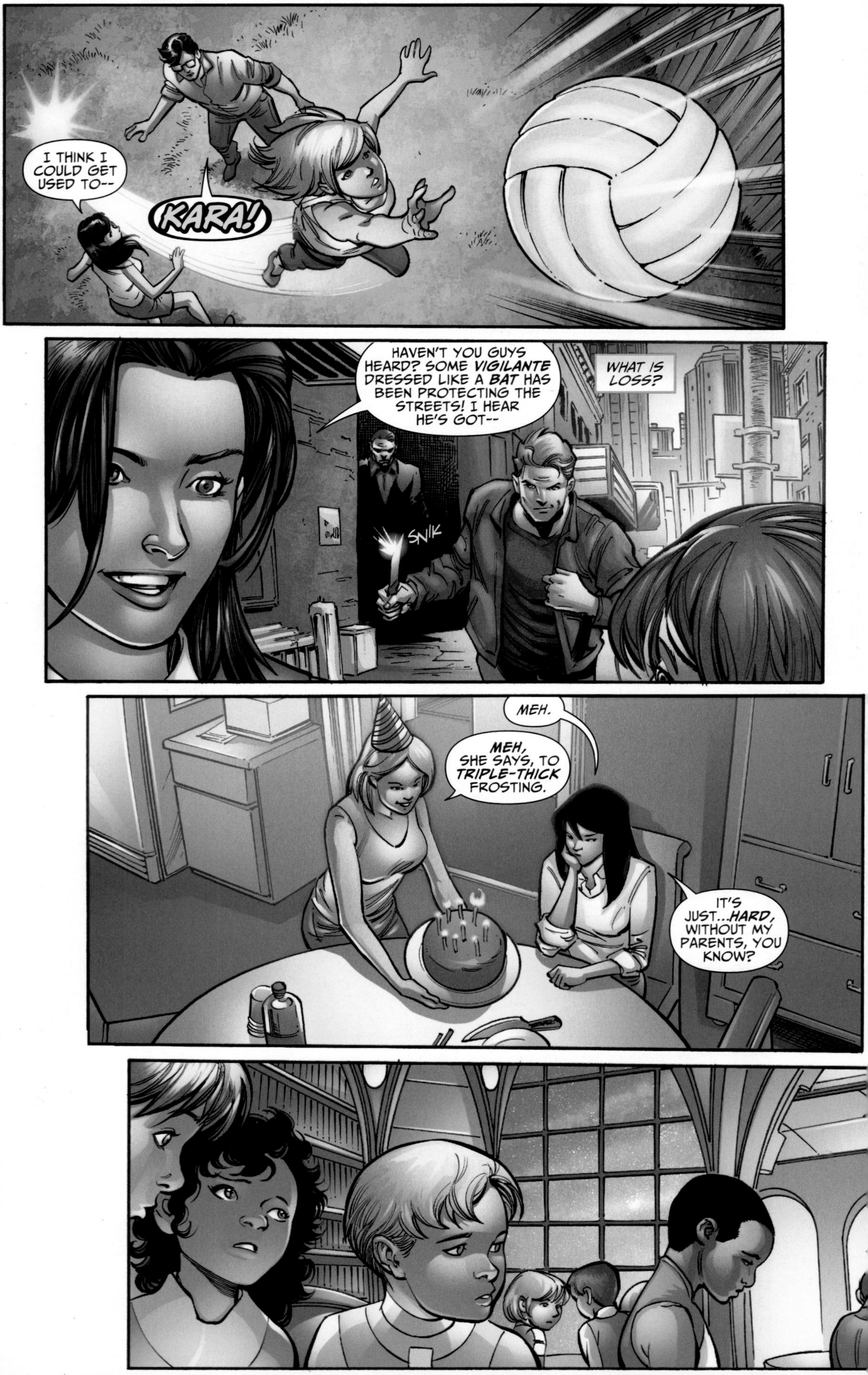

I THINK I COULD GET USED TO--
KARA!
HAVEN'T YOU GUYS HEARD? SOME VIGILANTE DRESSED LIKE A BAT HAS BEEN PROTECTING THE STREETS! I HEAR HE'S GOT--
WHAT IS LOSS?
SNIK
MEH.
MEH, SHE SAYS, TO TRIPLE-THICK FROSTING.
IT'S JUST...HARD, WITHOUT MY PARENTS, YOU KNOW?

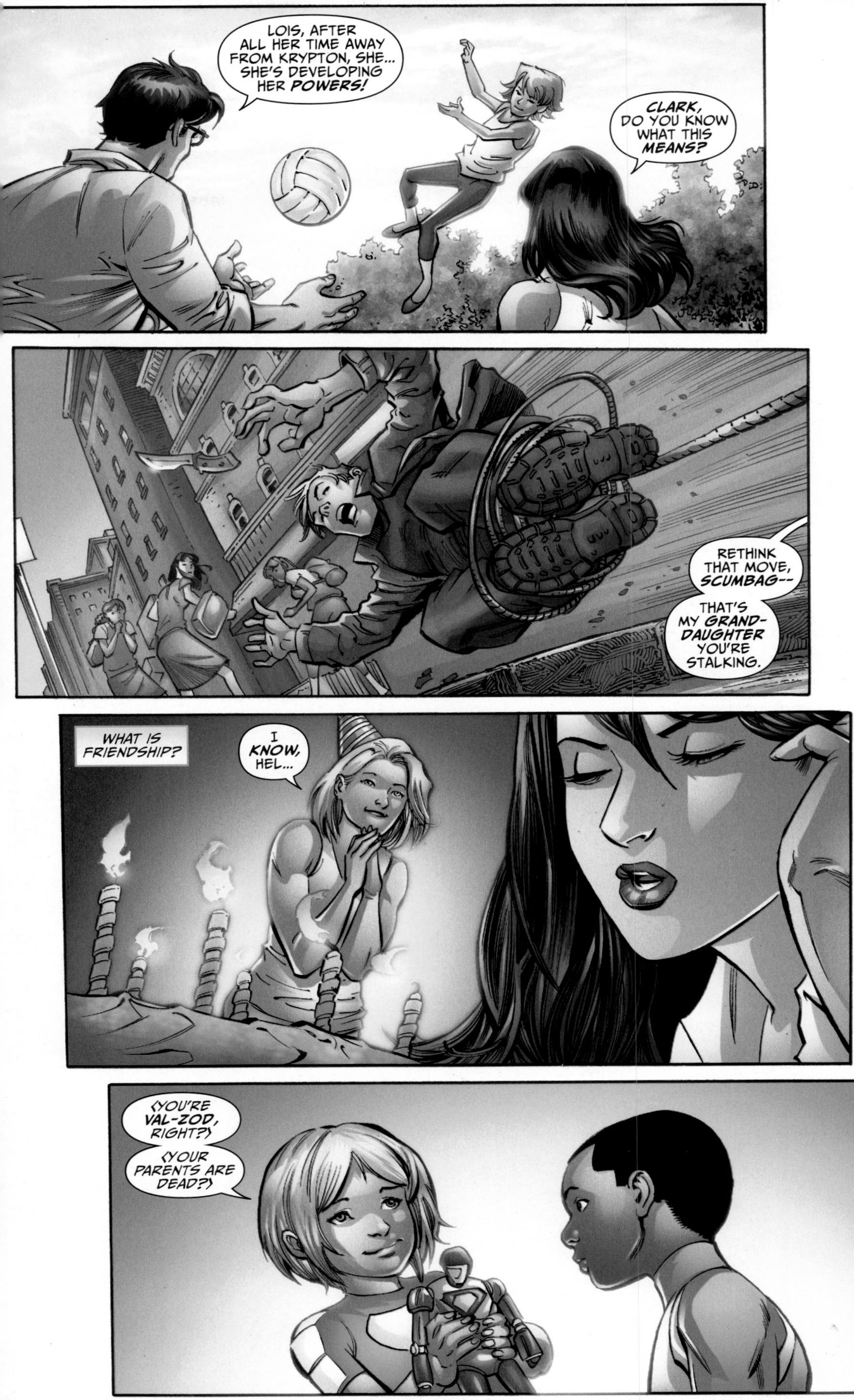
LOIS, AFTER ALL HER TIME AWAY FROM KRYPTON, SHE... SHE'S DEVELOPING HER POWERS!
CLARK, DO YOU KNOW WHAT THIS MEANS?
RETHINK THAT MOVE, SCUMBAG--
THAT'S MY GRAND-DAUGHTER YOU'RE STALKING.
WHAT IS FRIENDSHIP?
I KNOW, HEL...
‹YOU'RE VAL-ZOD, RIGHT?›
‹YOUR PARENTS ARE DEAD?›

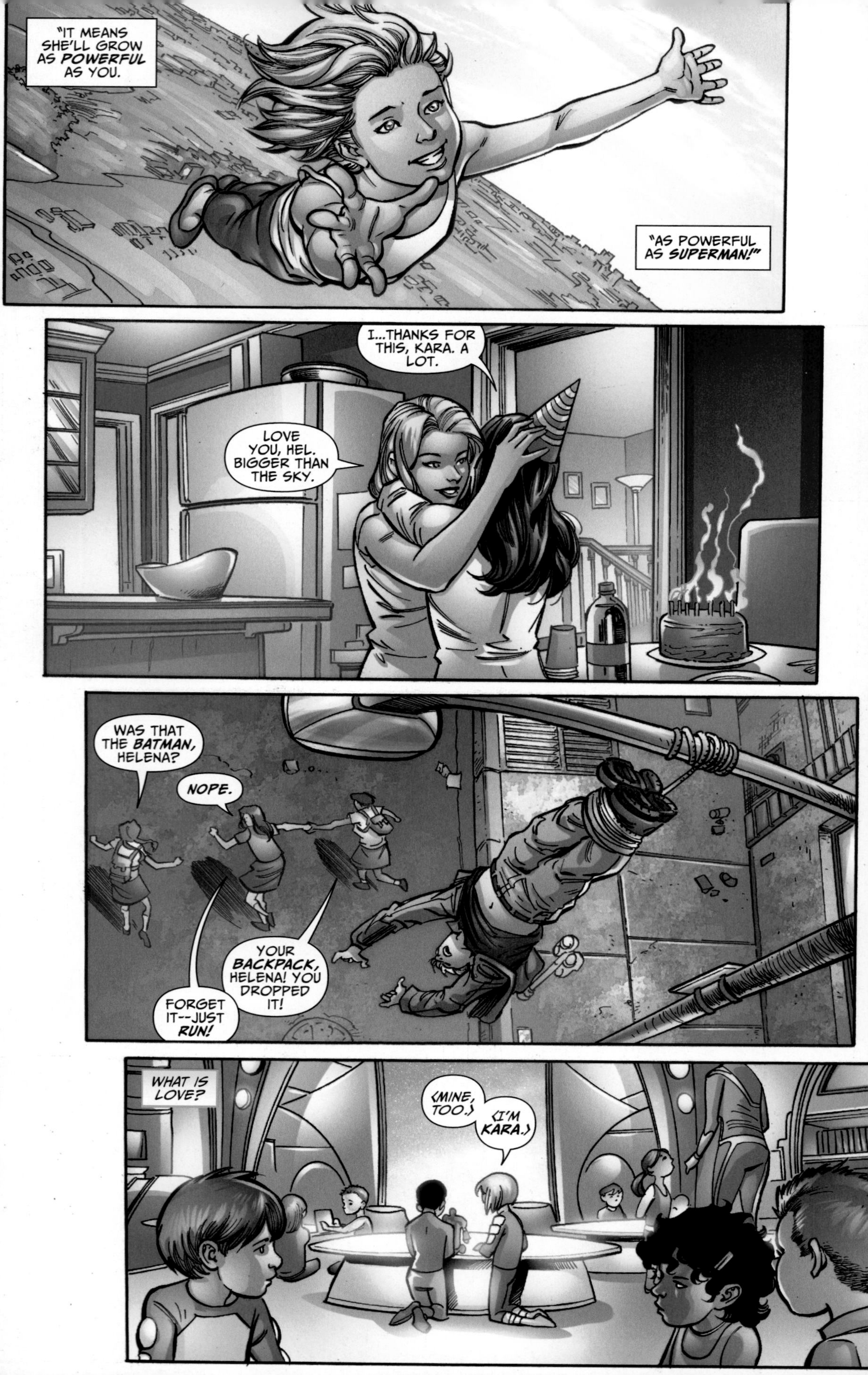
"IT MEANS SHE'LL GROW AS POWERFUL AS YOU.
"AS POWERFUL AS SUPERMAN!"
I...THANKS FOR THIS, KARA. A LOT.
LOVE YOU, HEL. BIGGER THAN THE SKY.
WAS THAT THE BATMAN, HELENA?
NOPE.
YOUR BACKPACK, HELENA! YOU DROPPED IT!
FORGET IT--JUST RUN!
WHAT IS LOVE?
<MINE, TOO.>
<I'M KARA.>

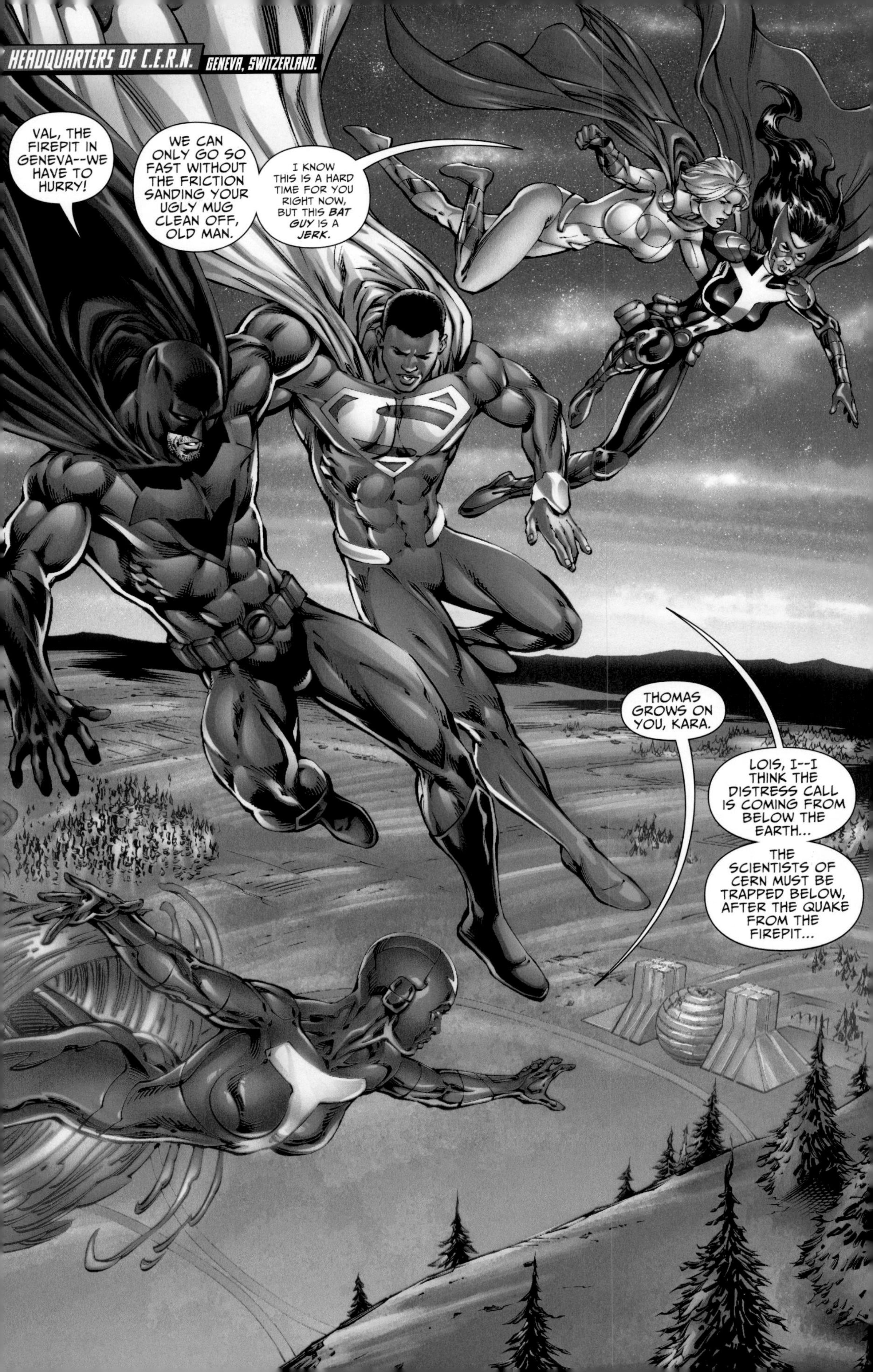
HEADQUARTERS OF C.E.R.N. GENEVA, SWITZERLAND.
VAL, THE FIREPIT IN GENEVA--WE HAVE TO HURRY!
WE CAN ONLY GO SO FAST WITHOUT THE FRICTION SANDING YOUR UGLY MUG CLEAN OFF, OLD MAN.
I KNOW THIS IS A HARD TIME FOR YOU RIGHT NOW, BUT THIS BAT GUY IS A JERK.
THOMAS GROWS ON YOU, KARA.
LOIS, I--I THINK THE DISTRESS CALL IS COMING FROM BELOW THE EARTH...
THE SCIENTISTS OF CERN MUST BE TRAPPED BELOW, AFTER THE QUAKE FROM THE FIREPIT...

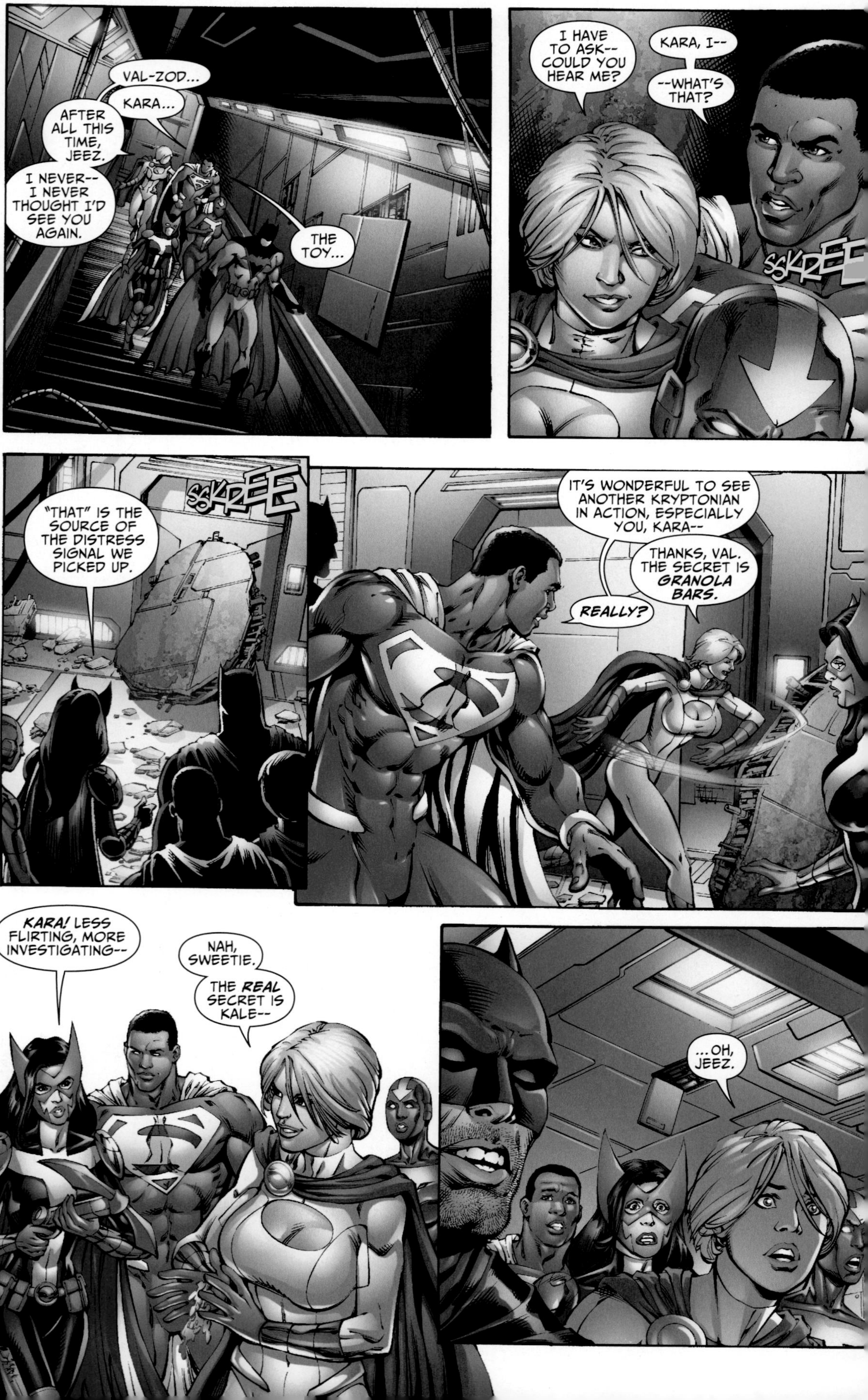
VAL-ZOD...
KARA...
AFTER ALL THIS TIME, JEEZ.
I NEVER-- I NEVER THOUGHT I'D SEE YOU AGAIN.
THE TOY...
I HAVE TO ASK-- COULD YOU HEAR ME?
KARA, I--
--WHAT'S THAT?
SSKREE
SSKREEE
"THAT" IS THE SOURCE OF THE DISTRESS SIGNAL WE PICKED UP.
IT'S WONDERFUL TO SEE ANOTHER KRYPTONIAN IN ACTION, ESPECIALLY YOU, KARA--
THANKS, VAL. THE SECRET IS GRANOLA BARS.
REALLY?
KARA! LESS FLIRTING, MORE INVESTIGATING--
NAH, SWEETIE.
THE REAL SECRET IS KALE--
...OH, JEEZ.

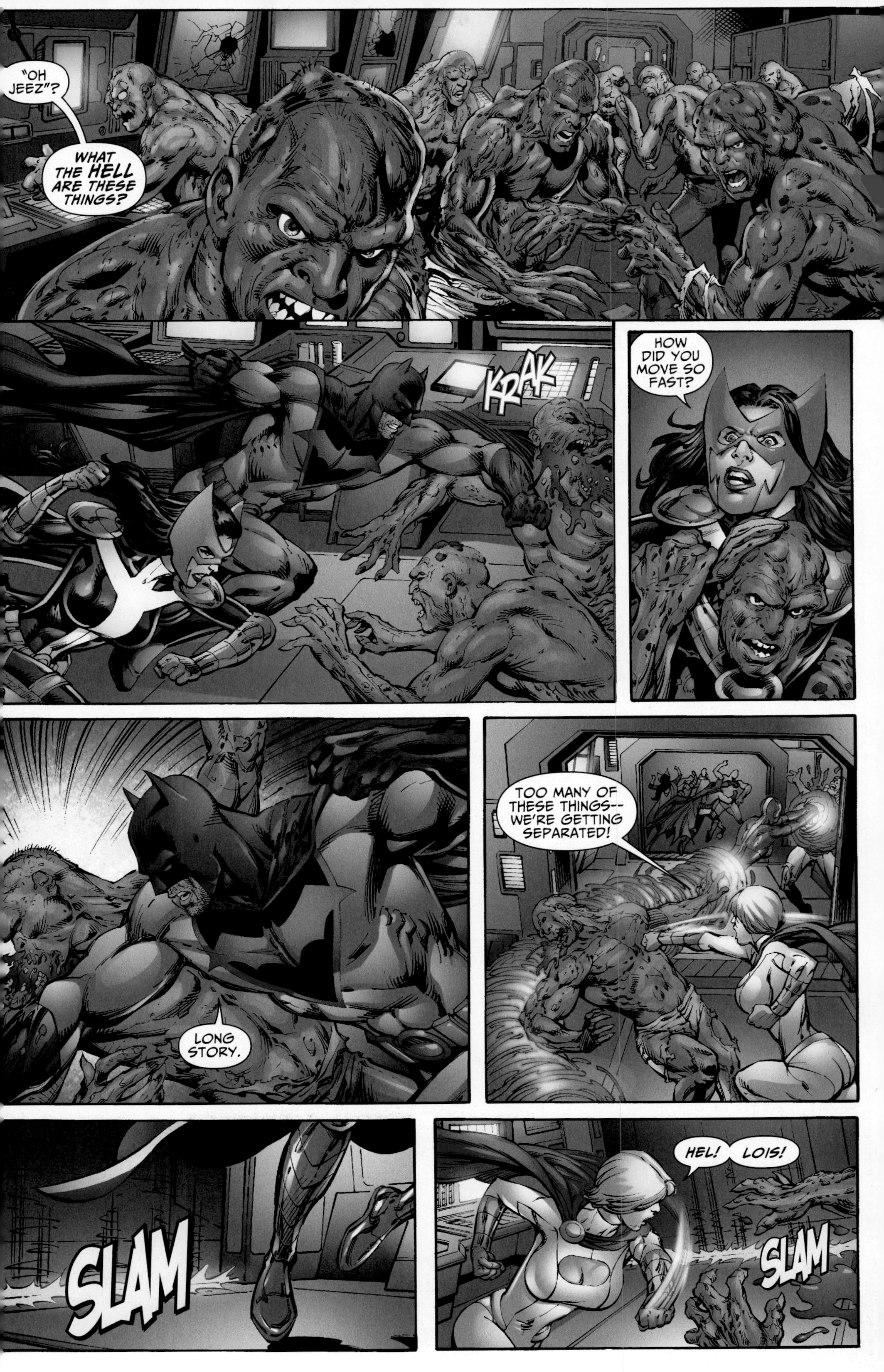
"OH JEEZ"?
WHAT THE HELL ARE THESE THINGS?
KRAK
HOW DID YOU MOVE SO FAST?
LONG STORY.
TOO MANY OF THESE THINGS-- WE'RE GETTING SEPARATED!
SLAM
HEL!
LOIS!
SLAM

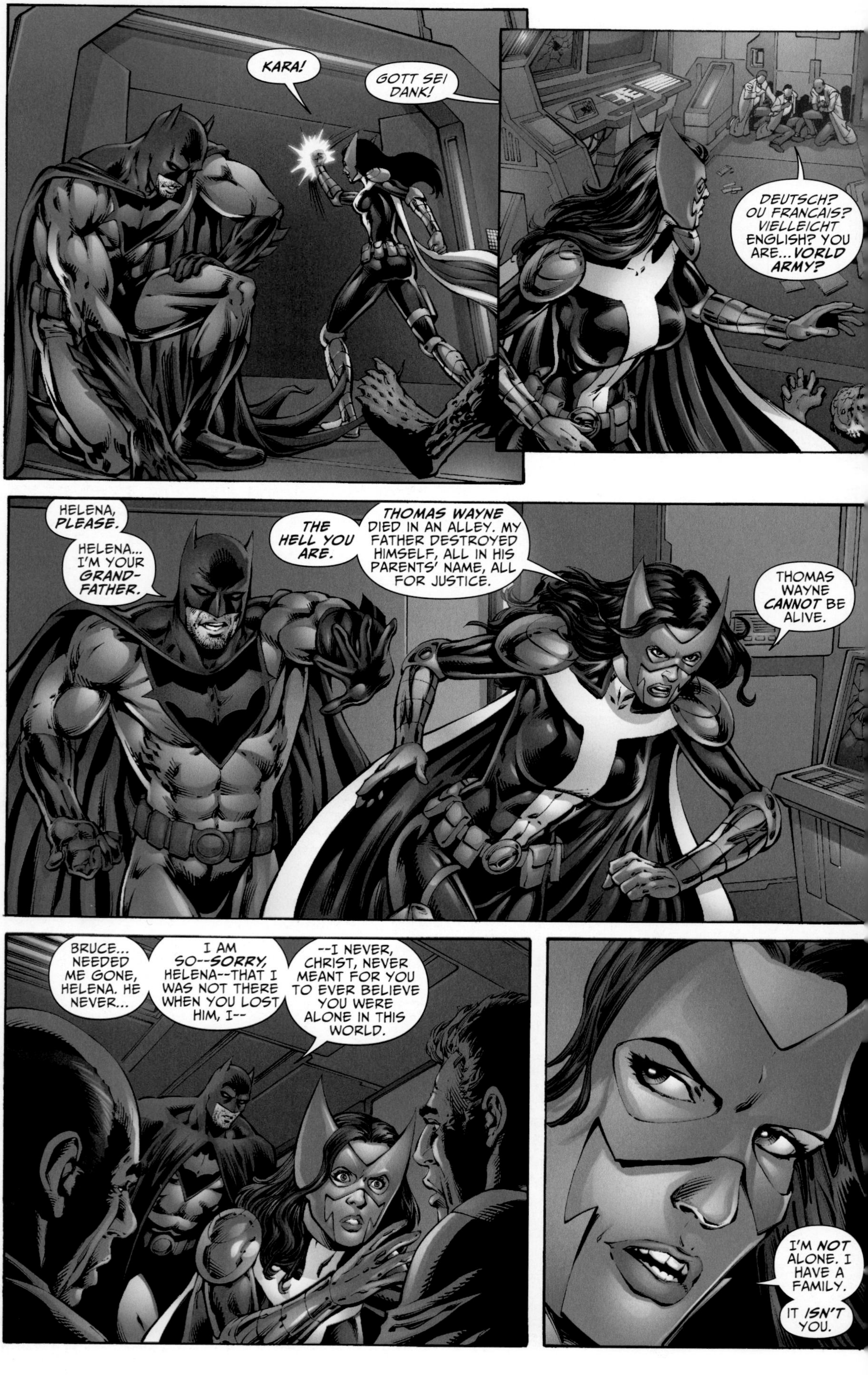
KARA!
GOTT SEI DANK!
DEUTSCH? OU FRANCAIS? VIELLEICHT ENGLISH? YOU ARE... VORLD ARMY?
HELENA, PLEASE.
HELENA... I'M YOUR GRAND-FATHER.
THE HELL YOU ARE.
THOMAS WAYNE DIED IN AN ALLEY. MY FATHER DESTROYED HIMSELF, ALL IN HIS PARENTS' NAME, ALL FOR JUSTICE.
THOMAS WAYNE CANNOT BE ALIVE.
BRUCE... NEEDED ME GONE, HELENA. HE NEVER...
I AM SO--SORRY, HELENA--THAT I WAS NOT THERE WHEN YOU LOST HIM, I--
--I NEVER, CHRIST, NEVER MEANT FOR YOU TO EVER BELIEVE YOU WERE ALONE IN THIS WORLD.
I'M NOT ALONE. I HAVE A FAMILY.
IT ISN'T YOU.

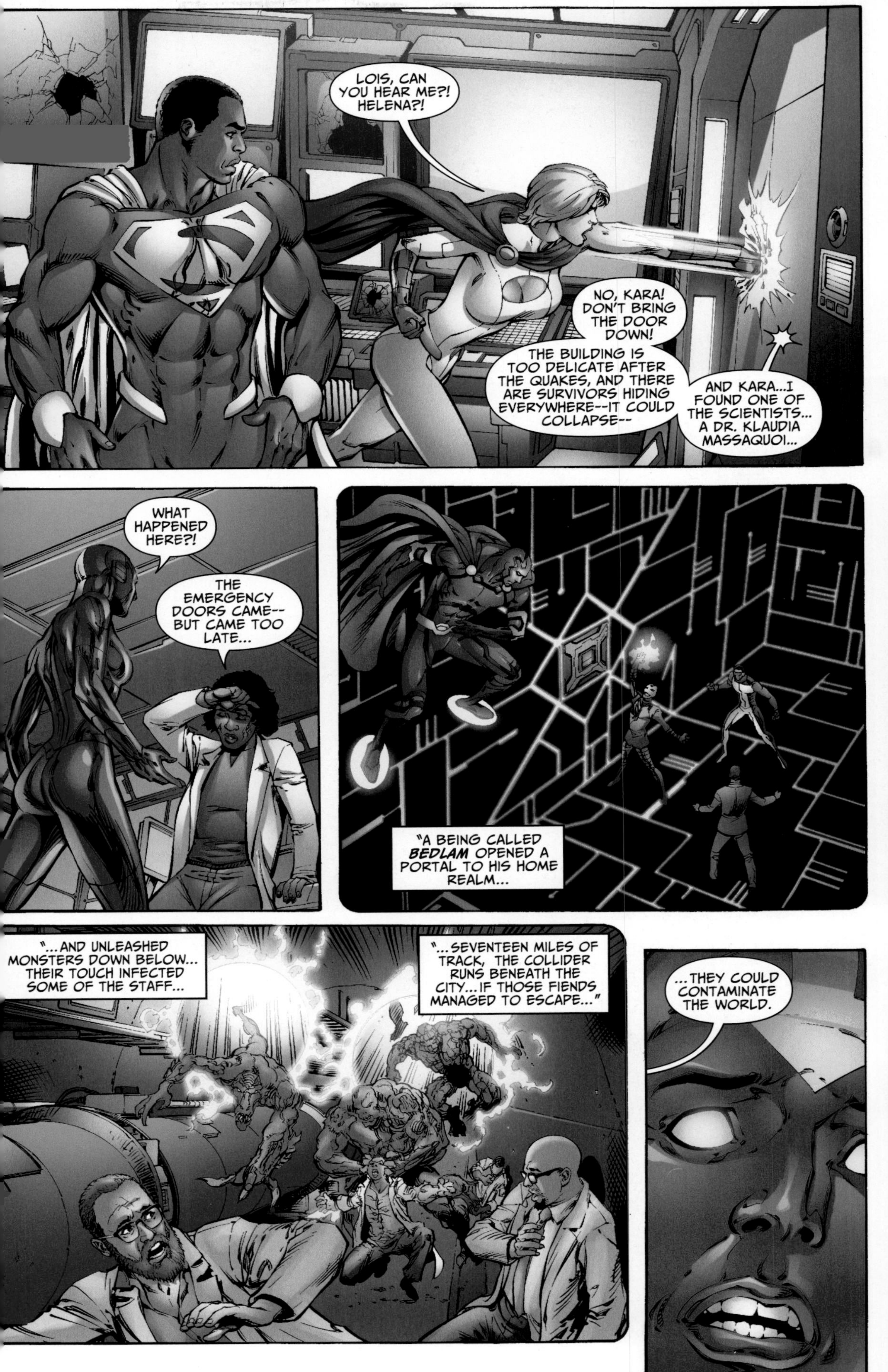
LOIS, CAN YOU HEAR ME?! HELENA?!
NO, KARA! DON'T BRING THE DOOR DOWN!
THE BUILDING IS TOO DELICATE AFTER THE QUAKES, AND THERE ARE SURVIVORS HIDING EVERYWHERE--IT COULD COLLAPSE--
AND KARA...I FOUND ONE OF THE SCIENTISTS... A DR. KLAUDIA MASSAQUOI...
WHAT HAPPENED HERE?!
THE EMERGENCY DOORS CAME--BUT CAME TOO LATE...
"A BEING CALLED BEDLAM OPENED A PORTAL TO HIS HOME REALM...
"...AND UNLEASHED MONSTERS DOWN BELOW... THEIR TOUCH INFECTED SOME OF THE STAFF...
"...SEVENTEEN MILES OF TRACK, THE COLLIDER RUNS BENEATH THE CITY... IF THOSE FIENDS MANAGED TO ESCAPE..."
...THEY COULD CONTAMINATE THE WORLD.

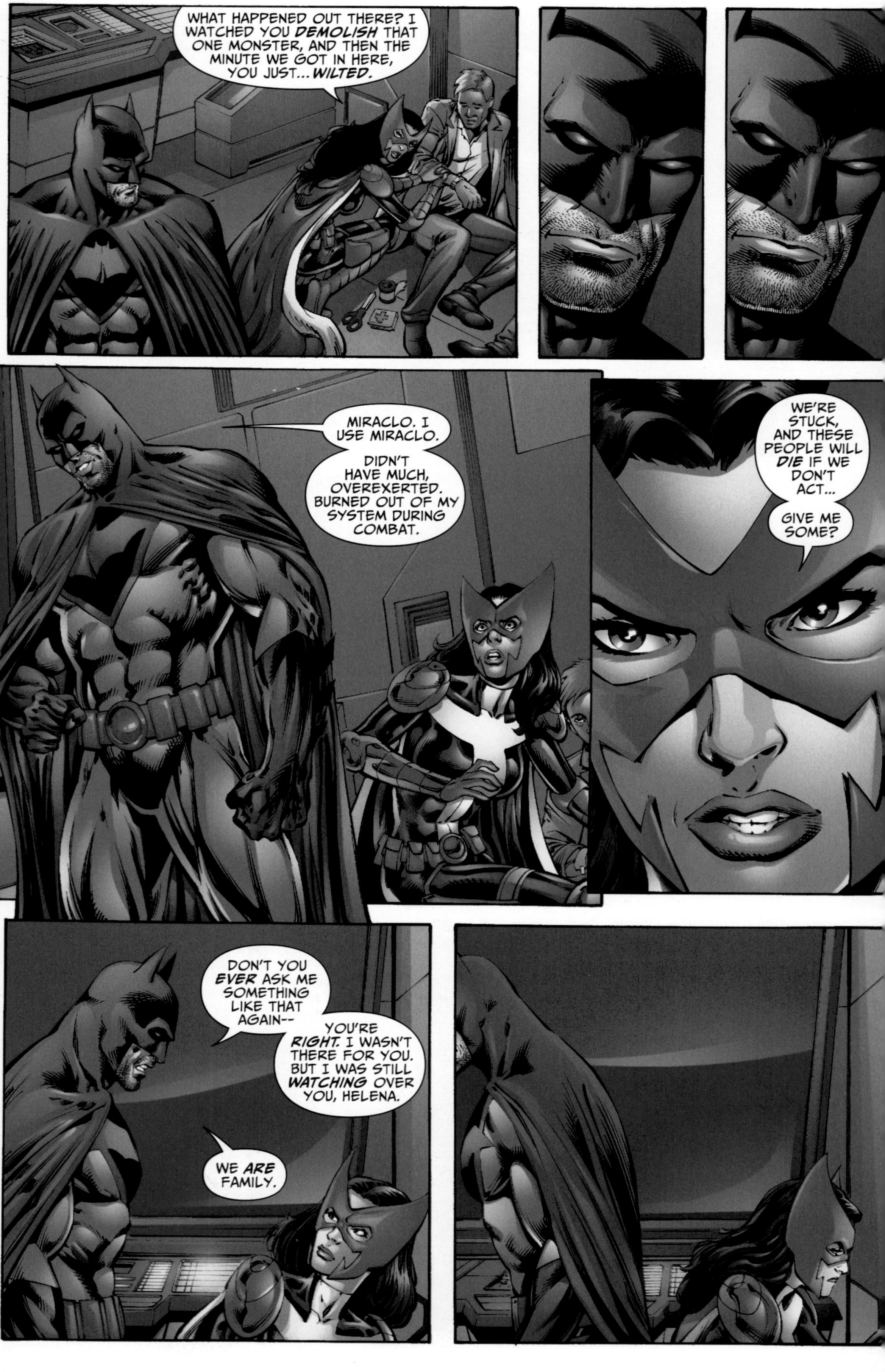
WHAT HAPPENED OUT THERE? I WATCHED YOU DEMOLISH THAT ONE MONSTER, AND THEN THE MINUTE WE GOT IN HERE, YOU JUST...WILTED.
MIRACLO. I USE MIRACLO.
DIDN'T HAVE MUCH, OVEREXERTED. BURNED OUT OF MY SYSTEM DURING COMBAT.
WE'RE STUCK, AND THESE PEOPLE WILL DIE IF WE DON'T ACT...
GIVE ME SOME?
DON'T YOU EVER ASK ME SOMETHING LIKE THAT AGAIN--
YOU'RE RIGHT. I WASN'T THERE FOR YOU. BUT I WAS STILL WATCHING OVER YOU, HELENA.
WE ARE FAMILY.

HERE, DR. MASSAQUOI...

...MY DAUGHTER AND HER FRIEND CAN HELP, THEY ARE KRYPTONIAN--

YOUNG MAN? YOUNG MISS?

YOUNG MAN, YOU WEAR THE SYMBOL OF THE MAN OF STEEL...IT WAS SAID HE COULD REACH SUCH SPEEDS, INCALCULABLE...

KRAK

...IF YOU WERE ABLE TO GENERATE SUCH A SPEED, AND COLLIDE, WITH SUCH AN EXPULSION OF ENERGY, YOU COULD CREATE AN EVENT SIMILAR TO THAT OF A NEUTRON BOMB--

--A FORCE POWERFUL ENOUGH TO DESTROY THE VIRUS LOOSE IN THE COLLIDER, TO SHRED THROUGH THE VERY MOLECULES OF THE DISEASE.

WILL YOU RISK THIS?

WHAM

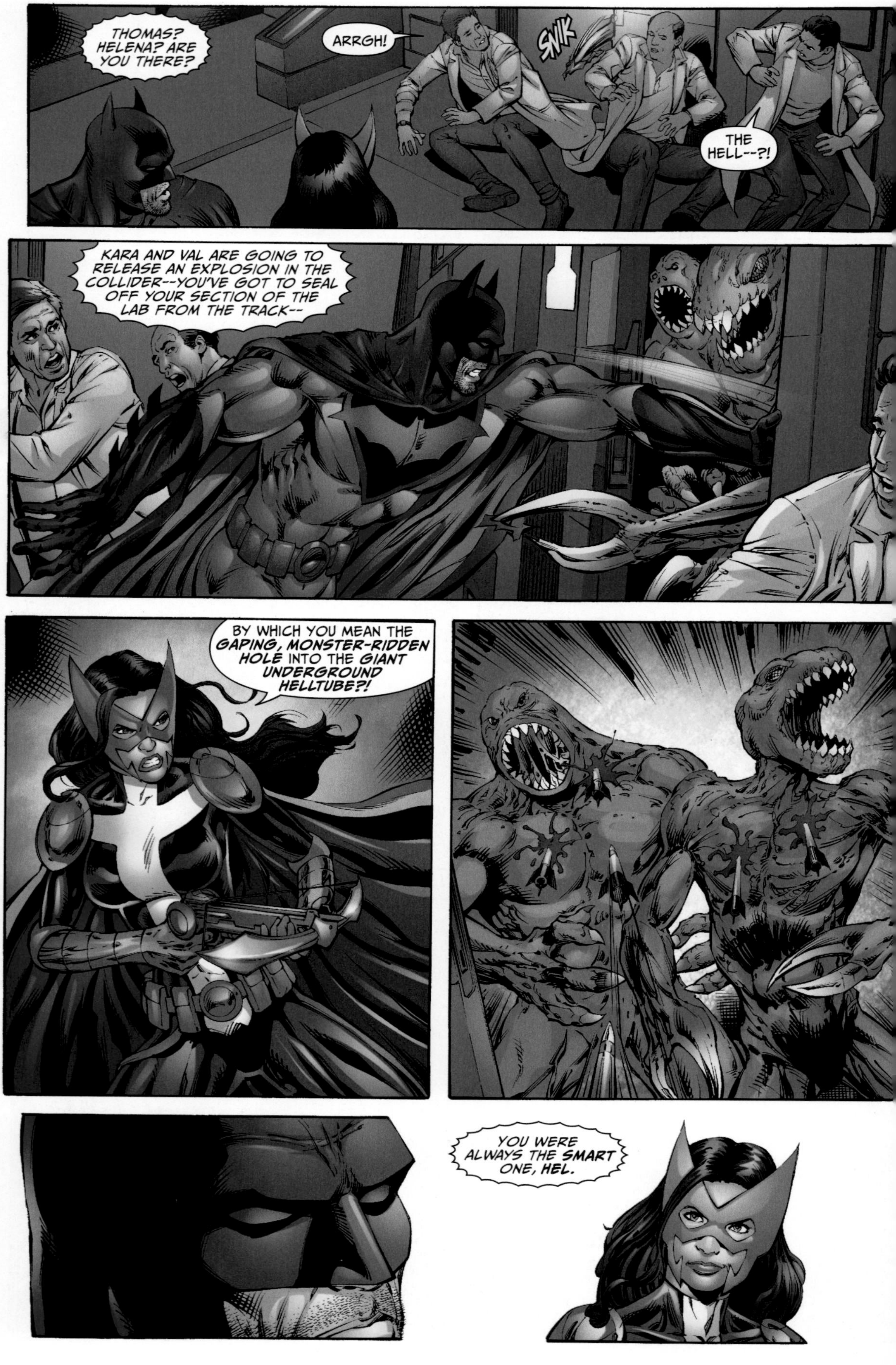
THOMAS? HELENA? ARE YOU THERE?
ARRGH!
SNIK
THE HELL--?!
KARA AND VAL ARE GOING TO RELEASE AN EXPLOSION IN THE COLLIDER--YOU'VE GOT TO SEAL OFF YOUR SECTION OF THE LAB FROM THE TRACK--
BY WHICH YOU MEAN THE GAPING, MONSTER-RIDDEN HOLE INTO THE GIANT UNDERGROUND HELLTUBE?!
YOU WERE ALWAYS THE SMART ONE, HEL.

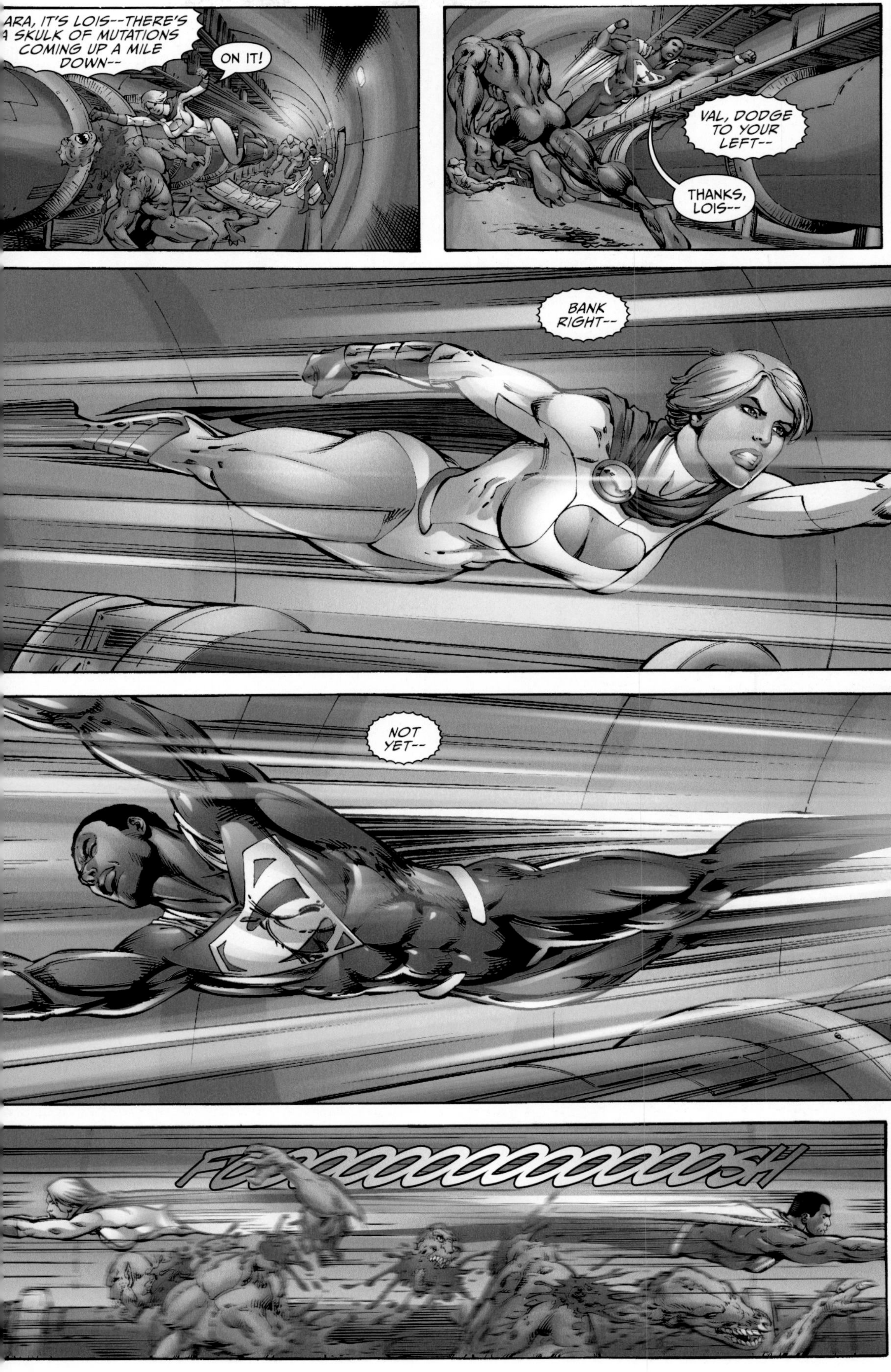
ARA, IT'S LOIS--THERE'S A SKULK OF MUTATIONS COMING UP A MILE DOWN--
ON IT!
VAL, DODGE TO YOUR LEFT--
THANKS, LOIS--
BANK RIGHT--
NOT YET--
FOOOOOOOOOOOOOSH

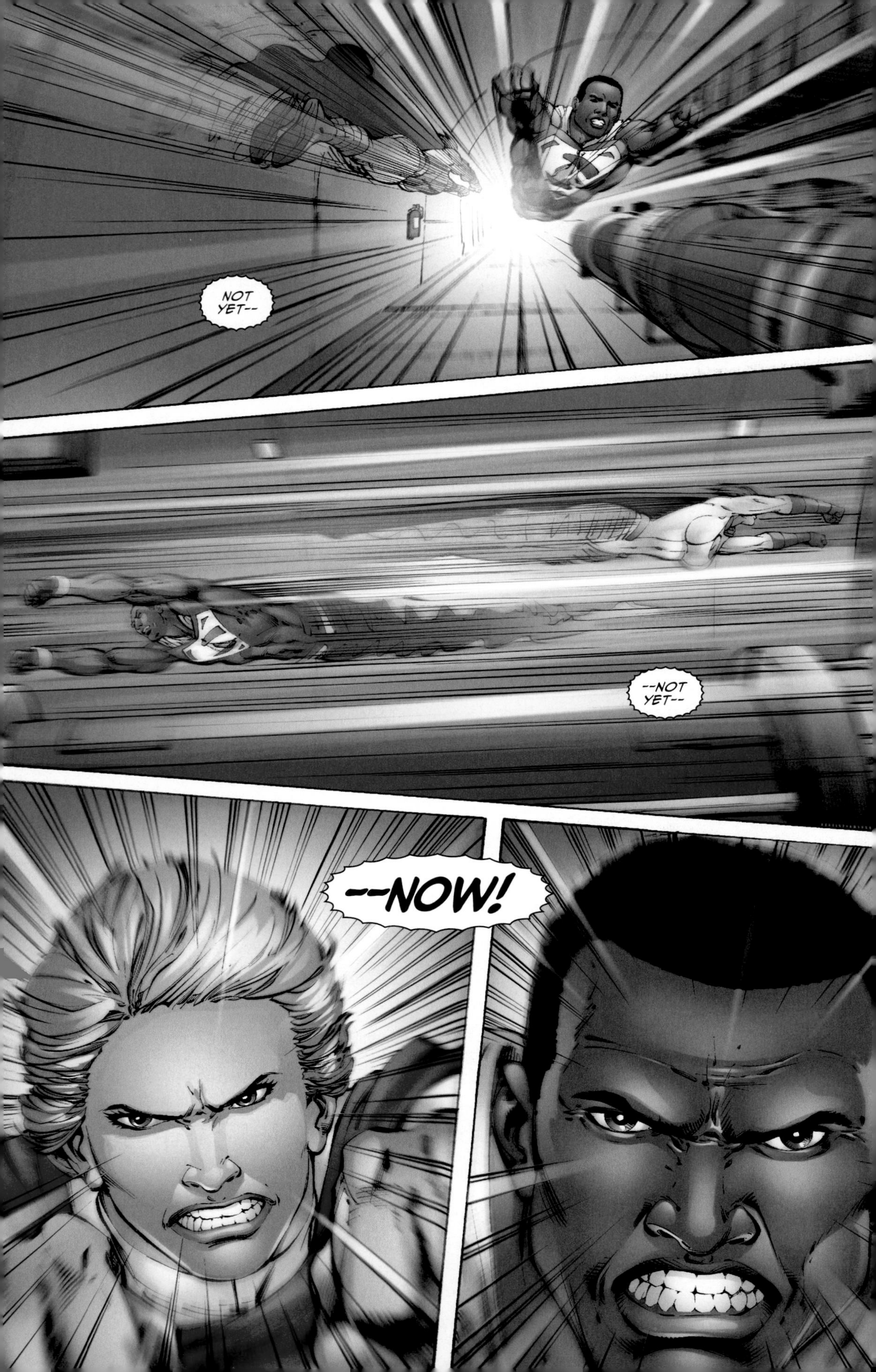
NOT YET--
--NOT YET--
--NOW!

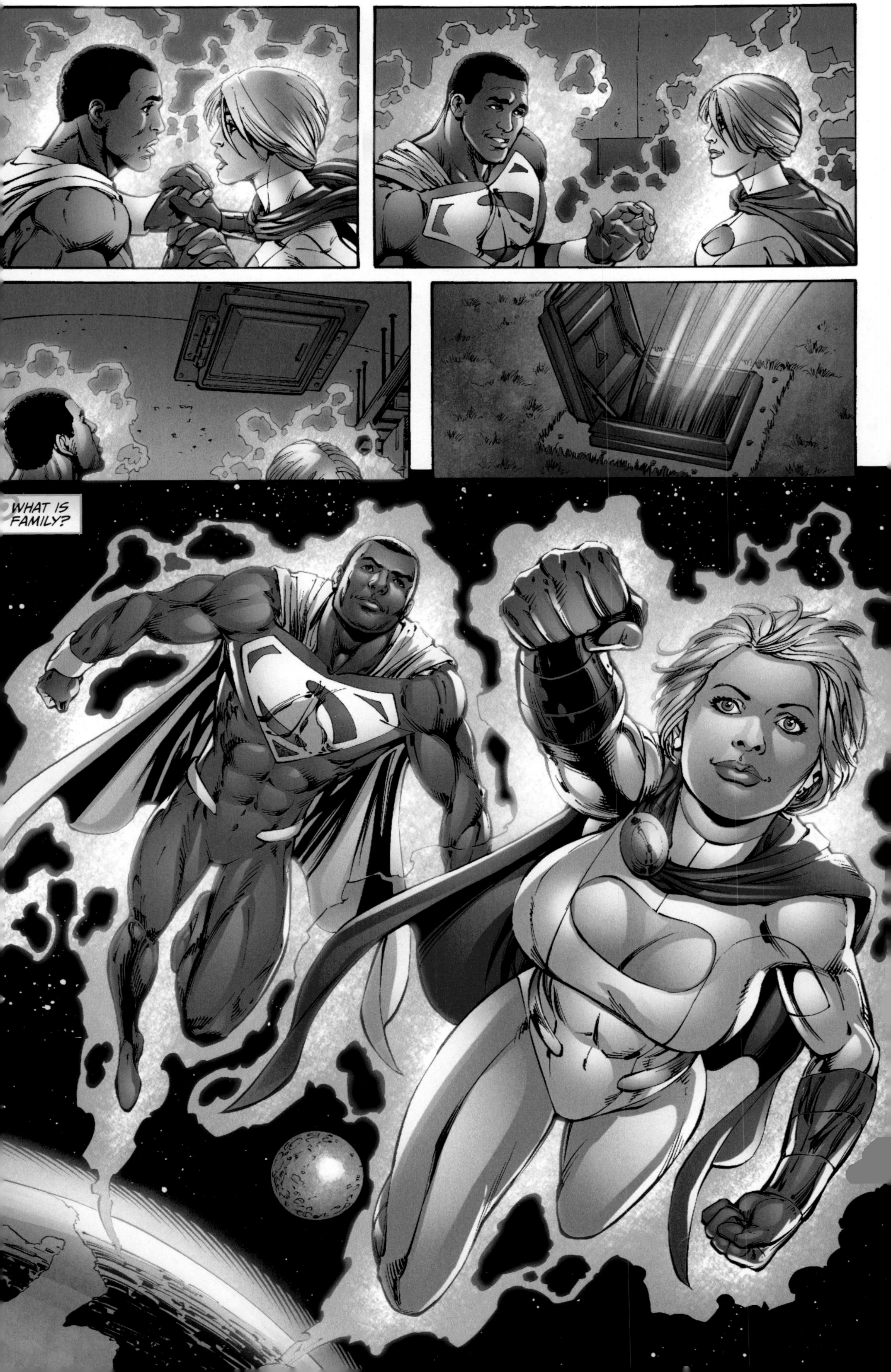
WHAT IS FAMILY?

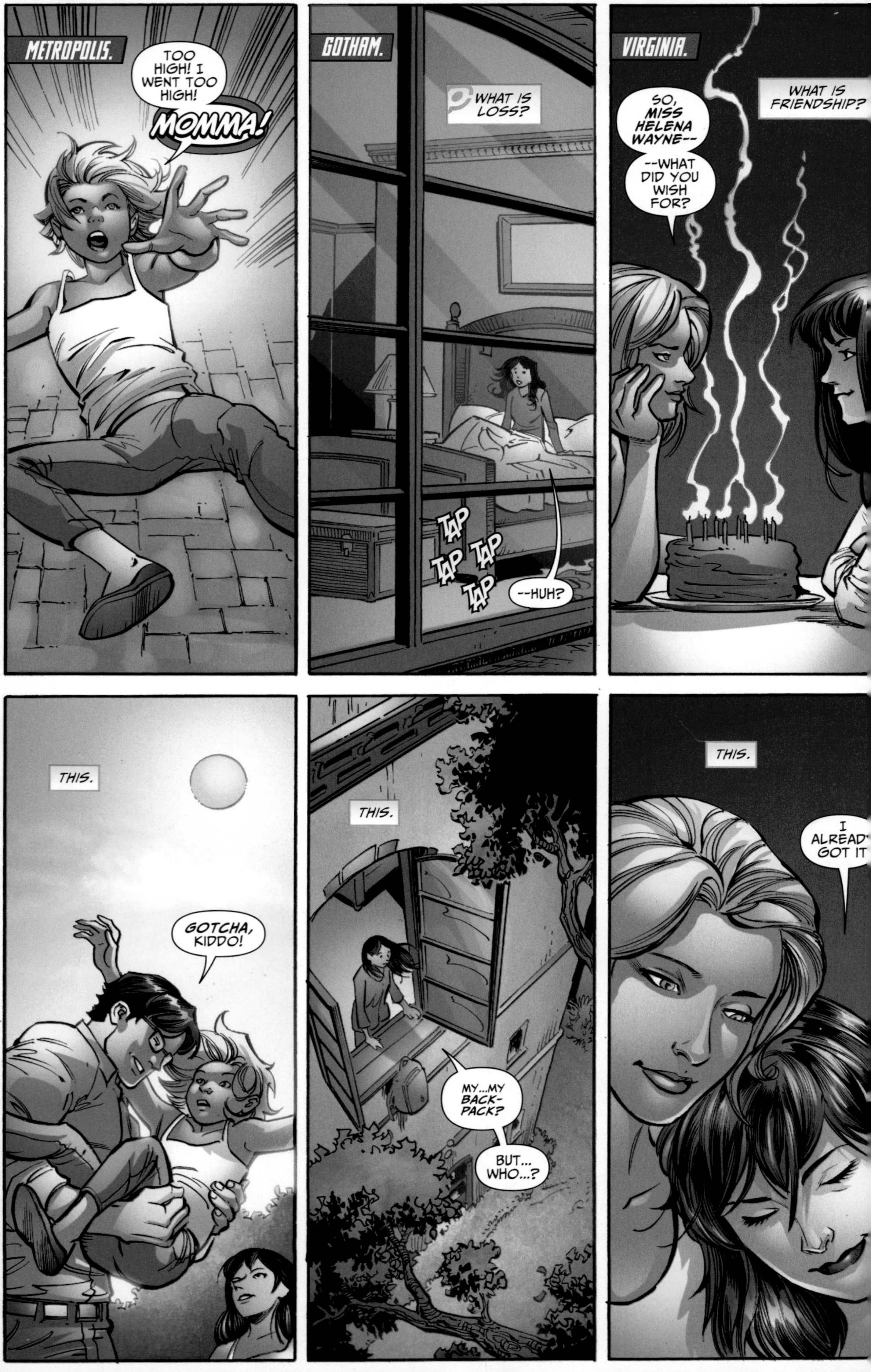

METROPOLIS.
TOO HIGH! I WENT TOO HIGH!
MOMMA!
GOTHAM.
WHAT IS LOSS?
TAP TAP TAP TAP
--HUH?
VIRGINIA.
WHAT IS FRIENDSHIP?
SO, MISS HELENA WAYNE--
--WHAT DID YOU WISH FOR?
THIS.
GOTCHA, KIDDO!
THIS.
MY...MY BACK-PACK?
BUT... WHO...?
THIS.
I ALREAD GOT IT

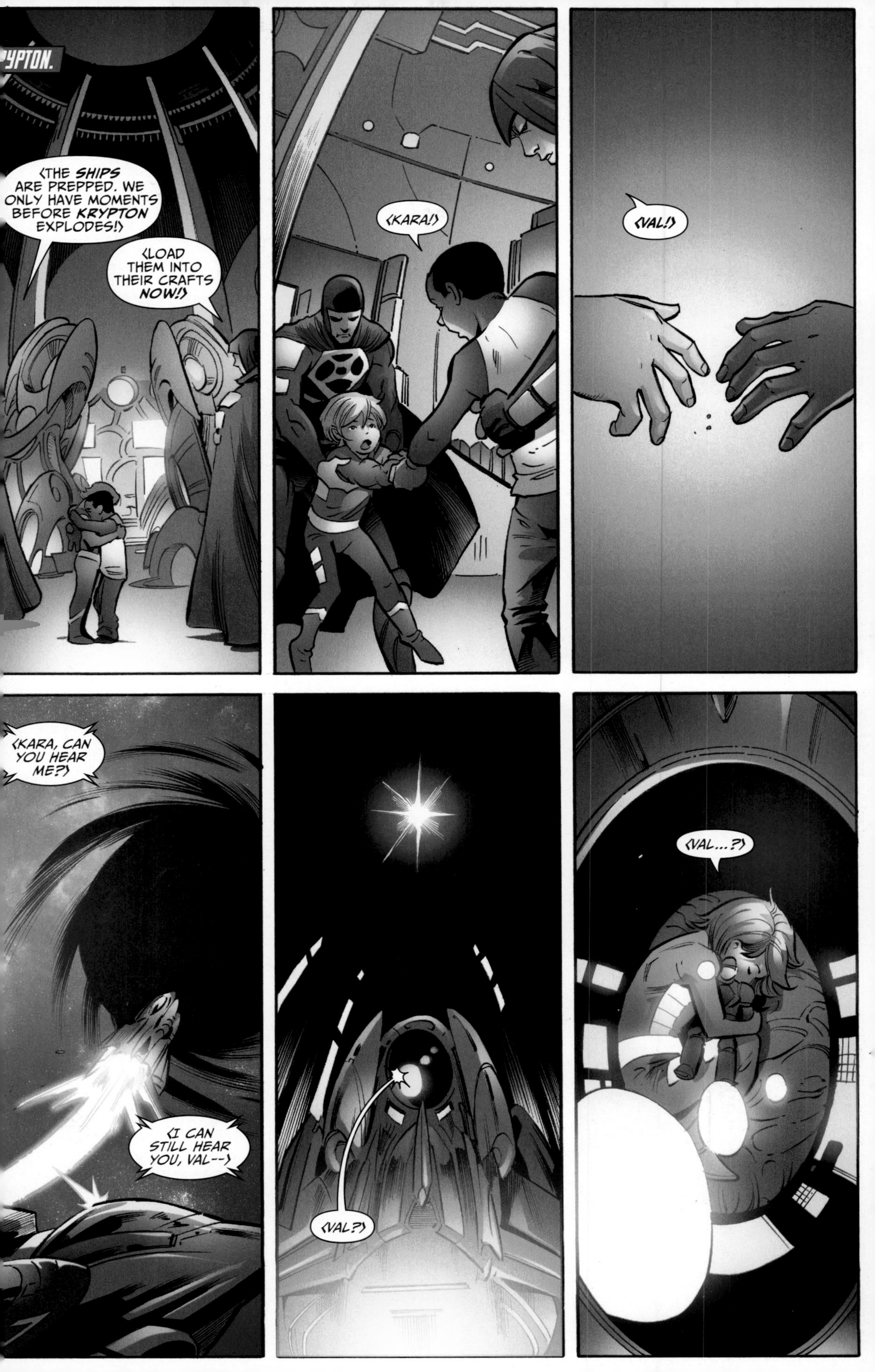
YPTON.
<THE SHIPS ARE PREPPED. WE ONLY HAVE MOMENTS BEFORE KRYPTON EXPLODES!>
<LOAD THEM INTO THEIR CRAFTS NOW!>
<KARA!>
<VAL!>
<KARA, CAN YOU HEAR ME?>
<I CAN STILL HEAR YOU, VAL-->
<VAL?>
<VAL...?>

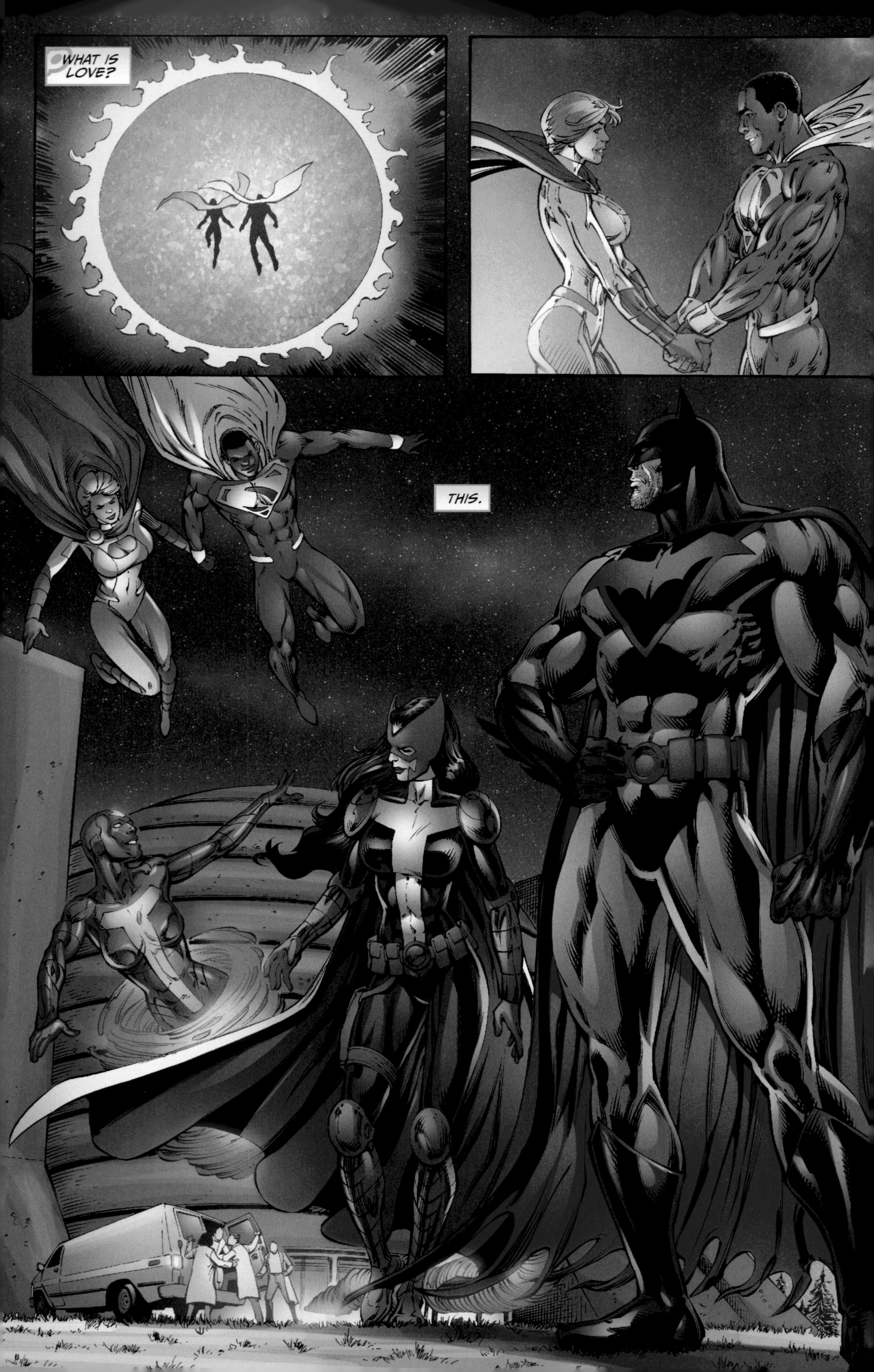
WHAT IS LOVE?
THIS.

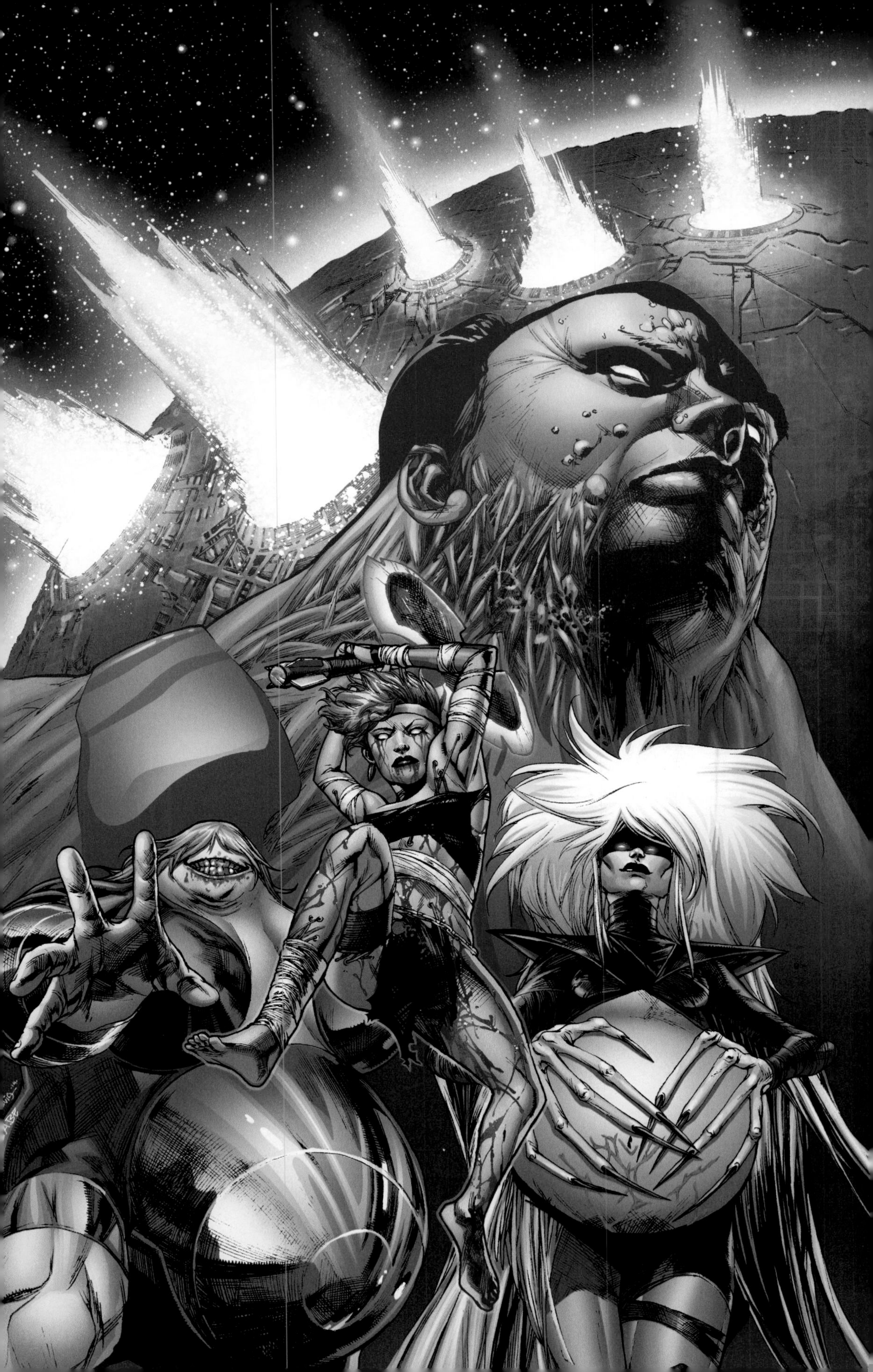

ORIGINS

TOM TAYLOR, MARGUERITE BENNETT story **MARGUERITE BENNETT** writer
ALISSON BORGES, ANDY SMITH, TREVOR SCOTT, JAVIER FERNANDEZ, DIOGENES NEVES, MARC DEERING artists
PETE PANTAZIS colorist **TAYLOR ESPOSITO** letterer cover by **STEPHEN SEGOVIA** and **GABE ELTAEB**

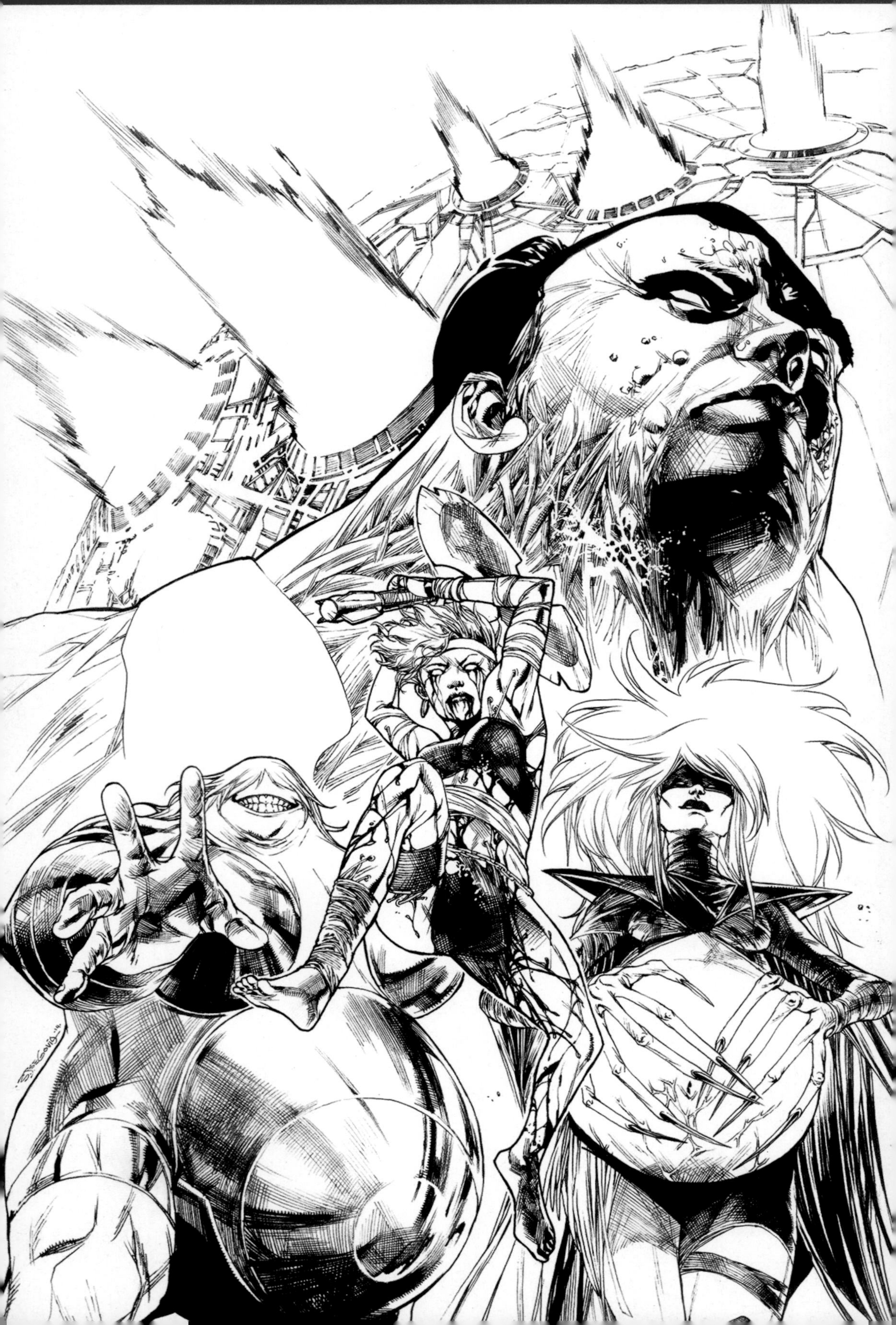

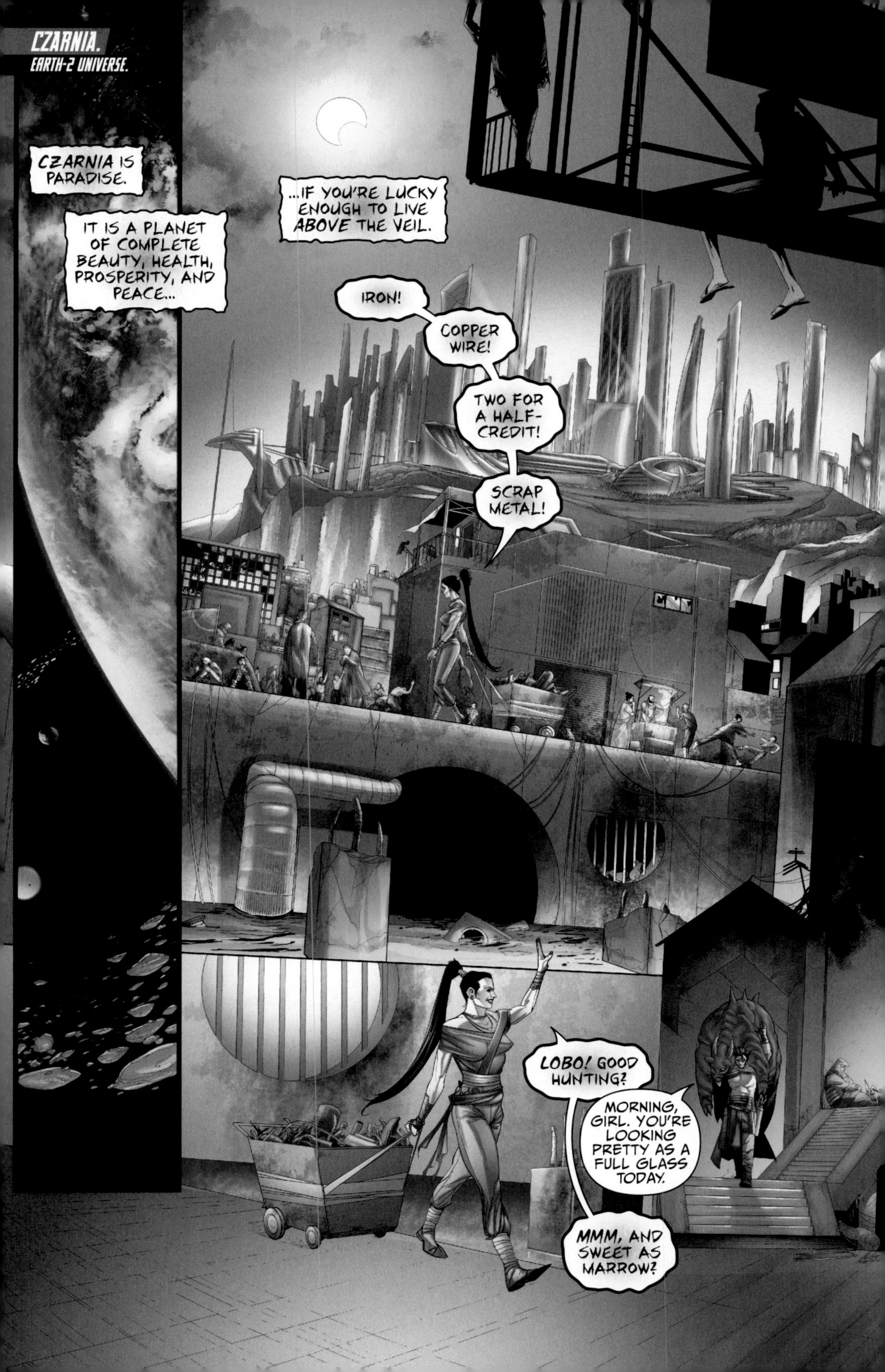
CZARNIA.
EARTH-2 UNIVERSE.
CZARNIA IS PARADISE.
IT IS A PLANET OF COMPLETE BEAUTY, HEALTH, PROSPERITY, AND PEACE...
...IF YOU'RE LUCKY ENOUGH TO LIVE ABOVE THE VEIL.
IRON!
COPPER WIRE!
TWO FOR A HALF-CREDIT!
SCRAP METAL!
LOBO! GOOD HUNTING?
MORNING, GIRL. YOU'RE LOOKING PRETTY AS A FULL GLASS TODAY.
MMM, AND SWEET AS MARROW?

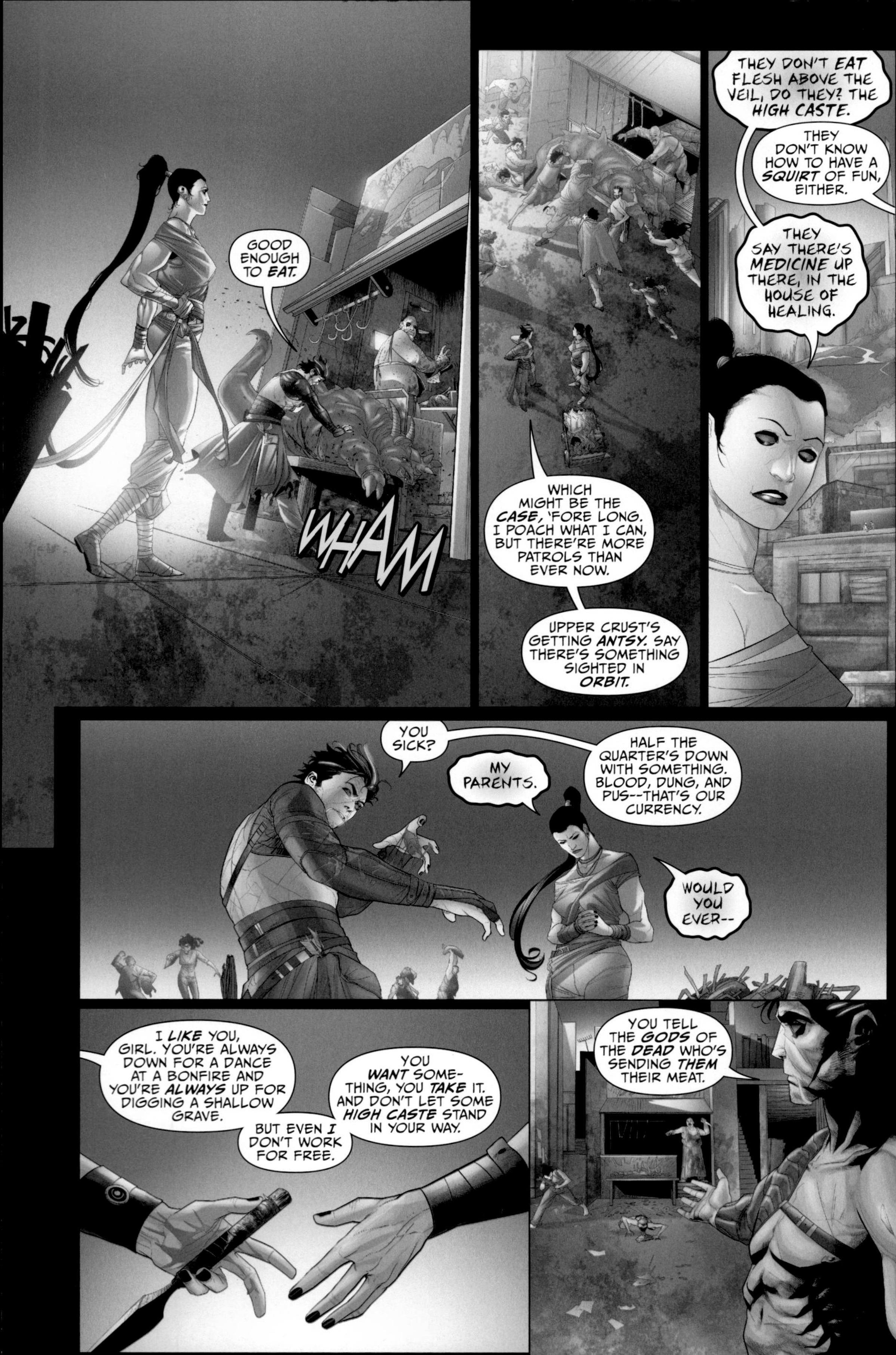
GOOD ENOUGH TO EAT.
WHAM
WHICH MIGHT BE THE CASE, 'FORE LONG. I POACH WHAT I CAN, BUT THERE'RE MORE PATROLS THAN EVER NOW.
UPPER CRUST'S GETTING ANTSY. SAY THERE'S SOMETHING SIGHTED IN ORBIT.
THEY DON'T EAT FLESH ABOVE THE VEIL, DO THEY? THE HIGH CASTE.
THEY DON'T KNOW HOW TO HAVE A SQUIRT OF FUN, EITHER.
THEY SAY THERE'S MEDICINE UP THERE, IN THE HOUSE OF HEALING.
YOU SICK?
MY PARENTS.
HALF THE QUARTER'S DOWN WITH SOMETHING. BLOOD, DUNG, AND PUS--THAT'S OUR CURRENCY.
WOULD YOU EVER--
I LIKE YOU, GIRL. YOU'RE ALWAYS DOWN FOR A DANCE AT A BONFIRE AND YOU'RE ALWAYS UP FOR DIGGING A SHALLOW GRAVE.
BUT EVEN I DON'T WORK FOR FREE.
YOU WANT SOME-THING, YOU TAKE IT. AND DON'T LET SOME HIGH CASTE STAND IN YOUR WAY.
YOU TELL THE GODS OF THE DEAD WHO'S SENDING THEM THEIR MEAT.

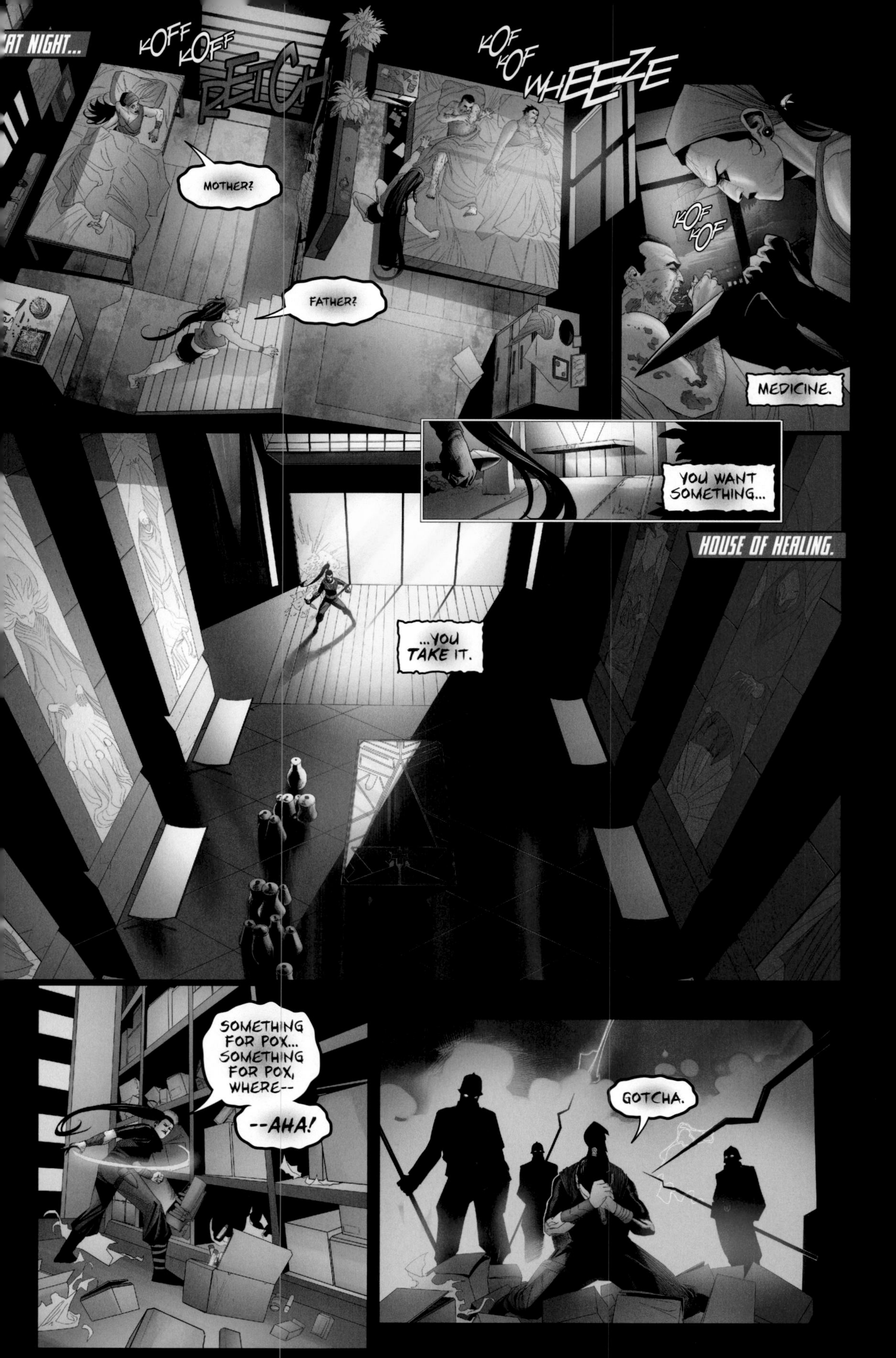
AT NIGHT...
KOFF KOFF RETCH
MOTHER?
FATHER?
KOF KOF WHEEZE
KOF KOF
MEDICINE.
YOU WANT SOMETHING...
HOUSE OF HEALING.
...YOU TAKE IT.
SOMETHING FOR POX... SOMETHING FOR POX, WHERE--
--AHA!
GOTCHA.

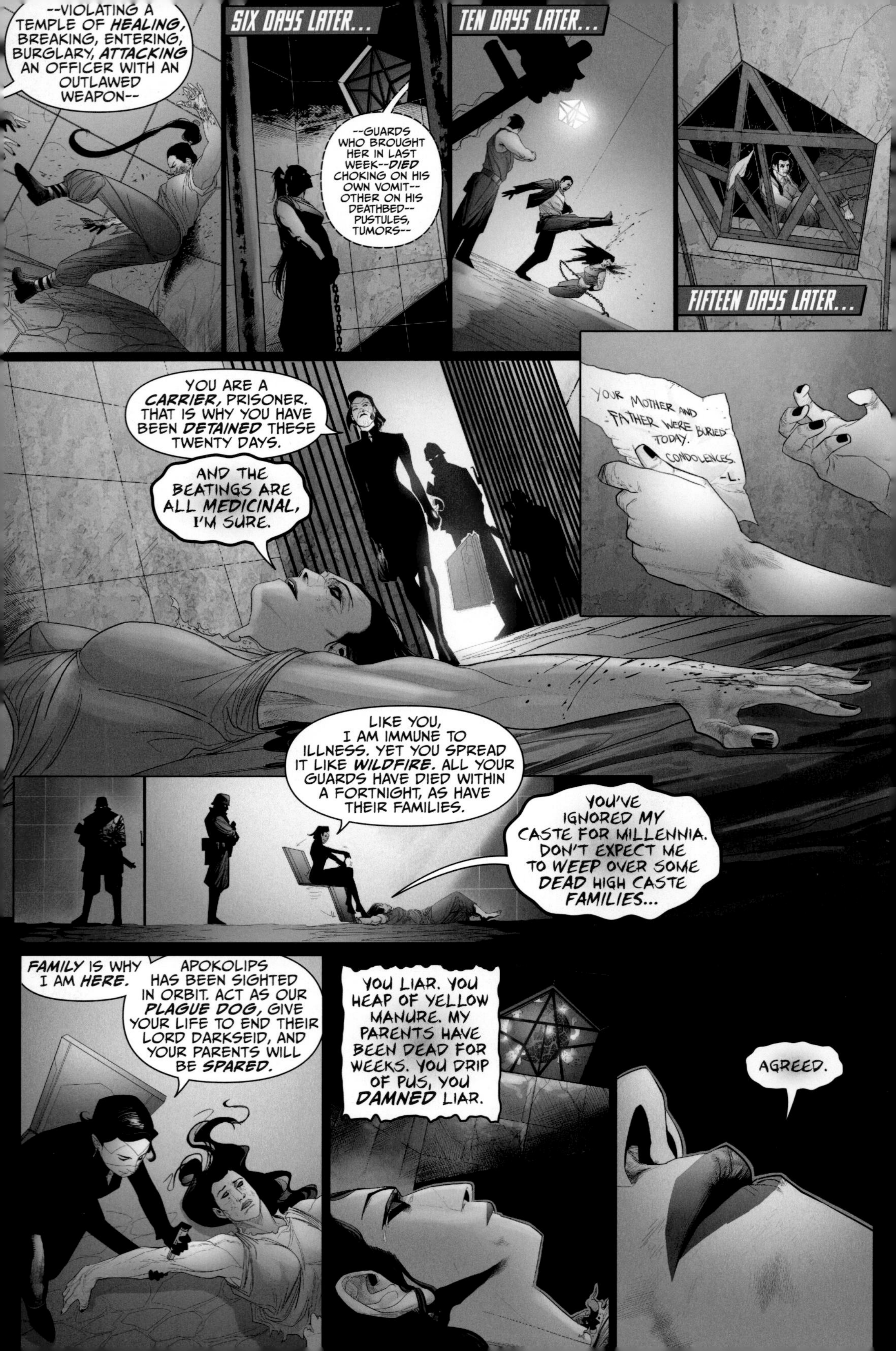
--VIOLATING A TEMPLE OF HEALING, BREAKING, ENTERING, BURGLARY, ATTACKING AN OFFICER WITH AN OUTLAWED WEAPON--
SIX DAYS LATER...
--GUARDS WHO BROUGHT HER IN LAST WEEK--DIED CHOKING ON HIS OWN VOMIT--OTHER ON HIS DEATHBED--PUSTULES, TUMORS--
TEN DAYS LATER...
FIFTEEN DAYS LATER...
YOU ARE A CARRIER, PRISONER. THAT IS WHY YOU HAVE BEEN DETAINED THESE TWENTY DAYS.
AND THE BEATINGS ARE ALL MEDICINAL, I'M SURE.
YOUR MOTHER AND FATHER WERE BURIED TODAY. CONDOLENCES. -L.
LIKE YOU, I AM IMMUNE TO ILLNESS. YET YOU SPREAD IT LIKE WILDFIRE. ALL YOUR GUARDS HAVE DIED WITHIN A FORTNIGHT, AS HAVE THEIR FAMILIES.
YOU'VE IGNORED MY CASTE FOR MILLENNIA. DON'T EXPECT ME TO WEEP OVER SOME DEAD HIGH CASTE FAMILIES...
FAMILY IS WHY I AM HERE.
APOKOLIPS HAS BEEN SIGHTED IN ORBIT. ACT AS OUR PLAGUE DOG, GIVE YOUR LIFE TO END THEIR LORD DARKSEID, AND YOUR PARENTS WILL BE SPARED.
YOU LIAR. YOU HEAP OF YELLOW MANURE. MY PARENTS HAVE BEEN DEAD FOR WEEKS. YOU DRIP OF PUS, YOU DAMNED LIAR.
AGREED.

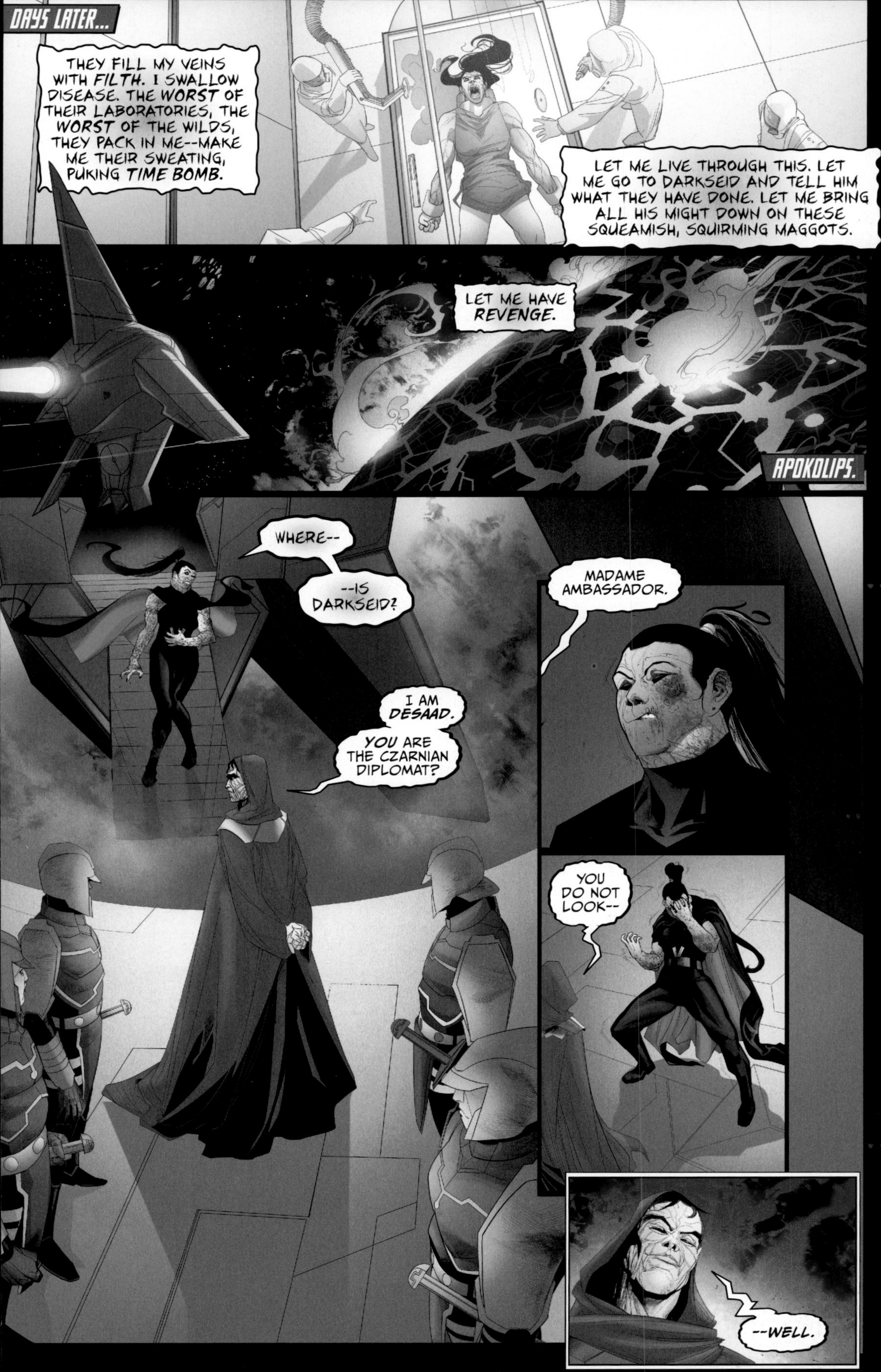
DAYS LATER...
THEY FILL MY VEINS WITH FILTH. I SWALLOW DISEASE. THE WORST OF THEIR LABORATORIES, THE WORST OF THE WILDS, THEY PACK IN ME--MAKE ME THEIR SWEATING, PUKING TIME BOMB.
LET ME LIVE THROUGH THIS. LET ME GO TO DARKSEID AND TELL HIM WHAT THEY HAVE DONE. LET ME BRING ALL HIS MIGHT DOWN ON THESE SQUEAMISH, SQUIRMING MAGGOTS.
LET ME HAVE REVENGE.
APOKOLIPS.
WHERE--
--IS DARKSEID?
I AM DESAAD.
YOU ARE THE CZARNIAN DIPLOMAT?
MADAME AMBASSADOR.
YOU DO NOT LOOK--
--WELL.

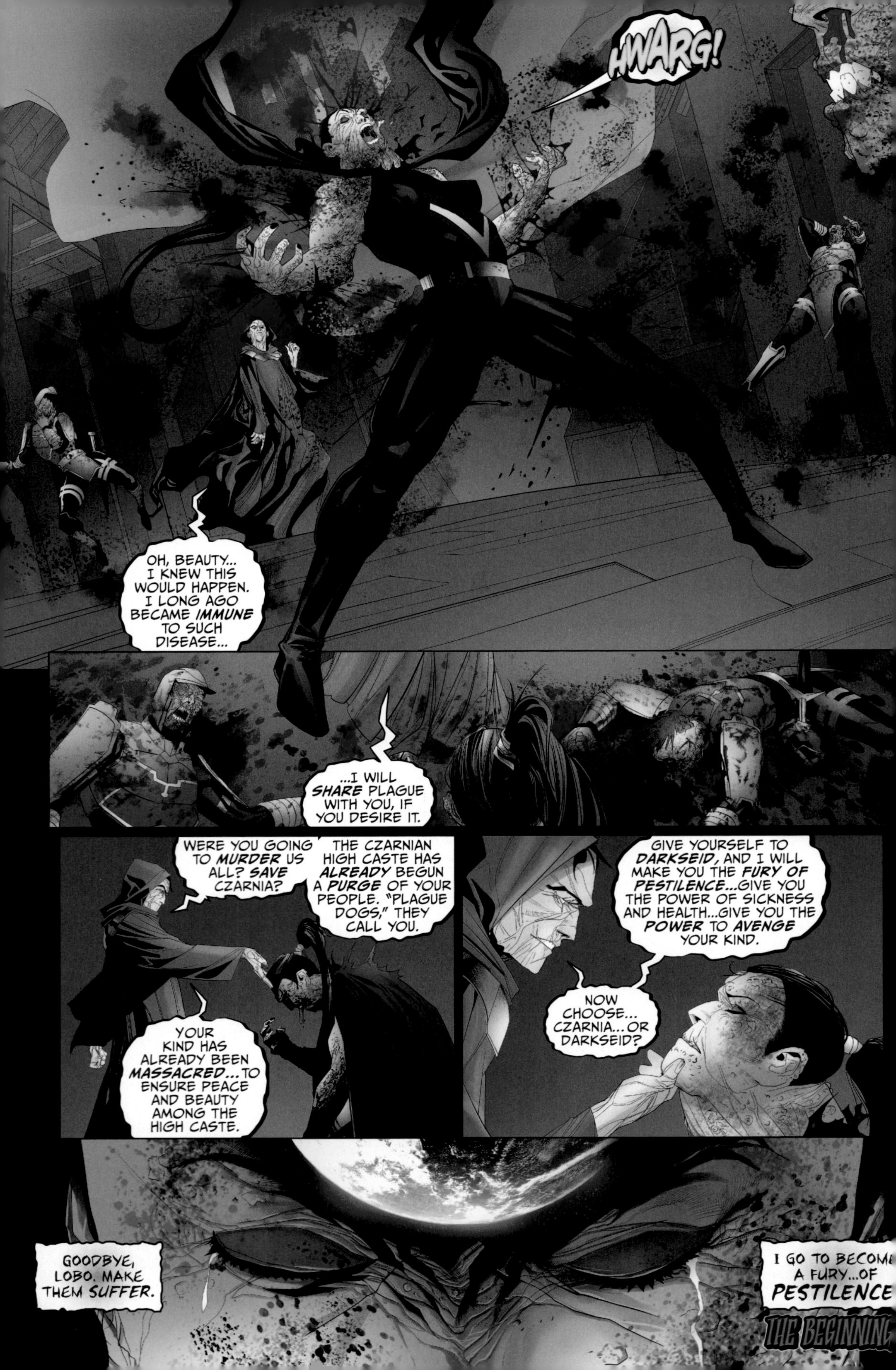
HWARG!
OH, BEAUTY... I KNEW THIS WOULD HAPPEN. I LONG AGO BECAME IMMUNE TO SUCH DISEASE...
...I WILL SHARE PLAGUE WITH YOU, IF YOU DESIRE IT.
WERE YOU GOING TO MURDER US ALL? SAVE CZARNIA?
THE CZARNIAN HIGH CASTE HAS ALREADY BEGUN A PURGE OF YOUR PEOPLE. "PLAGUE DOGS," THEY CALL YOU.
YOUR KIND HAS ALREADY BEEN MASSACRED...TO ENSURE PEACE AND BEAUTY AMONG THE HIGH CASTE.
GIVE YOURSELF TO DARKSEID, AND I WILL MAKE YOU THE FURY OF PESTILENCE...GIVE YOU THE POWER OF SICKNESS AND HEALTH...GIVE YOU THE POWER TO AVENGE YOUR KIND.
NOW CHOOSE... CZARNIA...OR DARKSEID?
GOODBYE, LOBO. MAKE THEM SUFFER.
I GO TO BECOME A FURY...OF PESTILENCE
THE BEGINNING

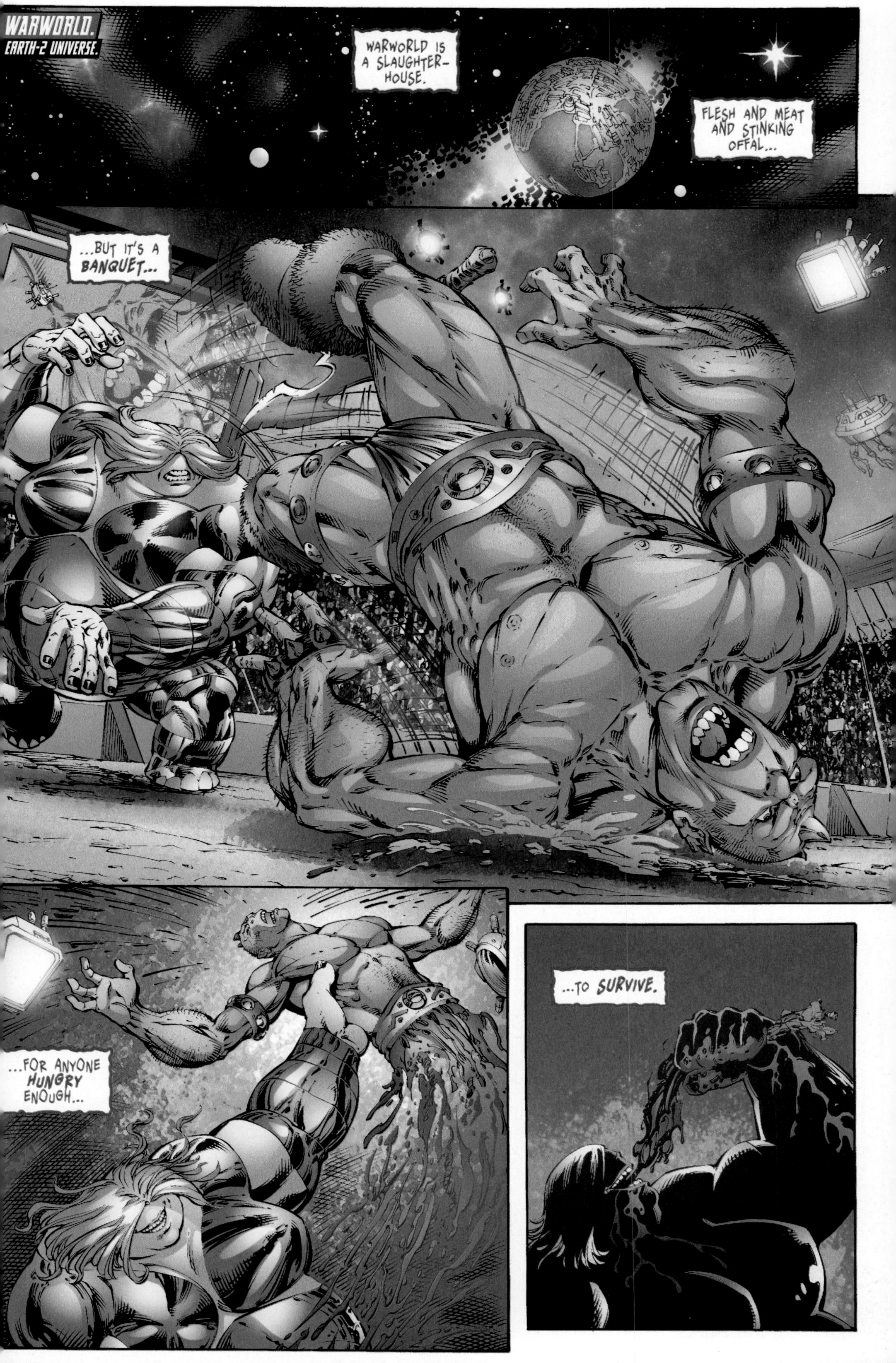
WARWORLD.
EARTH-2 UNIVERSE.
WARWORLD IS A SLAUGHTER-HOUSE.
FLESH AND MEAT AND STINKING OFFAL...
...BUT IT'S A BANQUET...
...FOR ANYONE HUNGRY ENOUGH...
...TO SURVIVE.

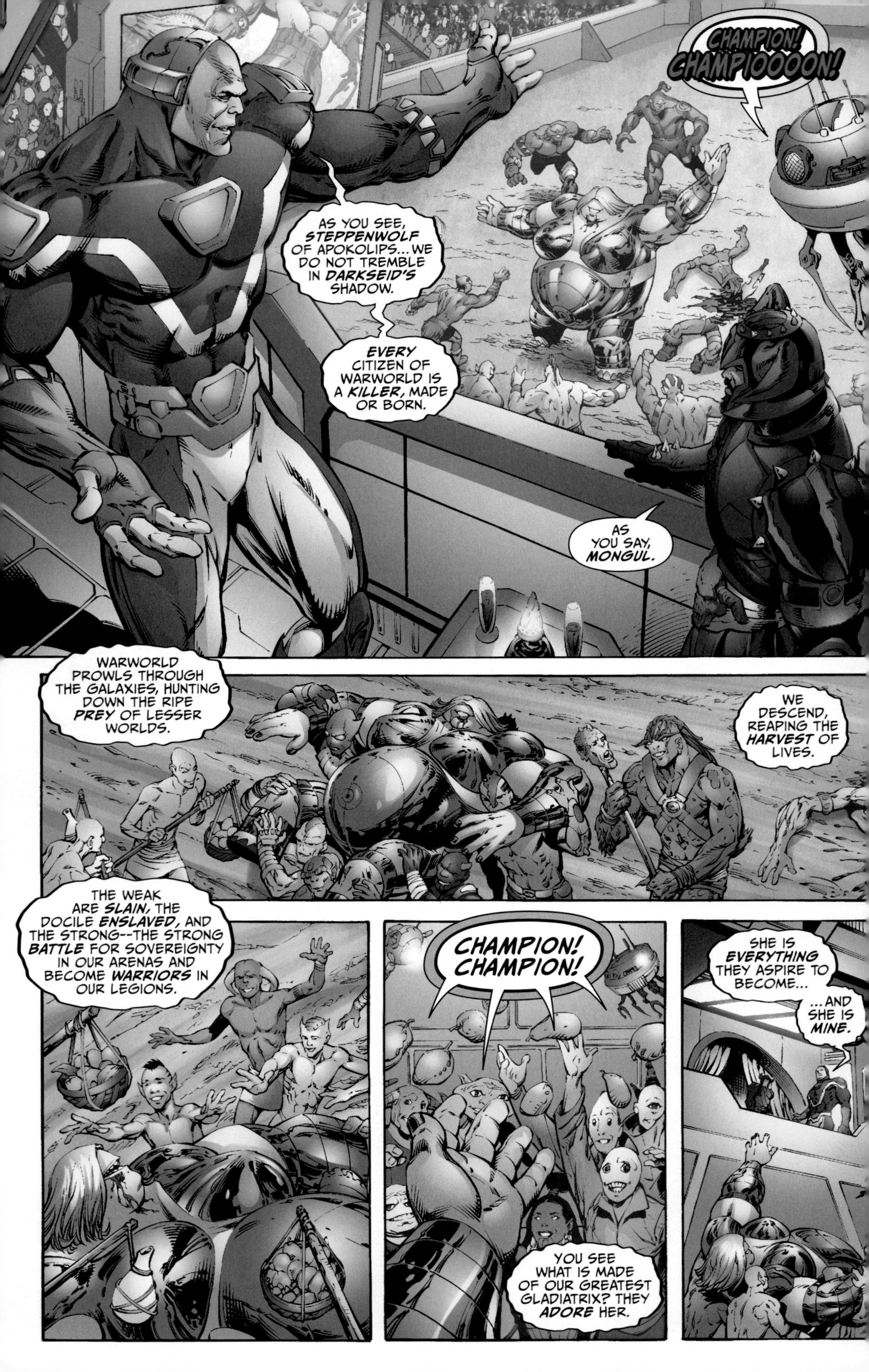
CHAMPION! CHAMPIOOOON!
AS YOU SEE, STEPPENWOLF OF APOKOLIPS... WE DO NOT TREMBLE IN DARKSEID'S SHADOW.
EVERY CITIZEN OF WARWORLD IS A KILLER, MADE OR BORN.
AS YOU SAY, MONGUL.
WARWORLD PROWLS THROUGH THE GALAXIES, HUNTING DOWN THE RIPE PREY OF LESSER WORLDS.
WE DESCEND, REAPING THE HARVEST OF LIVES.
THE WEAK ARE SLAIN, THE DOCILE ENSLAVED, AND THE STRONG--THE STRONG BATTLE FOR SOVEREIGNTY IN OUR ARENAS AND BECOME WARRIORS IN OUR LEGIONS.
CHAMPION! CHAMPION!
YOU SEE WHAT IS MADE OF OUR GREATEST GLADIATRIX? THEY ADORE HER.
SHE IS EVERYTHING THEY ASPIRE TO BECOME...
...AND SHE IS MINE.

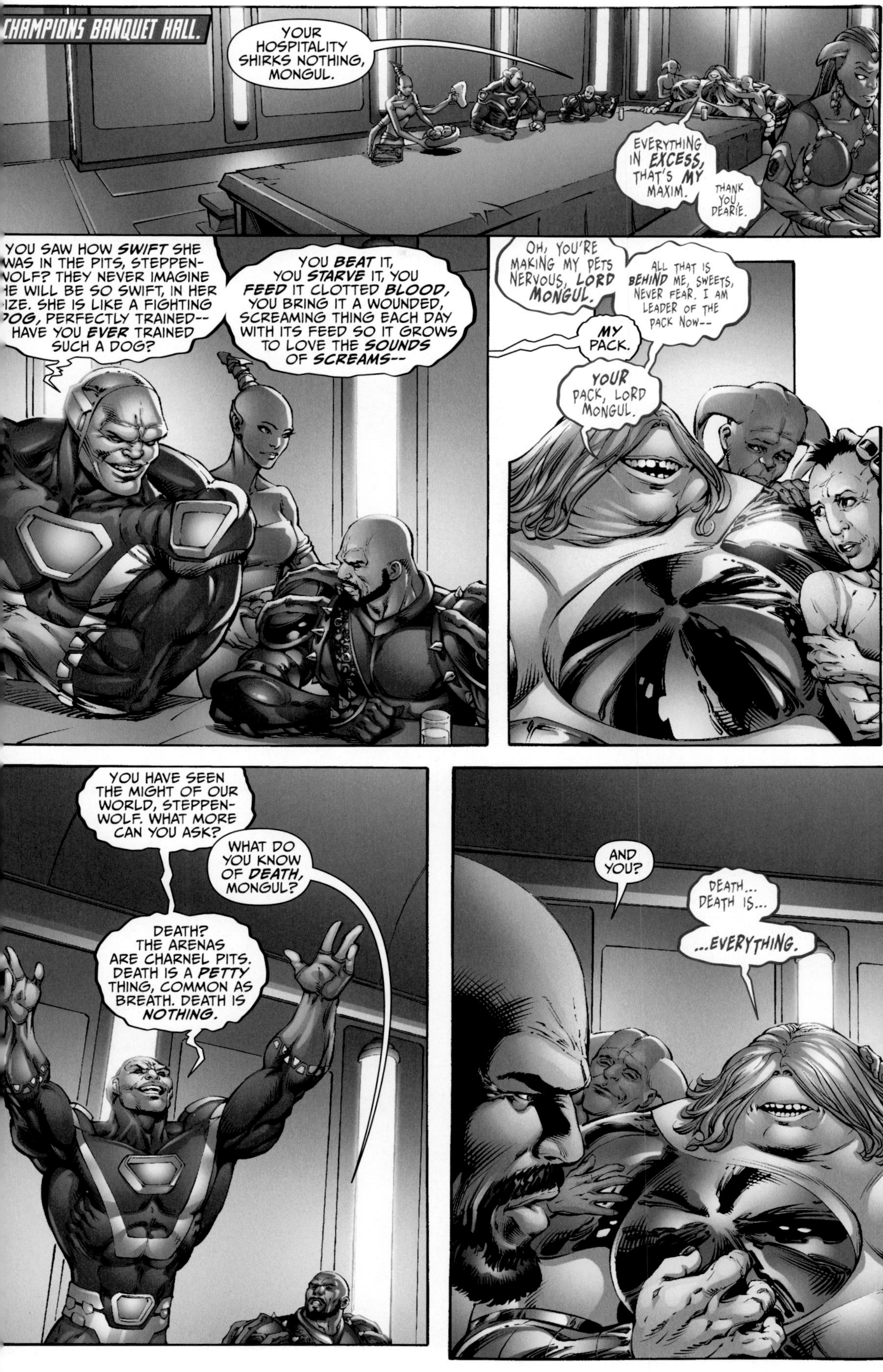
CHAMPIONS BANQUET HALL.
YOUR HOSPITALITY SHIRKS NOTHING, MONGUL.
EVERYTHING IN EXCESS, THAT'S MY MAXIM.
THANK YOU, DEARIE.
YOU SAW HOW SWIFT SHE WAS IN THE PITS, STEPPENWOLF? THEY NEVER IMAGINE SHE WILL BE SO SWIFT, IN HER SIZE. SHE IS LIKE A FIGHTING DOG, PERFECTLY TRAINED-- HAVE YOU EVER TRAINED SUCH A DOG?
YOU BEAT IT, YOU STARVE IT, YOU FEED IT CLOTTED BLOOD, YOU BRING IT A WOUNDED, SCREAMING THING EACH DAY WITH ITS FEED SO IT GROWS TO LOVE THE SOUNDS OF SCREAMS--
OH, YOU'RE MAKING MY PETS NERVOUS, LORD MONGUL.
ALL THAT IS BEHIND ME, SWEETS, NEVER FEAR. I AM LEADER OF THE PACK NOW--
MY PACK.
YOUR PACK, LORD MONGUL.
YOU HAVE SEEN THE MIGHT OF OUR WORLD, STEPPENWOLF. WHAT MORE CAN YOU ASK?
WHAT DO YOU KNOW OF DEATH, MONGUL?
DEATH? THE ARENAS ARE CHARNEL PITS. DEATH IS A PETTY THING, COMMON AS BREATH. DEATH IS NOTHING.
AND YOU?
DEATH... DEATH IS...
...EVERYTHING.

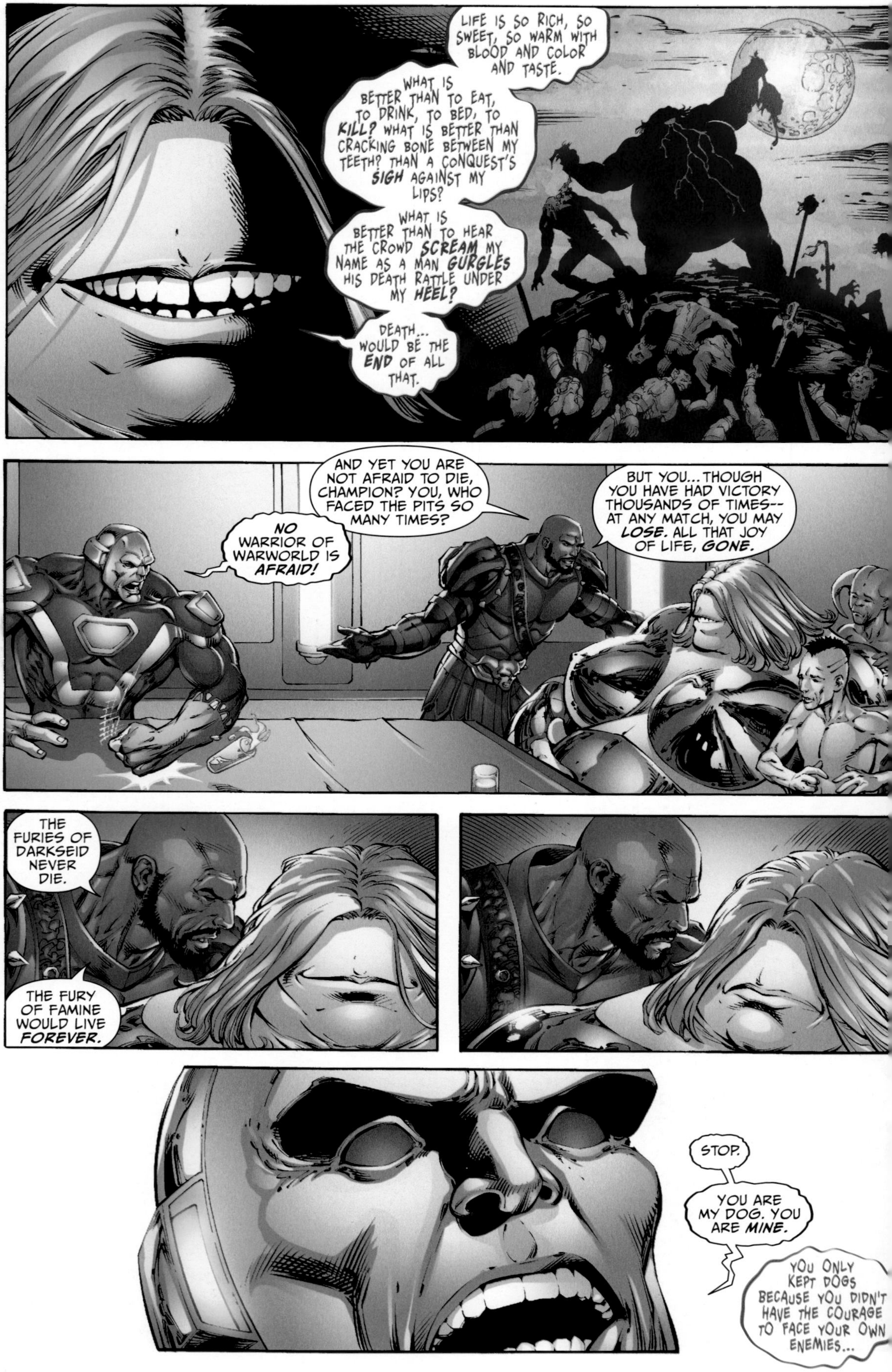
LIFE IS SO RICH, SO SWEET, SO WARM WITH BLOOD AND COLOR AND TASTE.
WHAT IS BETTER THAN TO EAT, TO DRINK, TO BED, TO KILL? WHAT IS BETTER THAN CRACKING BONE BETWEEN MY TEETH? THAN A CONQUEST'S SIGH AGAINST MY LIPS?
WHAT IS BETTER THAN TO HEAR THE CROWD SCREAM MY NAME AS A MAN GURGLES HIS DEATH RATTLE UNDER MY HEEL?
DEATH... WOULD BE THE END OF ALL THAT.
AND YET YOU ARE NOT AFRAID TO DIE, CHAMPION? YOU, WHO FACED THE PITS SO MANY TIMES?
NO WARRIOR OF WARWORLD IS AFRAID!
BUT YOU... THOUGH YOU HAVE HAD VICTORY THOUSANDS OF TIMES-- AT ANY MATCH, YOU MAY LOSE. ALL THAT JOY OF LIFE, GONE.
THE FURIES OF DARKSEID NEVER DIE.
THE FURY OF FAMINE WOULD LIVE FOREVER.
STOP.
YOU ARE MY DOG. YOU ARE MINE.
YOU ONLY KEPT DOGS BECAUSE YOU DIDN'T HAVE THE COURAGE TO FACE YOUR OWN ENEMIES...

...AND
BITE!

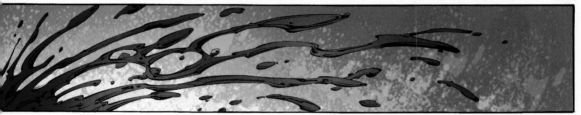

YOU BRED A *MAD DOG*. WHAT DID YOU *THINK* IT WOULD DO?

YOUR MAD DOG NOW. TAKE CARE, FOR YOU HAVE LEARNED HOW *FAITHFUL* SHE IS...

HOW AMBITIOUS...

YOUR *FURY* OF *FAMINE*...

...SO HUNGRY FOR LIFE.

THE BEGINNING...

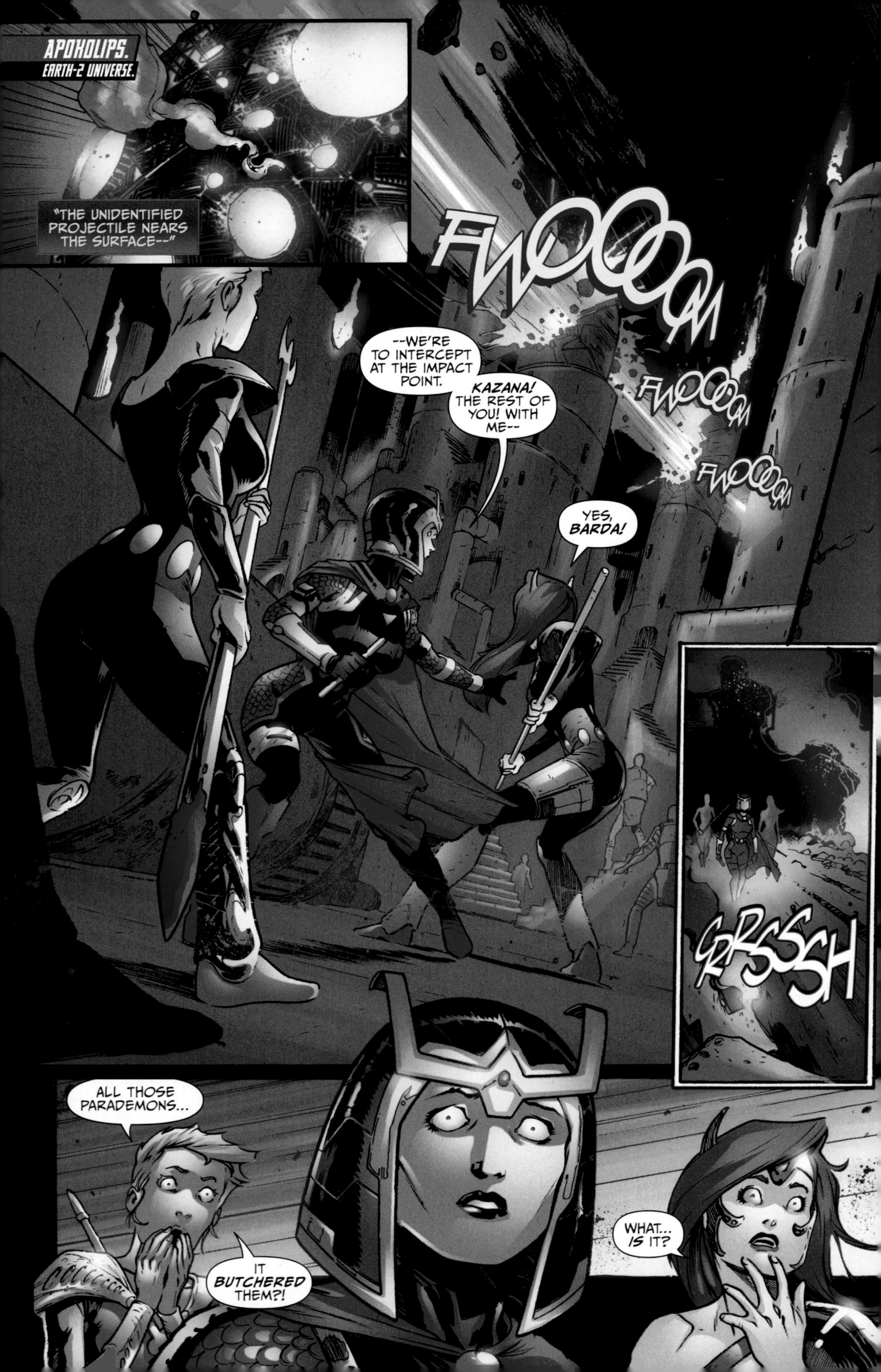
APOKOLIPS.
EARTH-2 UNIVERSE.
"THE UNIDENTIFIED PROJECTILE NEARS THE SURFACE--"
FWOOOOM
--WE'RE TO INTERCEPT AT THE IMPACT POINT.
KAZANA! THE REST OF YOU! WITH ME--
FWOOOOM
FWOOOOM
YES, BARDA!
CRRSSSH
ALL THOSE PARADEMONS...
IT BUTCHERED THEM?!
WHAT... IS IT?

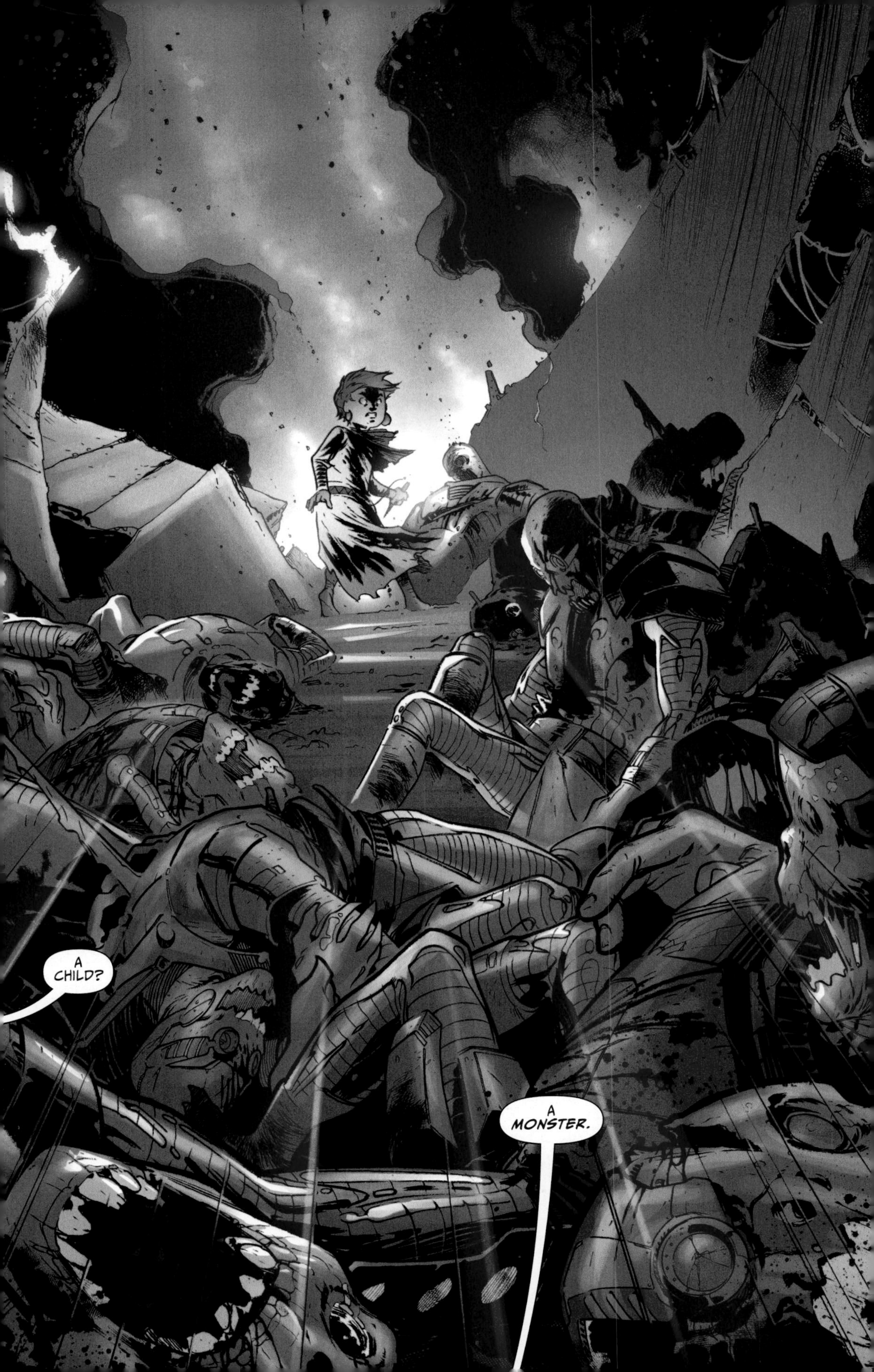
A CHILD?
A MONSTER.

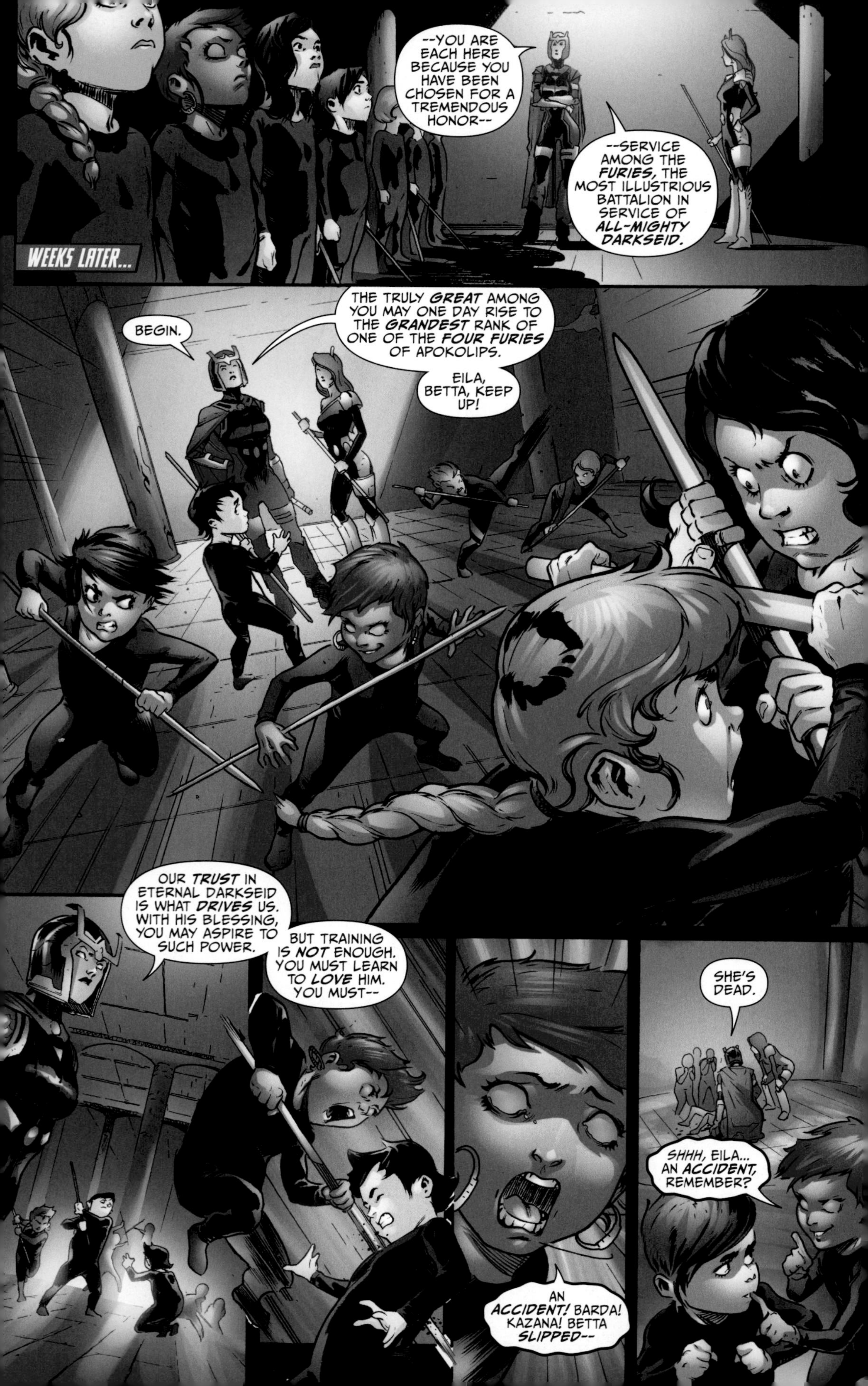

WEEKS LATER...
--YOU ARE EACH HERE BECAUSE YOU HAVE BEEN CHOSEN FOR A TREMENDOUS HONOR--
--SERVICE AMONG THE FURIES, THE MOST ILLUSTRIOUS BATTALION IN SERVICE OF ALL-MIGHTY DARKSEID.
BEGIN.
THE TRULY GREAT AMONG YOU MAY ONE DAY RISE TO THE GRANDEST RANK OF ONE OF THE FOUR FURIES OF APOKOLIPS.
EILA, BETTA, KEEP UP!
OUR TRUST IN ETERNAL DARKSEID IS WHAT DRIVES US. WITH HIS BLESSING, YOU MAY ASPIRE TO SUCH POWER.
BUT TRAINING IS NOT ENOUGH. YOU MUST LEARN TO LOVE HIM. YOU MUST--
AN ACCIDENT! BARDA! KAZANA! BETTA SLIPPED--
SHE'S DEAD.
SHHH, EILA... AN ACCIDENT, REMEMBER?

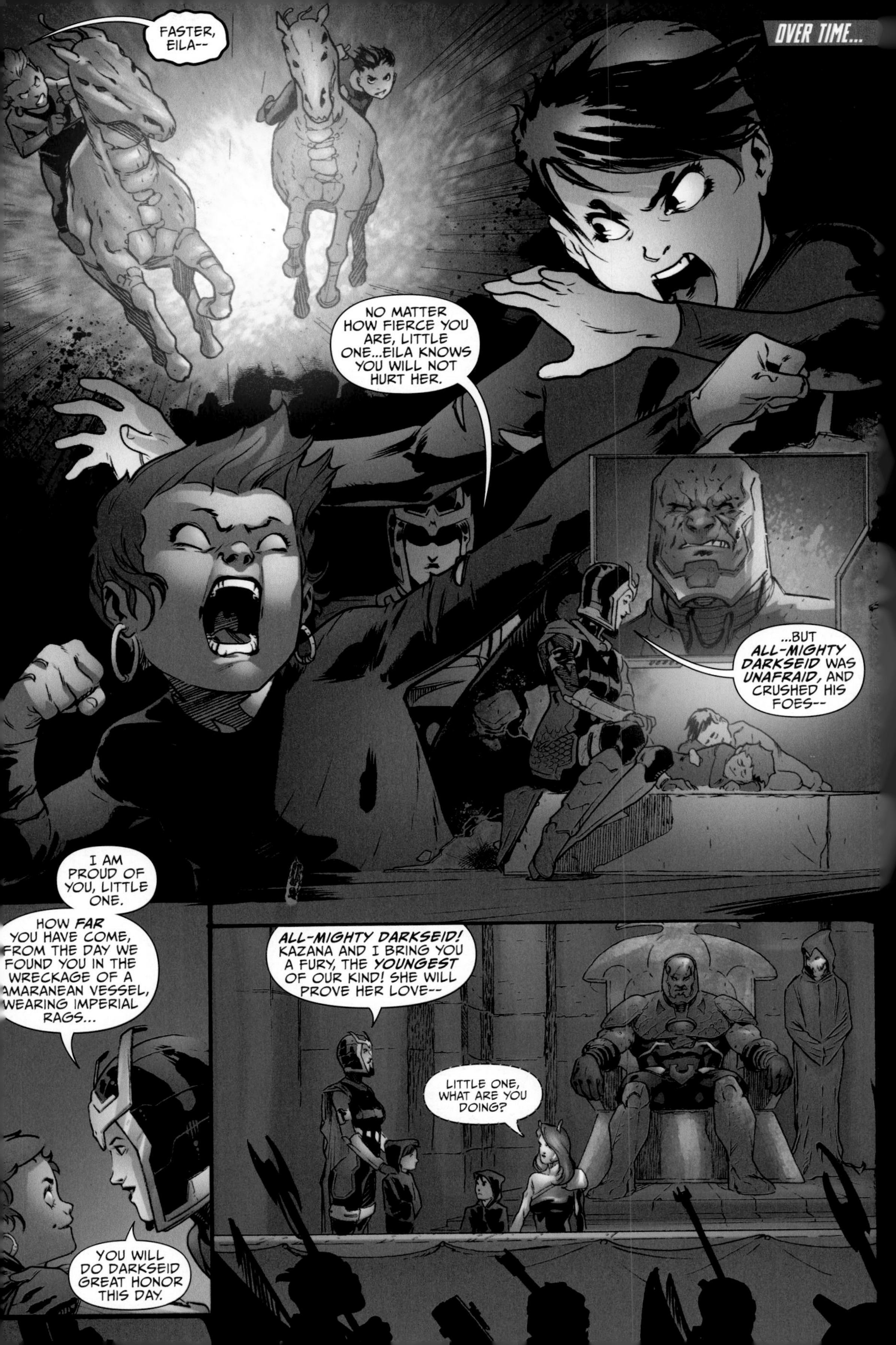
OVER TIME...
FASTER, EILA--
NO MATTER HOW FIERCE YOU ARE, LITTLE ONE...EILA KNOWS YOU WILL NOT HURT HER.
...BUT ALL-MIGHTY DARKSEID WAS UNAFRAID, AND CRUSHED HIS FOES--
I AM PROUD OF YOU, LITTLE ONE.
HOW FAR YOU HAVE COME, FROM THE DAY WE FOUND YOU IN THE WRECKAGE OF A AMARANEAN VESSEL, WEARING IMPERIAL RAGS...
YOU WILL DO DARKSEID GREAT HONOR THIS DAY.
ALL-MIGHTY DARKSEID! KAZANA AND I BRING YOU A FURY, THE YOUNGEST OF OUR KIND! SHE WILL PROVE HER LOVE--
LITTLE ONE, WHAT ARE YOU DOING?

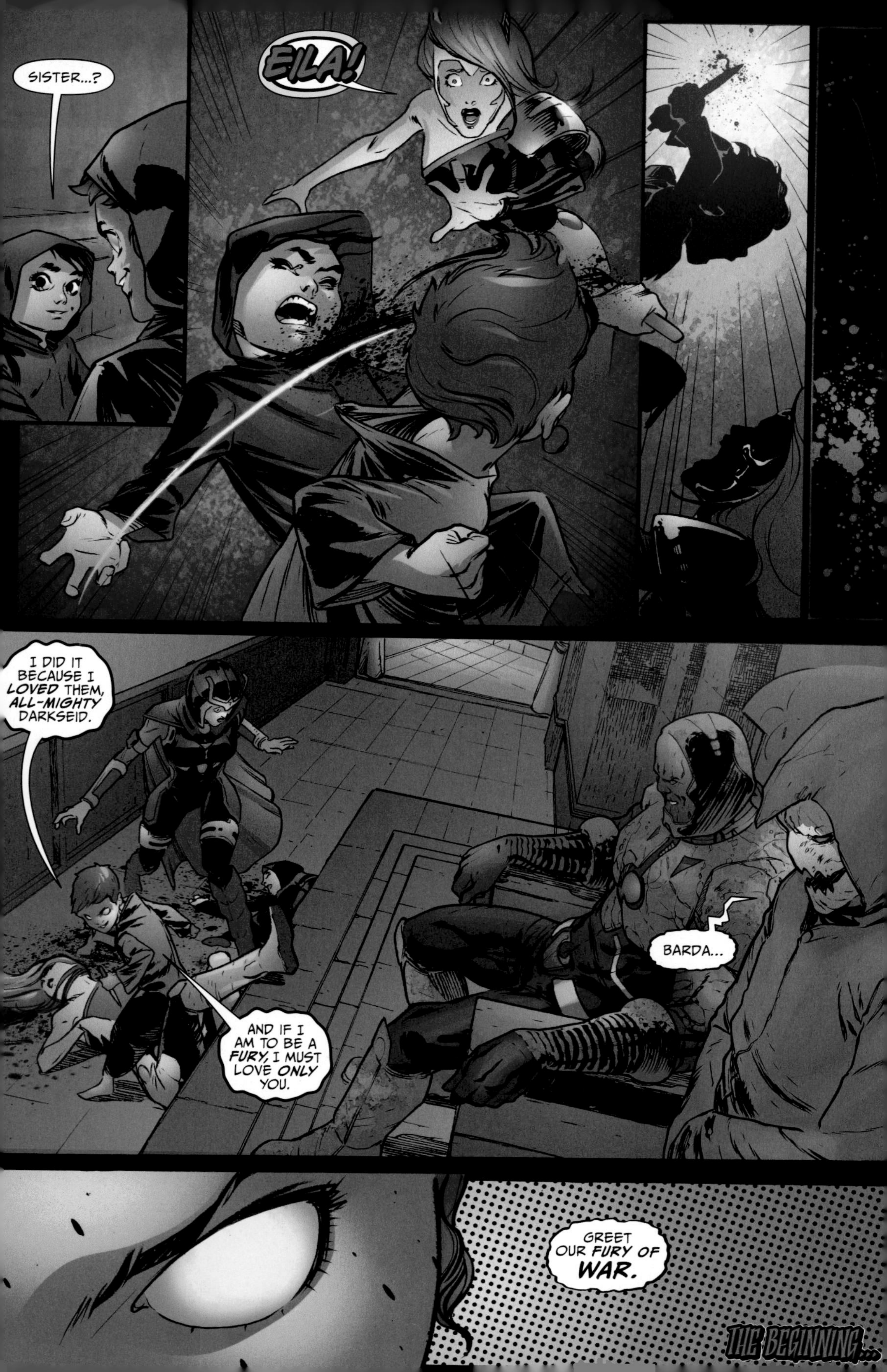
SISTER...?
EILA!
I DID IT BECAUSE I LOVED THEM, ALL-MIGHTY DARKSEID.
AND IF I AM TO BE A FURY, I MUST LOVE ONLY YOU.
BARDA...
GREET OUR FURY OF WAR.
THE BEGINNING...

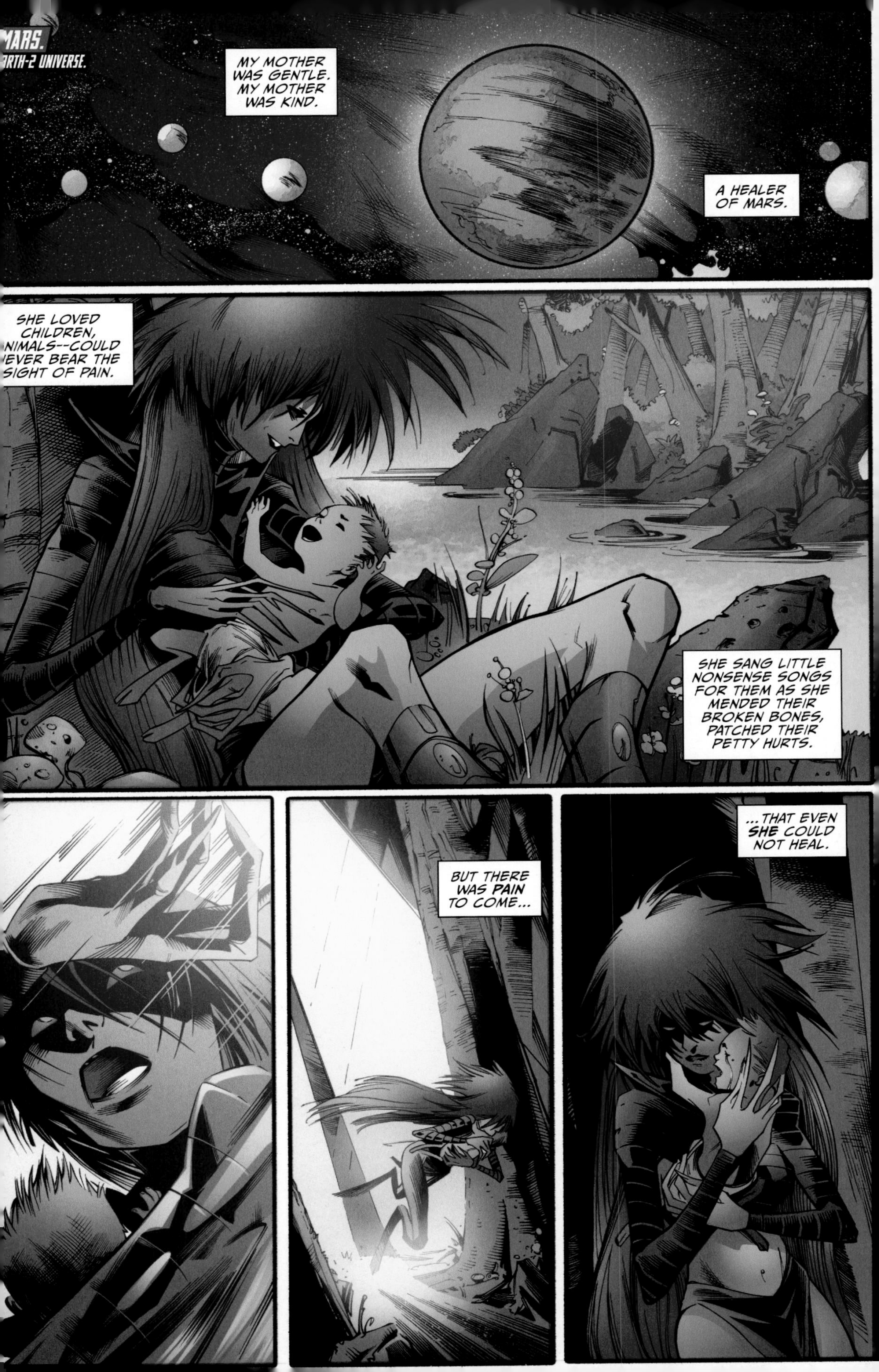
MARS.
ARTH-2 UNIVERSE.
MY MOTHER WAS GENTLE. MY MOTHER WAS KIND.
A HEALER OF MARS.
SHE LOVED CHILDREN, NIMALS--COULD NEVER BEAR THE SIGHT OF PAIN.
SHE SANG LITTLE NONSENSE SONGS FOR THEM AS SHE MENDED THEIR BROKEN BONES, PATCHED THEIR PETTY HURTS.
BUT THERE WAS PAIN TO COME...
...THAT EVEN SHE COULD NOT HEAL.

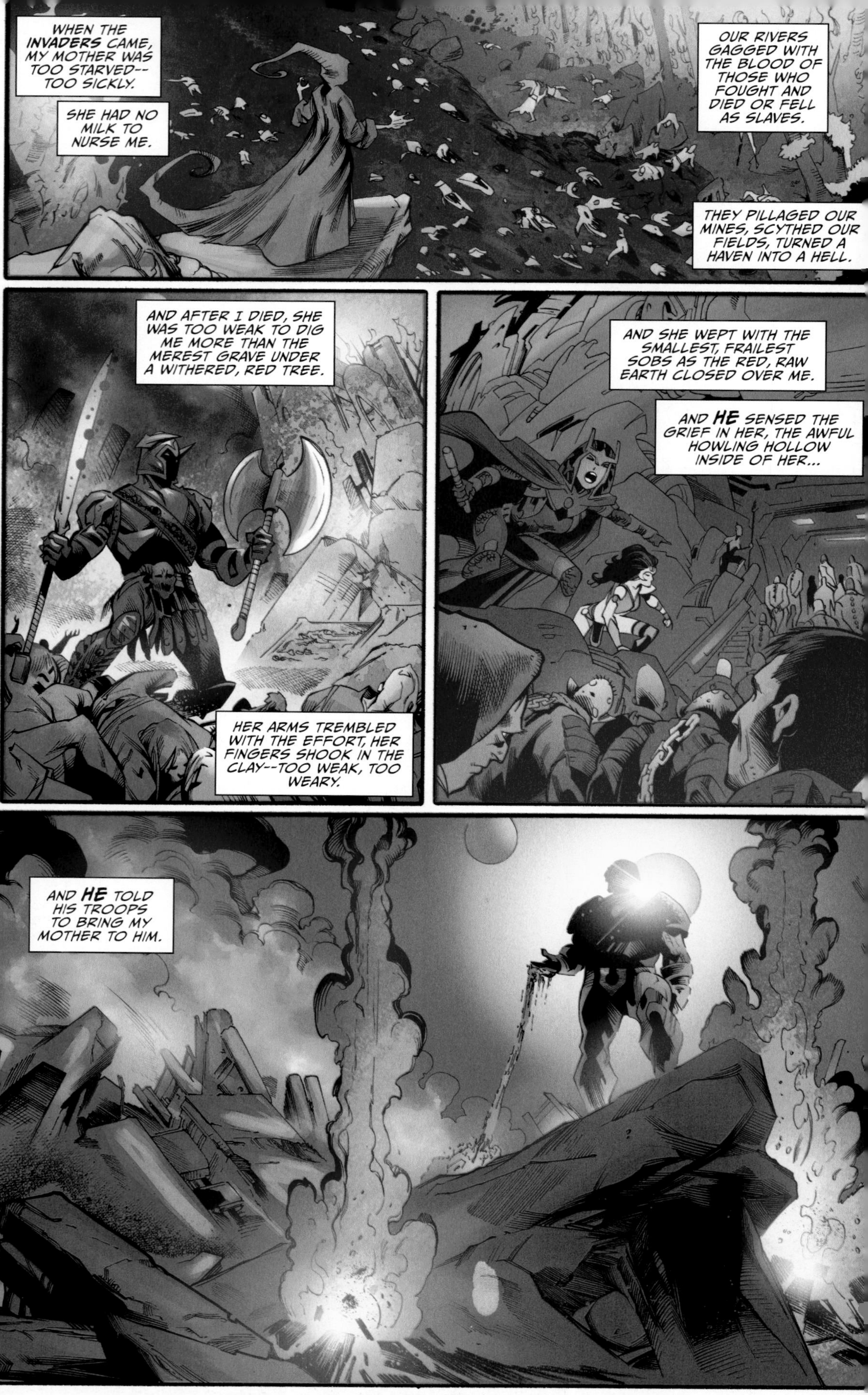

WHEN THE INVADERS CAME, MY MOTHER WAS TOO STARVED--TOO SICKLY.
SHE HAD NO MILK TO NURSE ME.
OUR RIVERS GAGGED WITH THE BLOOD OF THOSE WHO FOUGHT AND DIED OR FELL AS SLAVES.
THEY PILLAGED OUR MINES, SCYTHED OUR FIELDS, TURNED A HAVEN INTO A HELL.
AND AFTER I DIED, SHE WAS TOO WEAK TO DIG ME MORE THAN THE MEREST GRAVE UNDER A WITHERED, RED TREE.
HER ARMS TREMBLED WITH THE EFFORT, HER FINGERS SHOOK IN THE CLAY--TOO WEAK, TOO WEARY.
AND SHE WEPT WITH THE SMALLEST, FRAILEST SOBS AS THE RED, RAW EARTH CLOSED OVER ME.
AND HE SENSED THE GRIEF IN HER, THE AWFUL HOWLING HOLLOW INSIDE OF HER...
AND HE TOLD HIS TROOPS TO BRING MY MOTHER TO HIM.

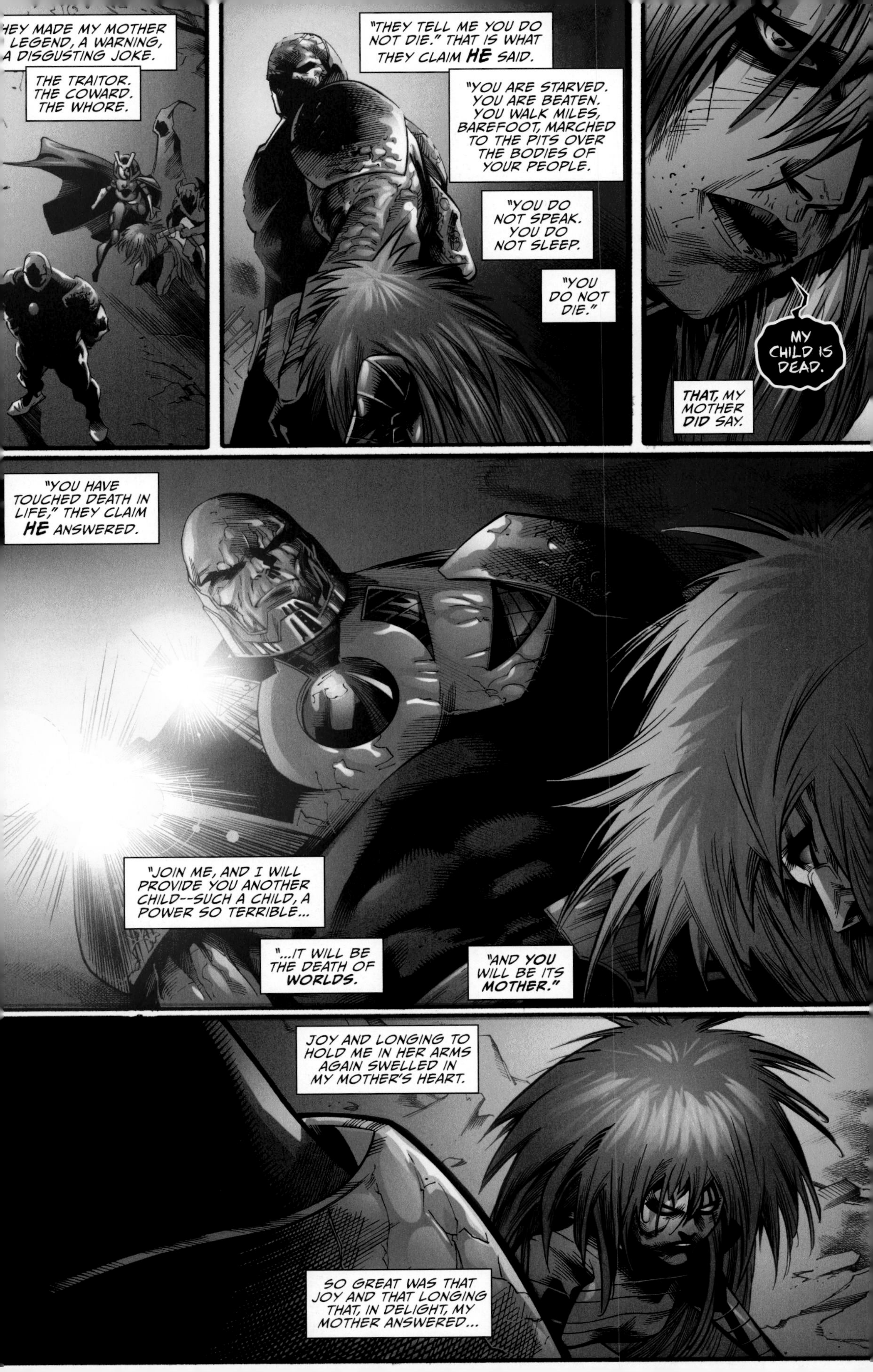

HEY MADE MY MOTHER
LEGEND, A WARNING,
A DISGUSTING JOKE.
THE TRAITOR. THE COWARD. THE WHORE.
"THEY TELL ME YOU DO NOT DIE." THAT IS WHAT THEY CLAIM HE SAID.
"YOU ARE STARVED. YOU ARE BEATEN. YOU WALK MILES, BAREFOOT, MARCHED TO THE PITS OVER THE BODIES OF YOUR PEOPLE.
"YOU DO NOT SPEAK. YOU DO NOT SLEEP.
"YOU DO NOT DIE."
MY CHILD IS DEAD.
THAT, MY MOTHER DID SAY.
"YOU HAVE TOUCHED DEATH IN LIFE," THEY CLAIM HE ANSWERED.
"JOIN ME, AND I WILL PROVIDE YOU ANOTHER CHILD--SUCH A CHILD, A POWER SO TERRIBLE...
"...IT WILL BE THE DEATH OF WORLDS.
"AND YOU WILL BE ITS MOTHER."
JOY AND LONGING TO HOLD ME IN HER ARMS AGAIN SWELLED IN MY MOTHER'S HEART.
SO GREAT WAS THAT JOY AND THAT LONGING THAT, IN DELIGHT, MY MOTHER ANSWERED...

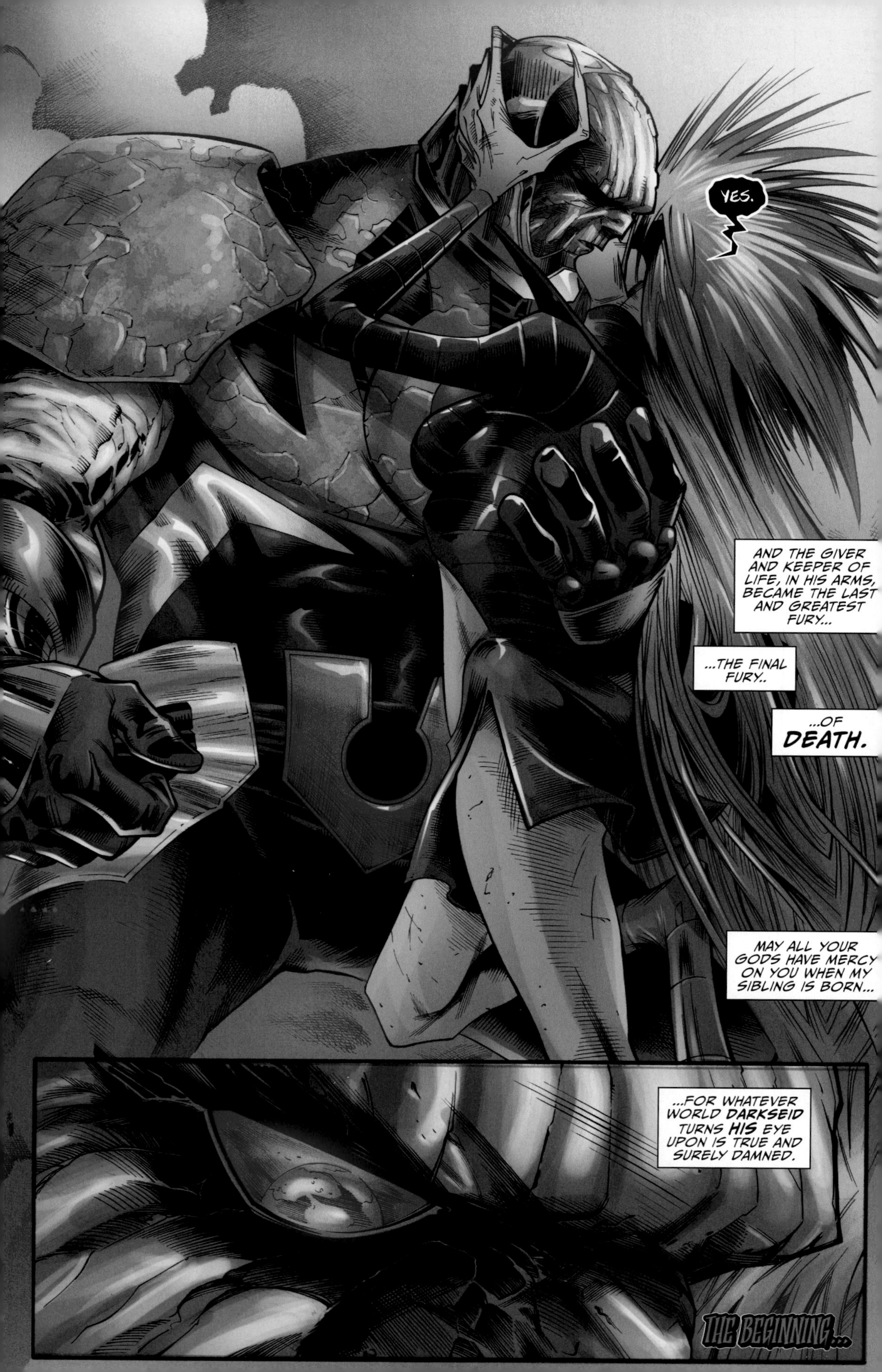
YES.
AND THE GIVER AND KEEPER OF LIFE, IN HIS ARMS, BECAME THE LAST AND GREATEST FURY...
...THE FINAL FURY..
...OF DEATH.
MAY ALL YOUR GODS HAVE MERCY ON YOU WHEN MY SIBLING IS BORN...
...FOR WHATEVER WORLD DARKSEID TURNS HIS EYE UPON IS TRUE AND SURELY DAMNED.
THE BEGINNING...

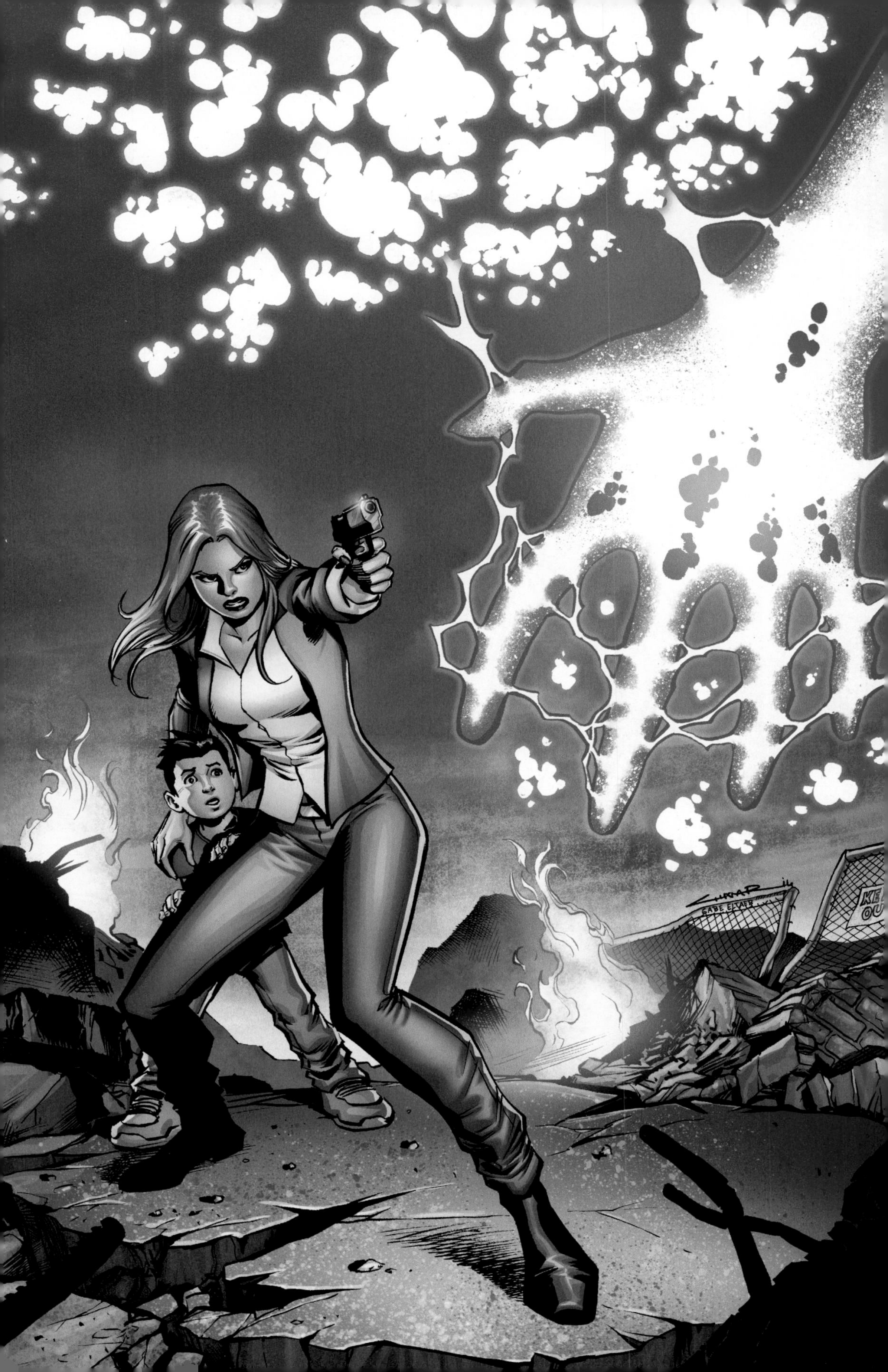
GABE ELTAEB

FLAGITIOUS

MARGUERITE BENNETT, MIKE JOHNSON writers ANDY SMITH penciller TREVOR SCOTT inker
PETER PANTAZIS, MATT YACKEY, ANDREW DALHOUSE colorists CARLOS M. MANGUAL letterer cover by YILDIRAY CINAR and GABE ELTAE

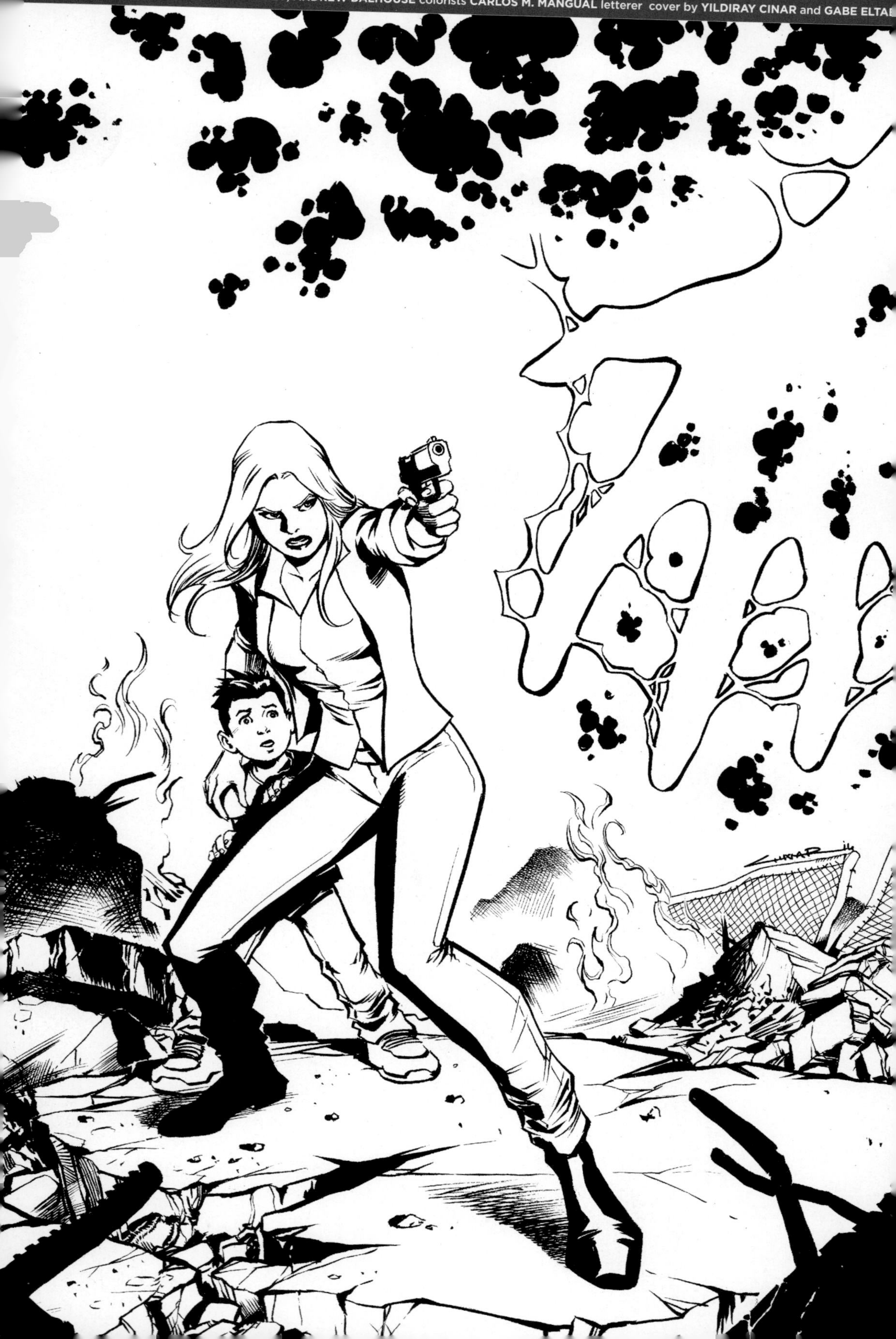

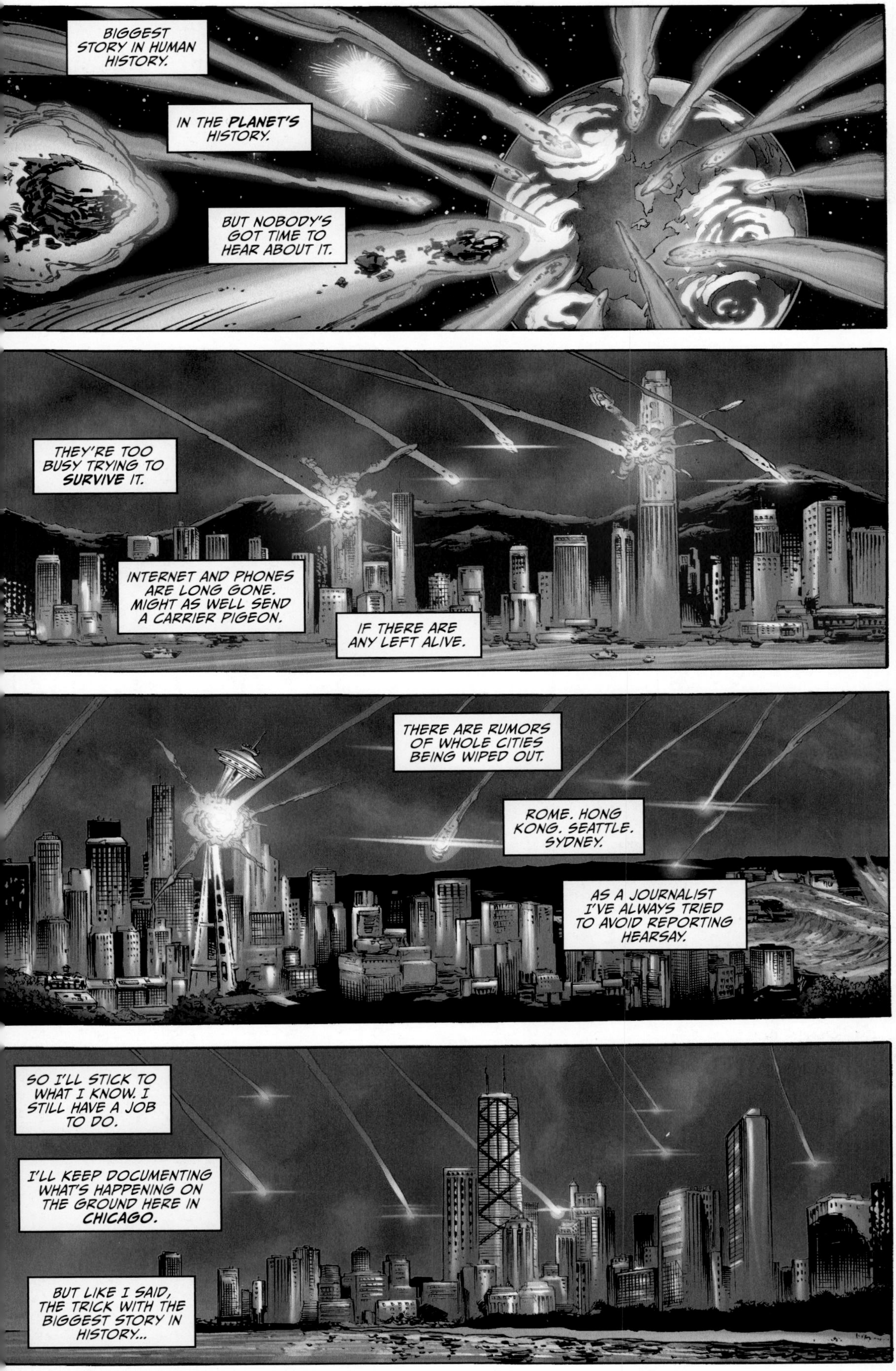
BIGGEST STORY IN HUMAN HISTORY.
IN THE **PLANET'S** HISTORY.
BUT NOBODY'S GOT TIME TO HEAR ABOUT IT.
THEY'RE TOO BUSY TRYING TO **SURVIVE** IT.
INTERNET AND PHONES ARE LONG GONE. MIGHT AS WELL SEND A CARRIER PIGEON.
IF THERE ARE ANY LEFT ALIVE.
THERE ARE RUMORS OF WHOLE CITIES BEING WIPED OUT.
ROME. HONG KONG. SEATTLE. SYDNEY.
AS A JOURNALIST I'VE ALWAYS TRIED TO AVOID REPORTING HEARSAY.
SO I'LL STICK TO WHAT I KNOW. I STILL HAVE A JOB TO DO.
I'LL KEEP DOCUMENTING WHAT'S HAPPENING ON THE GROUND HERE IN **CHICAGO.**
BUT LIKE I SAID, THE TRICK WITH THE BIGGEST STORY IN HISTORY...

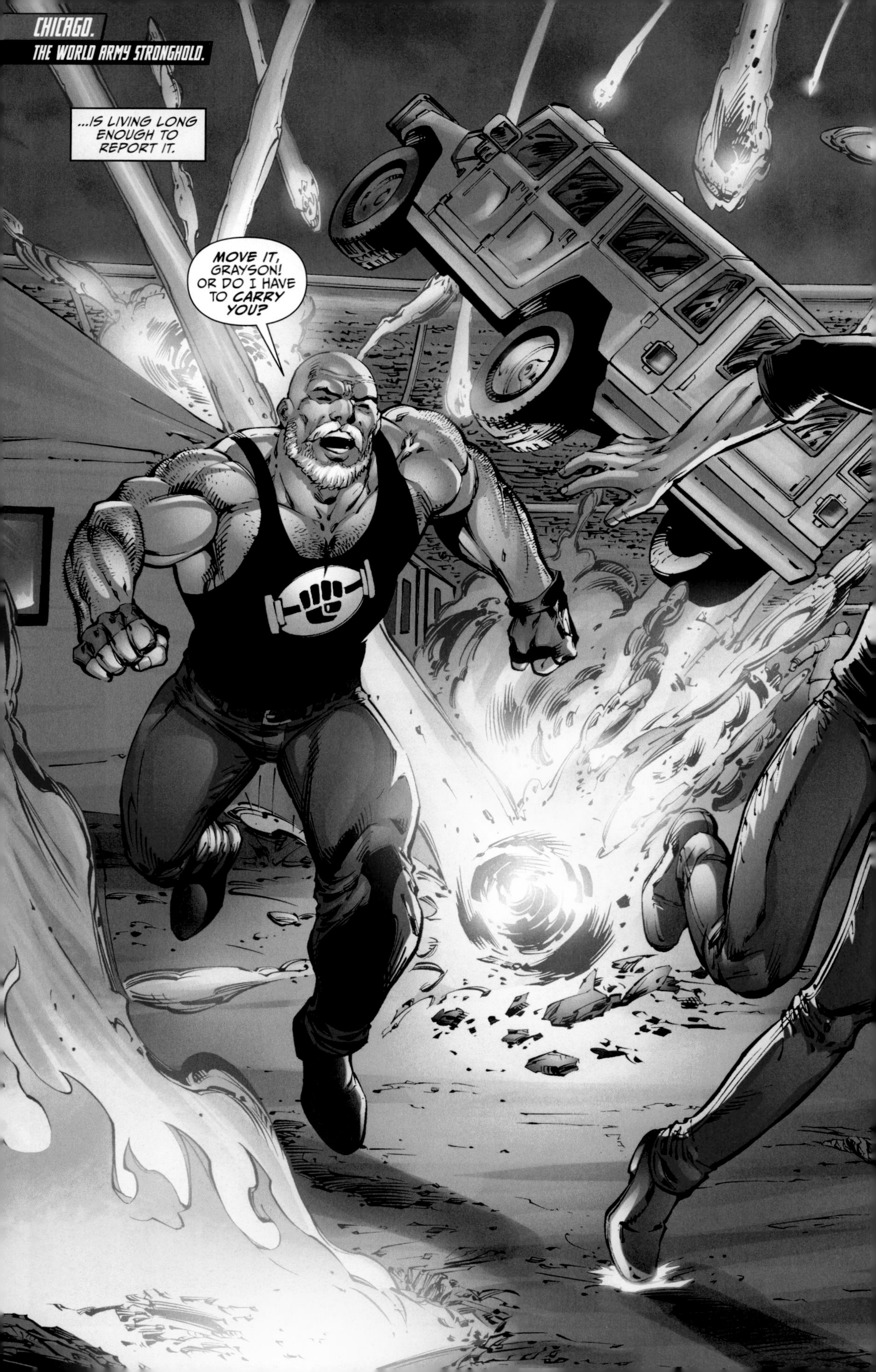
CHICAGO.
THE WORLD ARMY STRONGHOLD.
...IS LIVING LONG ENOUGH TO REPORT IT.
MOVE IT, GRAYSON! OR DO I HAVE TO CARRY YOU?

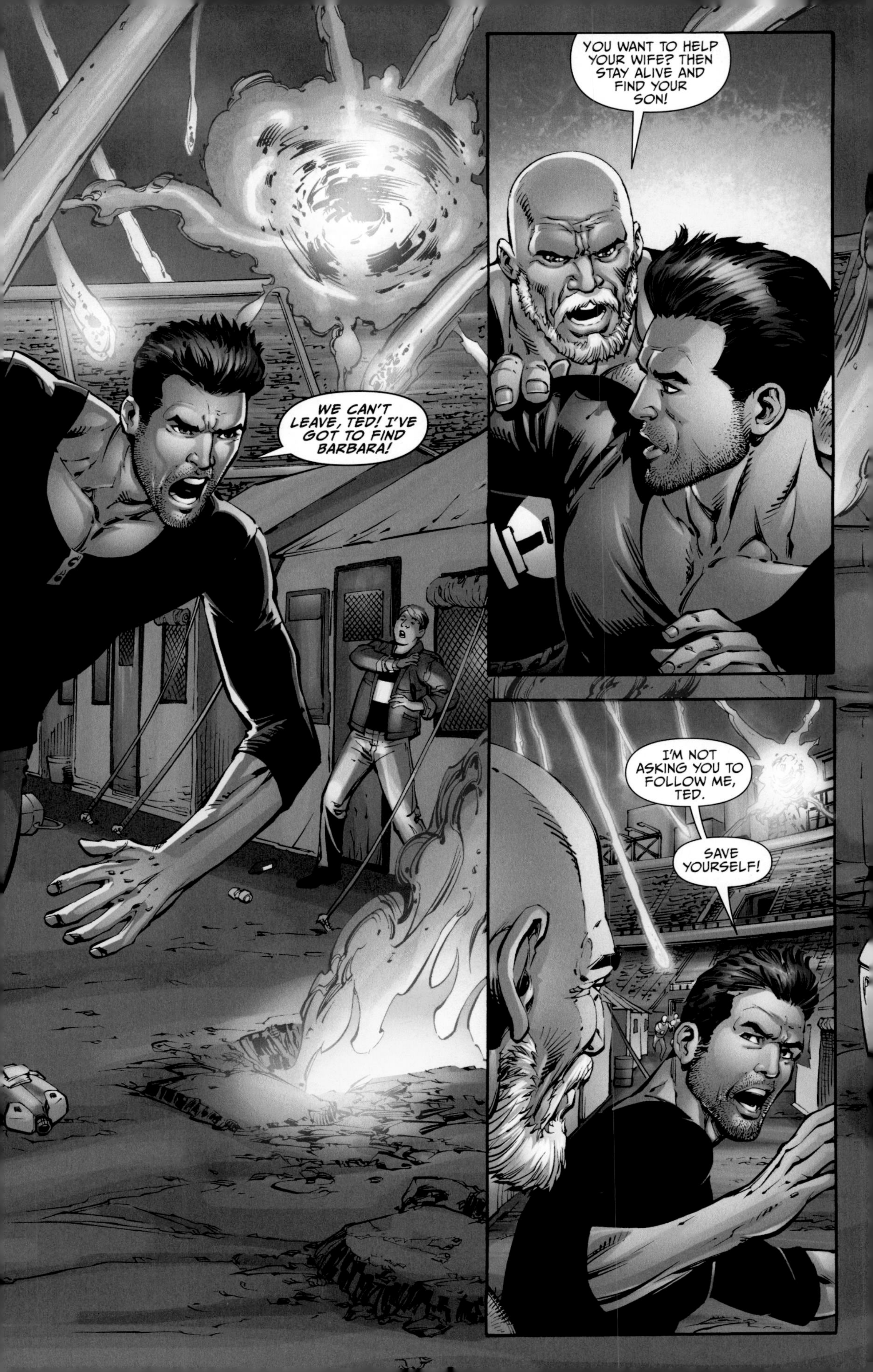
WE CAN'T LEAVE, TED! I'VE GOT TO FIND BARBARA!
YOU WANT TO HELP YOUR WIFE? THEN STAY ALIVE AND FIND YOUR SON!
I'M NOT ASKING YOU TO FOLLOW ME, TED.
SAVE YOURSELF!

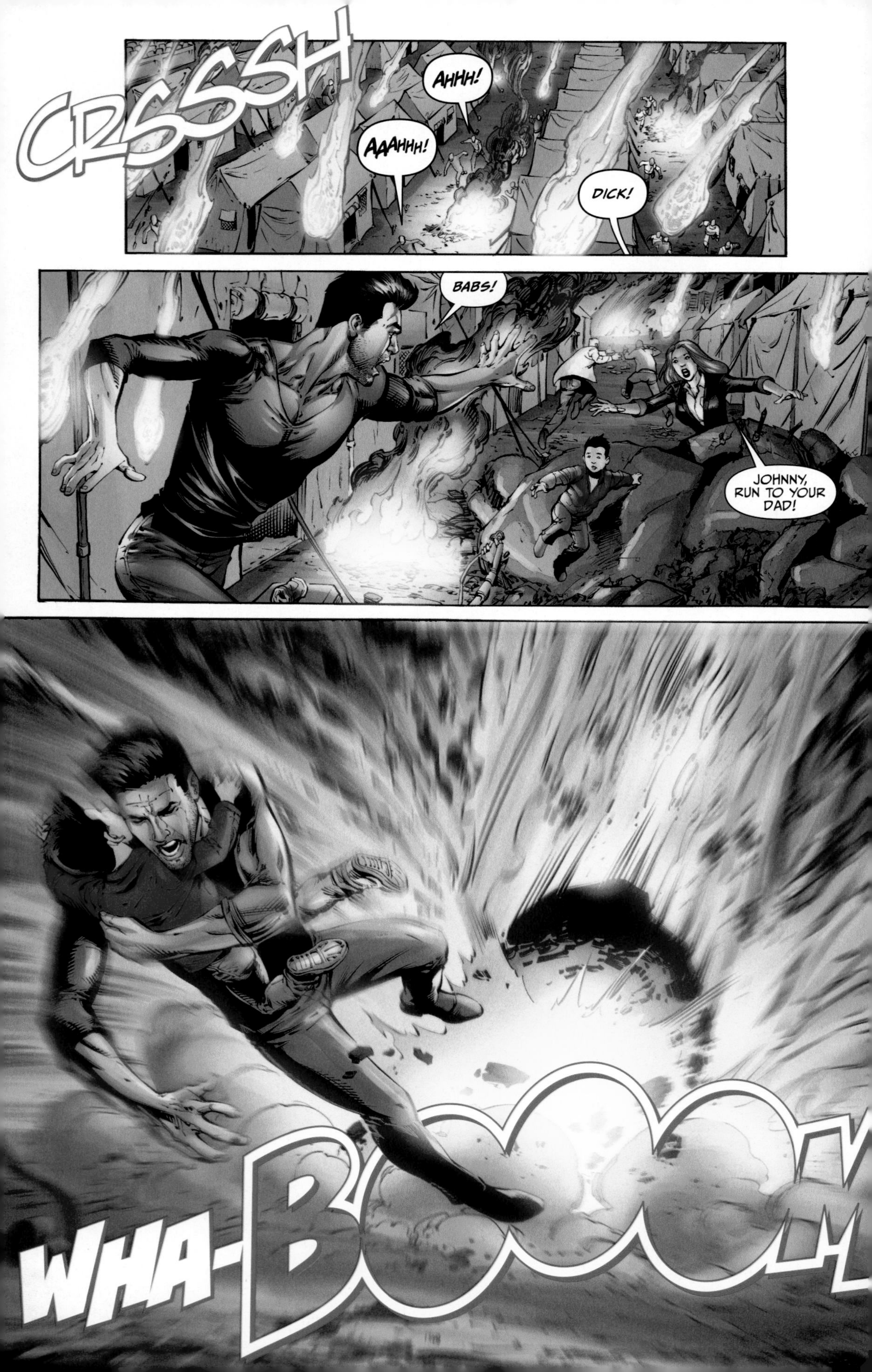
CRSSSH
AHHH!
AAAHHH!
DICK!
BABS!
JOHNNY, RUN TO YOUR DAD!
WHA-BOOOM

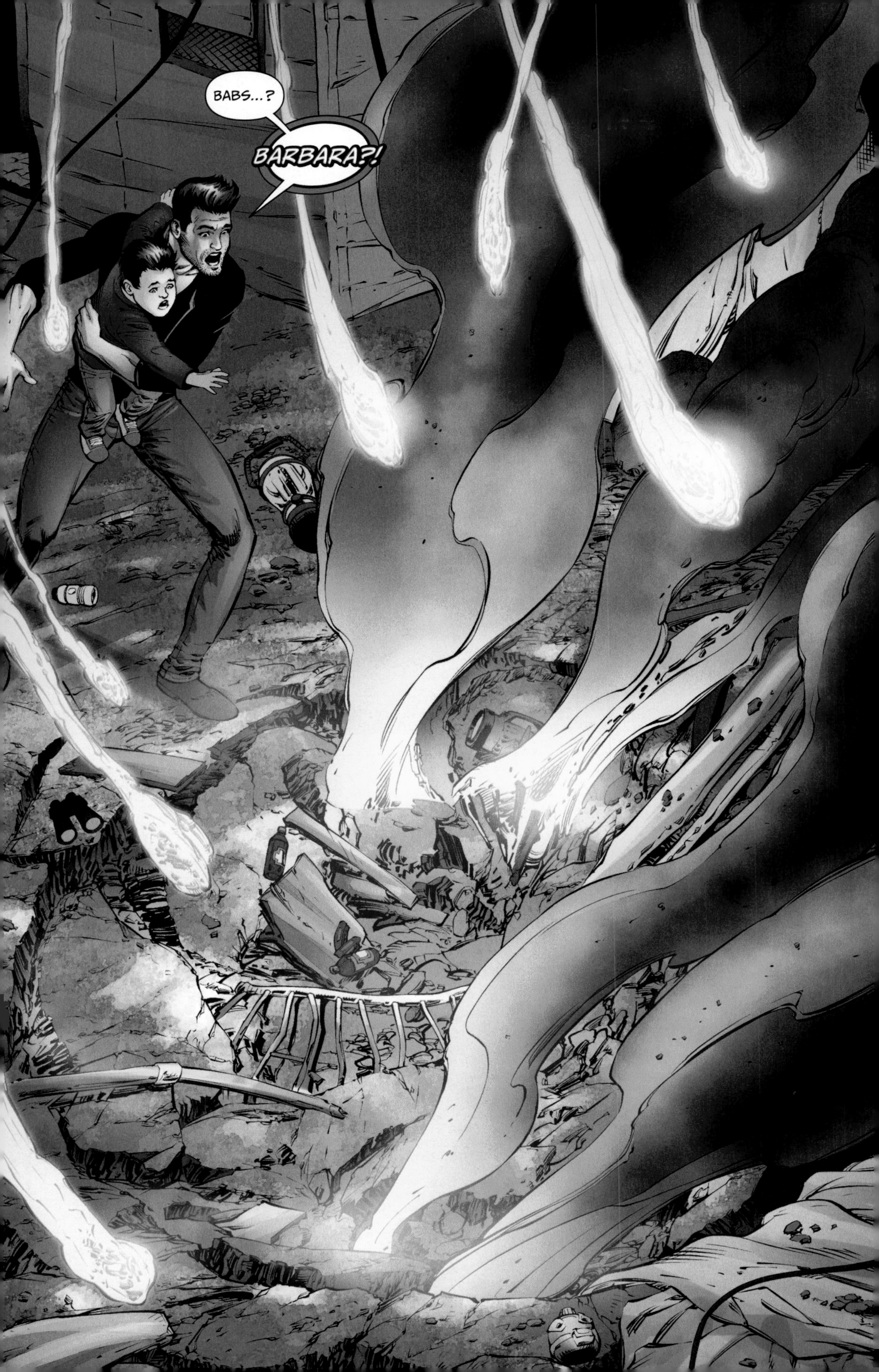
BABS...?
BARBARA?!

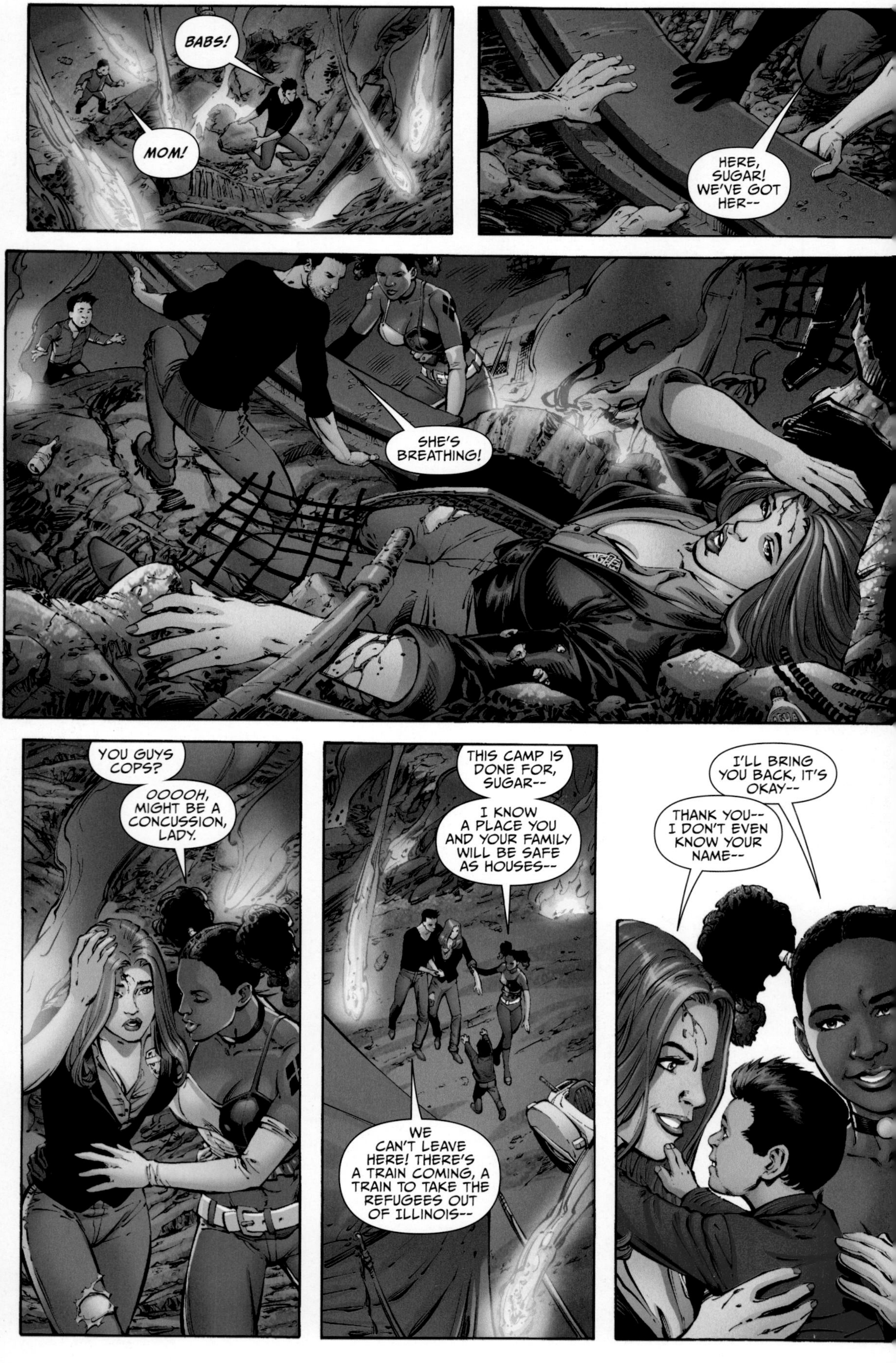
BABS!
MOM!
HERE, SUGAR! WE'VE GOT HER--
SHE'S BREATHING!
YOU GUYS COPS?
OOOOH, MIGHT BE A CONCUSSION, LADY.
THIS CAMP IS DONE FOR, SUGAR--
I KNOW A PLACE YOU AND YOUR FAMILY WILL BE SAFE AS HOUSES--
WE CAN'T LEAVE HERE! THERE'S A TRAIN COMING, A TRAIN TO TAKE THE REFUGEES OUT OF ILLINOIS--
THANK YOU-- I DON'T EVEN KNOW YOUR NAME--
I'LL BRING YOU BACK, IT'S OKAY--

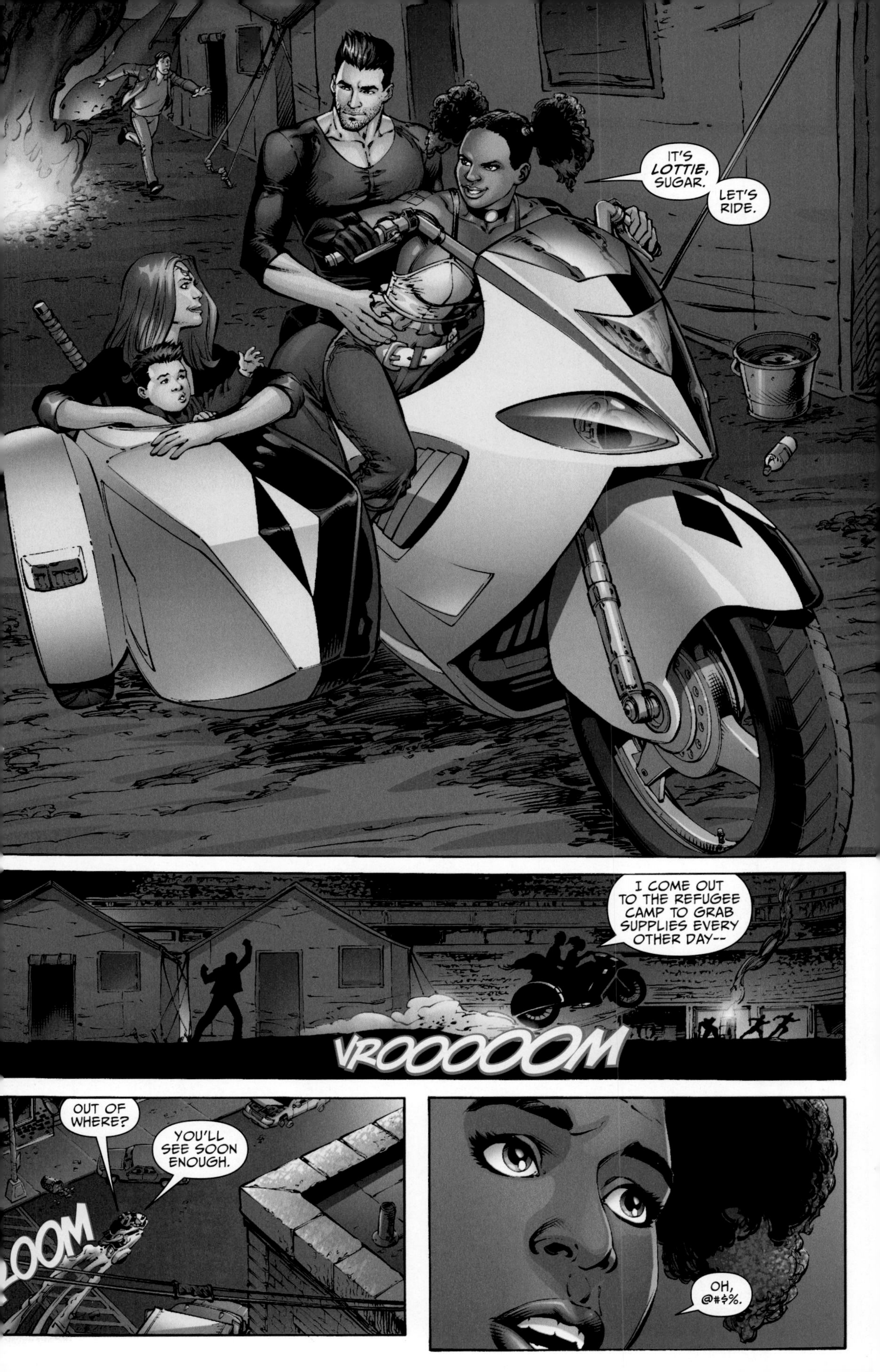
IT'S *LOTTIE*, SUGAR.
LET'S RIDE.
I COME OUT TO THE REFUGEE CAMP TO GRAB SUPPLIES EVERY OTHER DAY--
VROOOOOOM
OUT OF WHERE?
YOU'LL SEE SOON ENOUGH.
OOM
OH, @#$%.

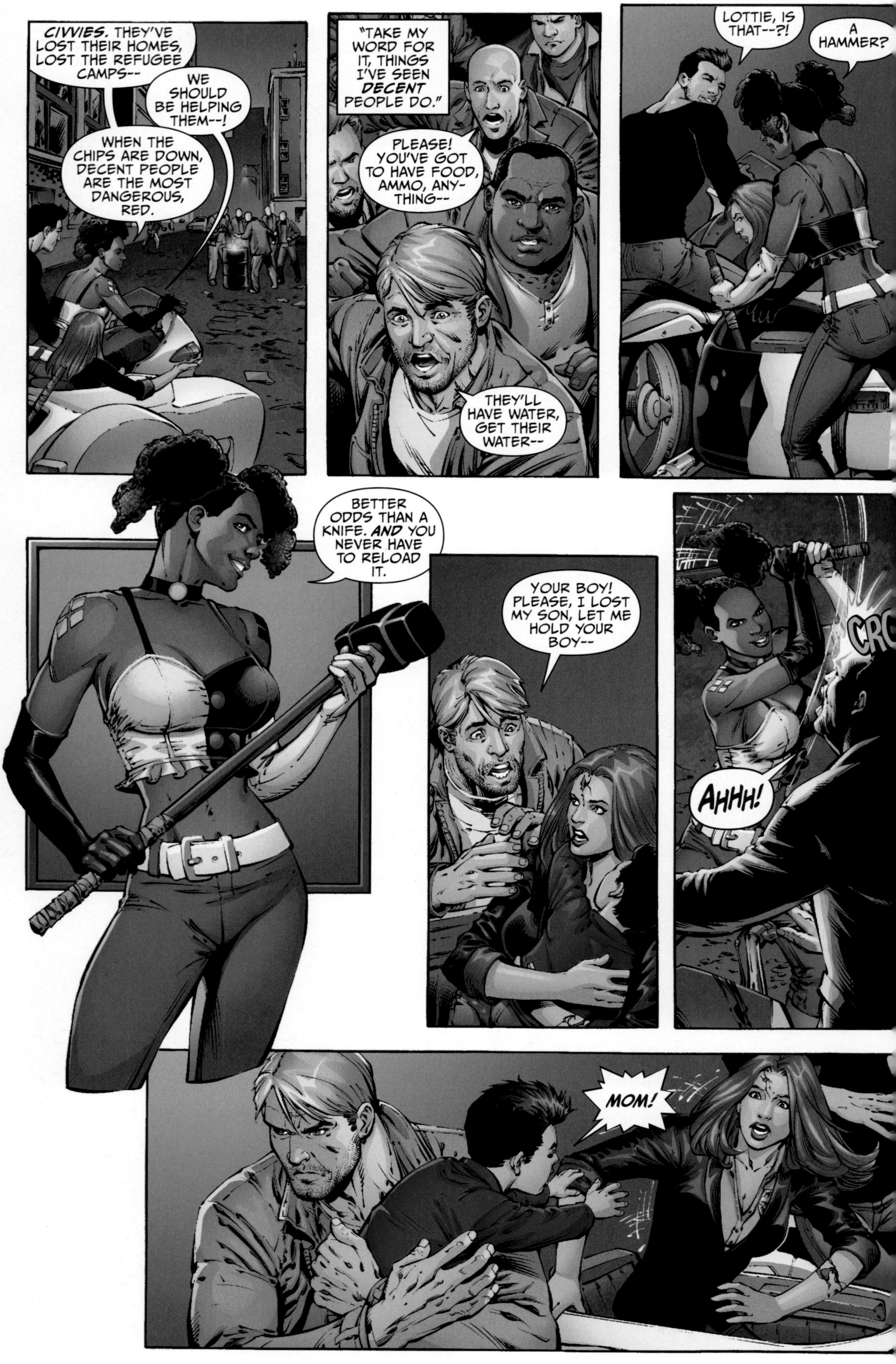
CIVVIES. THEY'VE LOST THEIR HOMES, LOST THE REFUGEE CAMPS--
WE SHOULD BE HELPING THEM--!
WHEN THE CHIPS ARE DOWN, DECENT PEOPLE ARE THE MOST DANGEROUS, RED.
"TAKE MY WORD FOR IT, THINGS I'VE SEEN DECENT PEOPLE DO."
PLEASE! YOU'VE GOT TO HAVE FOOD, AMMO, ANYTHING--
THEY'LL HAVE WATER, GET THEIR WATER--
LOTTIE, IS THAT--?!
A HAMMER?
BETTER ODDS THAN A KNIFE. AND YOU NEVER HAVE TO RELOAD IT.
YOUR BOY! PLEASE, I LOST MY SON, LET ME HOLD YOUR BOY--
AHHH!
MOM!

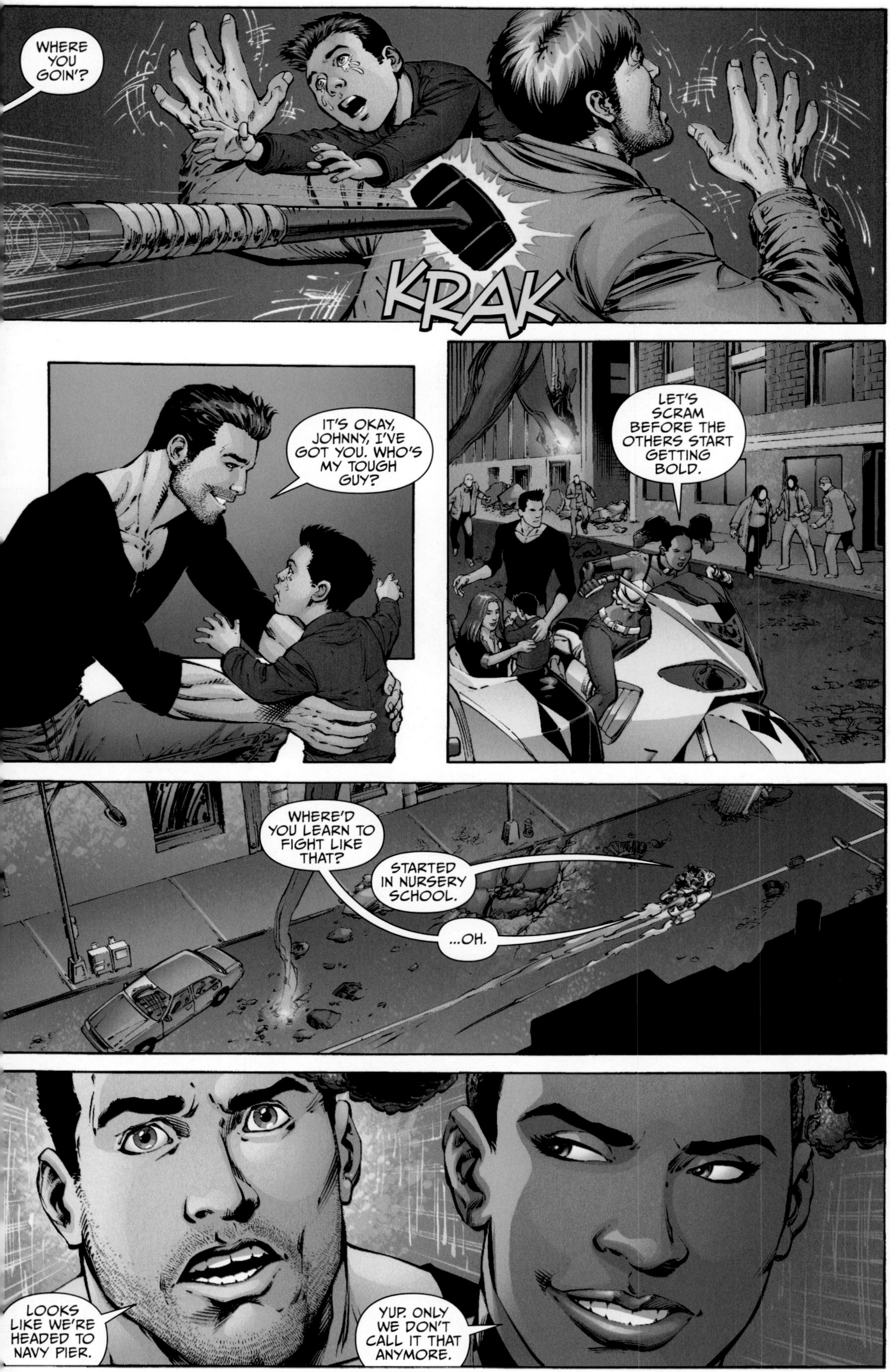
WHERE YOU GOIN'?
KRAK
IT'S OKAY, JOHNNY, I'VE GOT YOU. WHO'S MY TOUGH GUY?
LET'S SCRAM BEFORE THE OTHERS START GETTING BOLD.
WHERE'D YOU LEARN TO FIGHT LIKE THAT?
STARTED IN NURSERY SCHOOL.
...OH.
LOOKS LIKE WE'RE HEADED TO NAVY PIER.
YUP. ONLY WE DON'T CALL IT THAT ANYMORE.

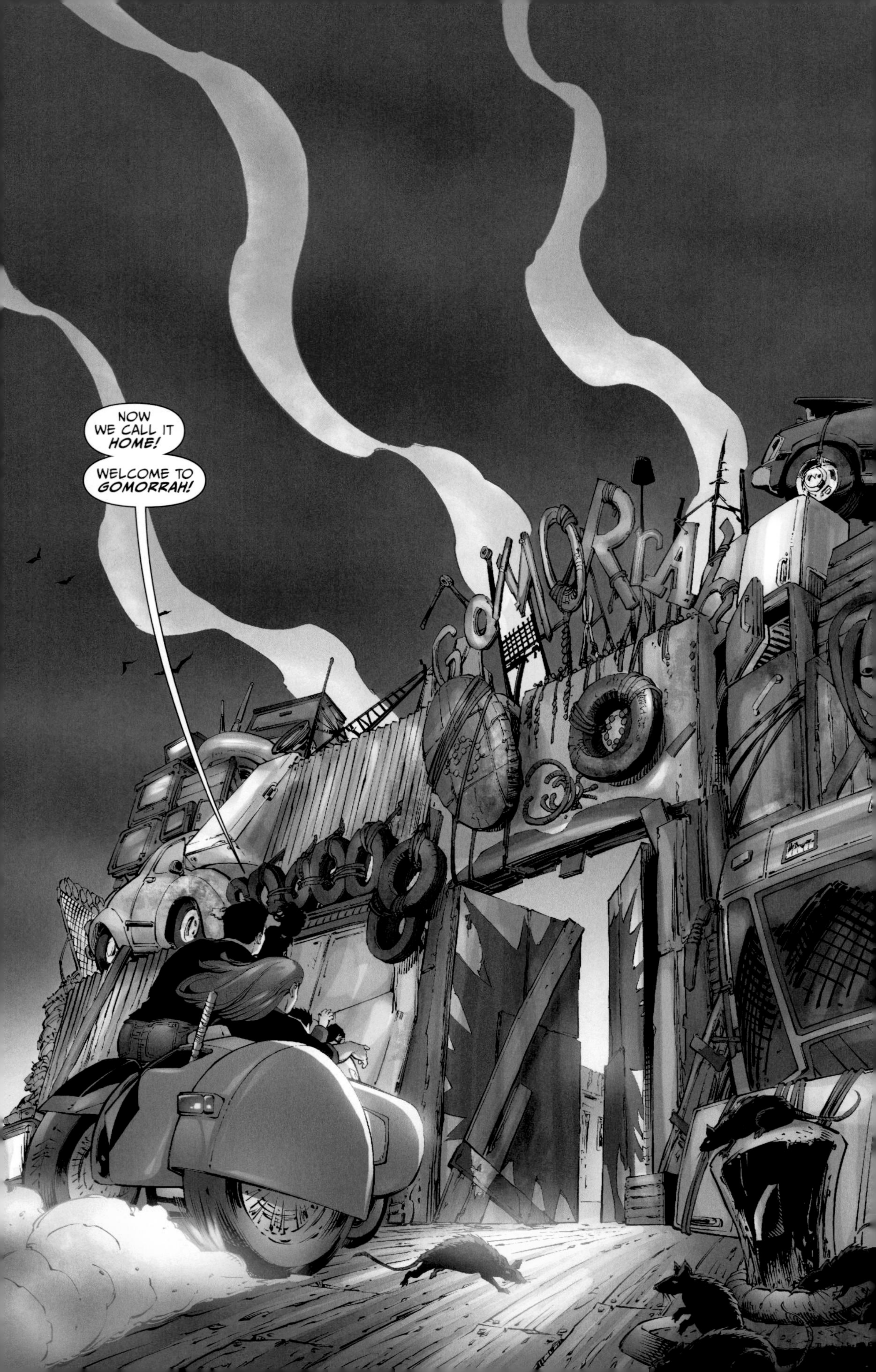
NOW WE CALL IT HOME!
WELCOME TO GOMORRAH!

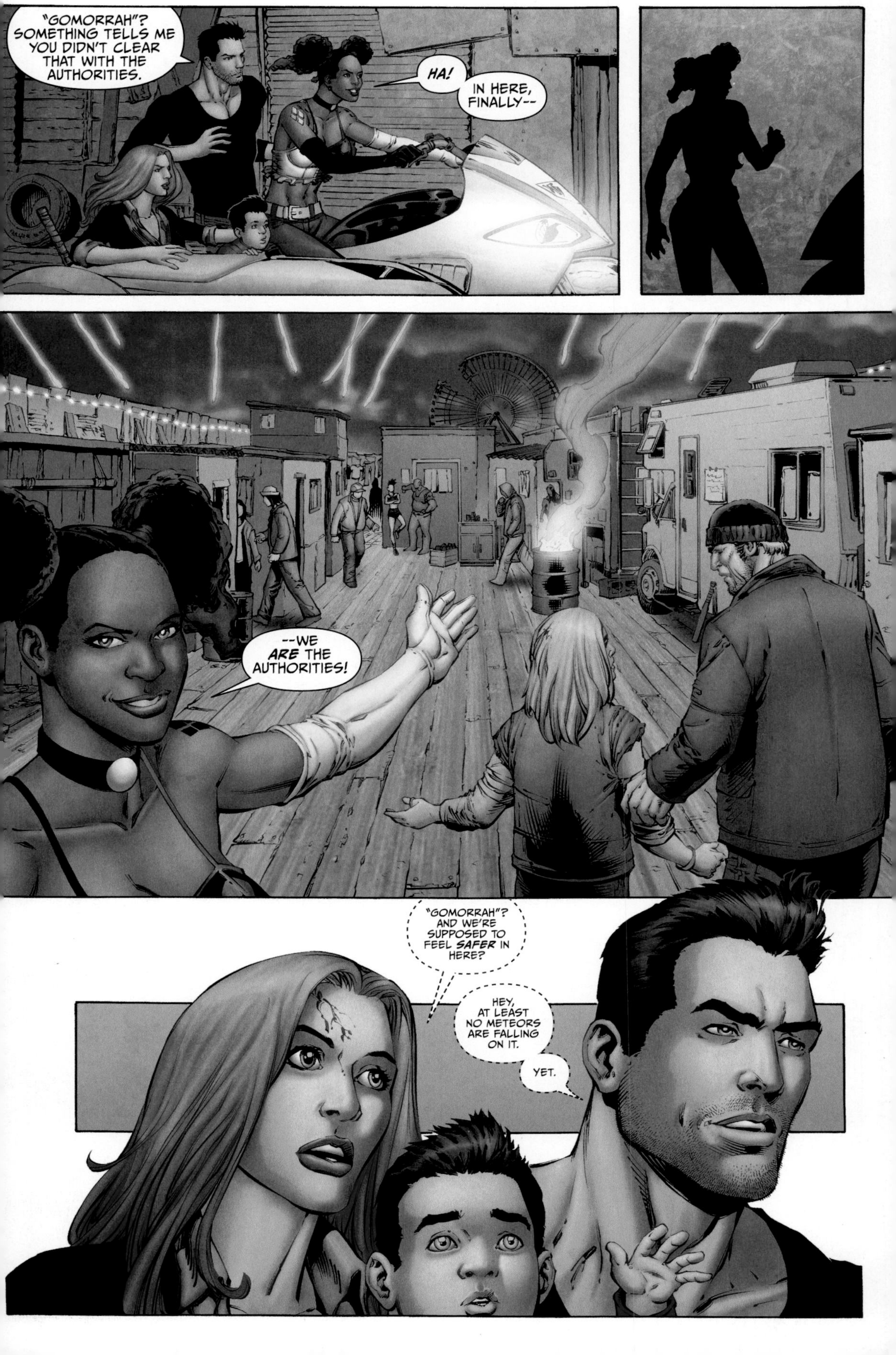
"GOMORRAH"? SOMETHING TELLS ME YOU DIDN'T CLEAR THAT WITH THE AUTHORITIES.
HA!
IN HERE, FINALLY--
--WE ARE THE AUTHORITIES!
"GOMORRAH"? AND WE'RE SUPPOSED TO FEEL SAFER IN HERE?
HEY, AT LEAST NO METEORS ARE FALLING ON IT.
YET.

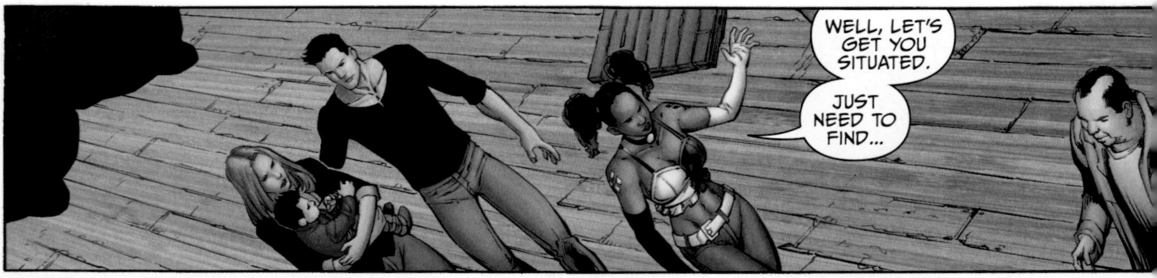
WELL, LET'S GET YOU SITUATED.
JUST NEED TO FIND...
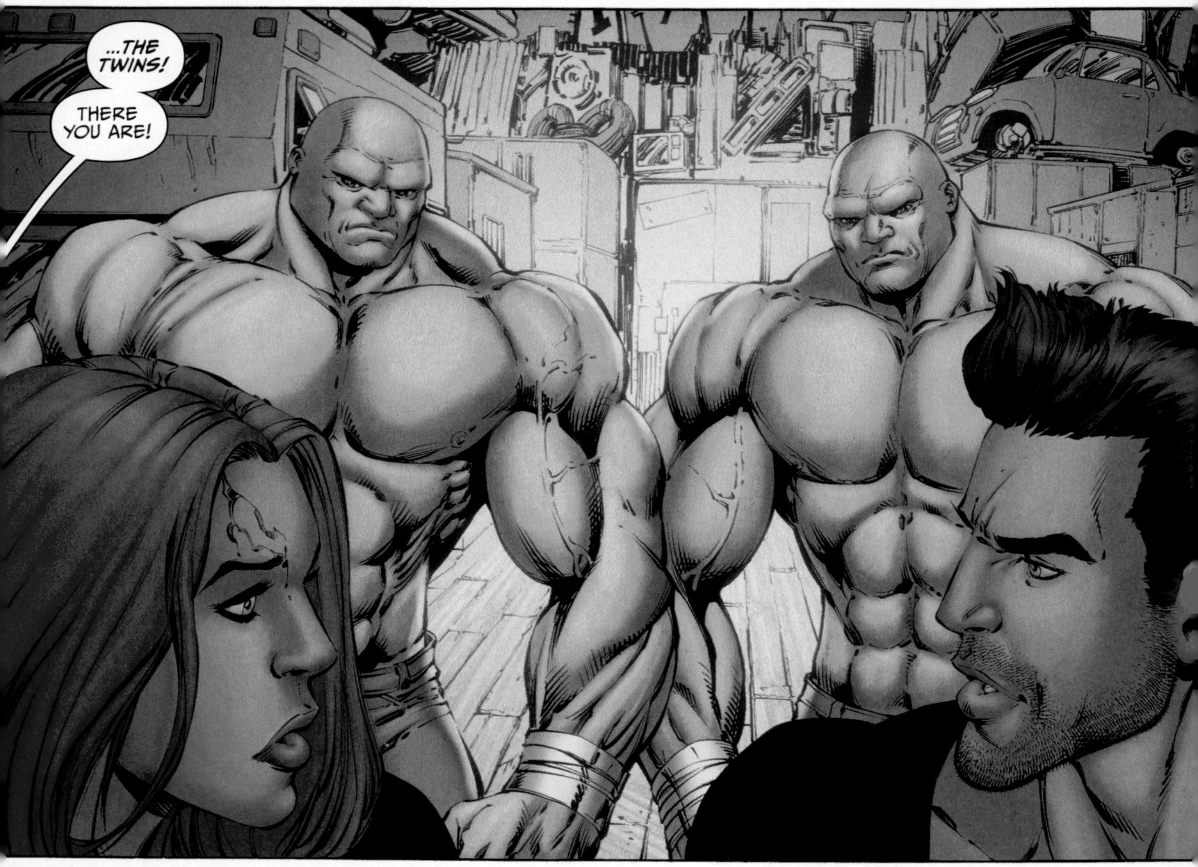
...THE TWINS!
THERE YOU ARE!
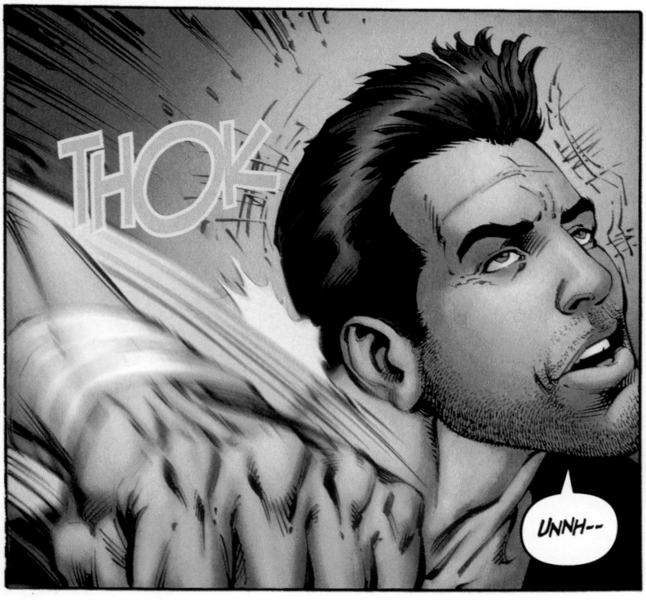
THOK
UNNH--
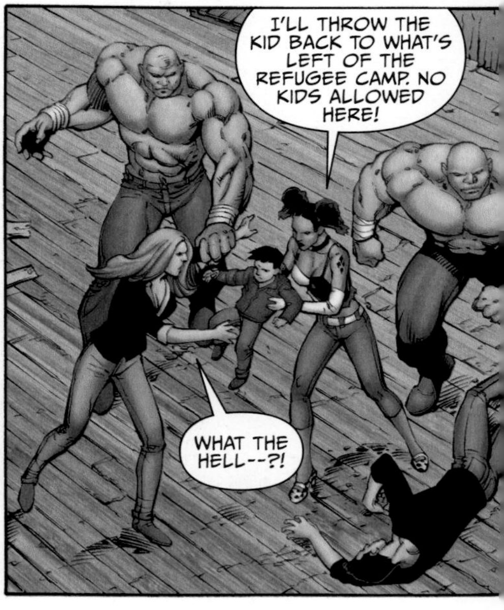
I'LL THROW THE KID BACK TO WHAT'S LEFT OF THE REFUGEE CAMP. NO KIDS ALLOWED HERE!
WHAT THE HELL--?!

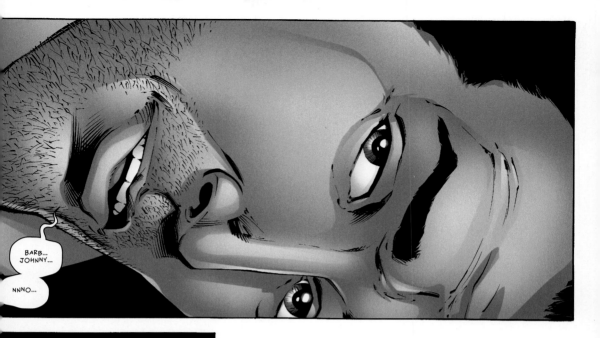

BARB... JOHNNY...

NNNO...

DON'T WORRY, "BARB." WE JUST *LOVE COPS* HERE!

HEY, DICK, DON'T WORRY...

THE FUN'S JUST GETTING STARTED!

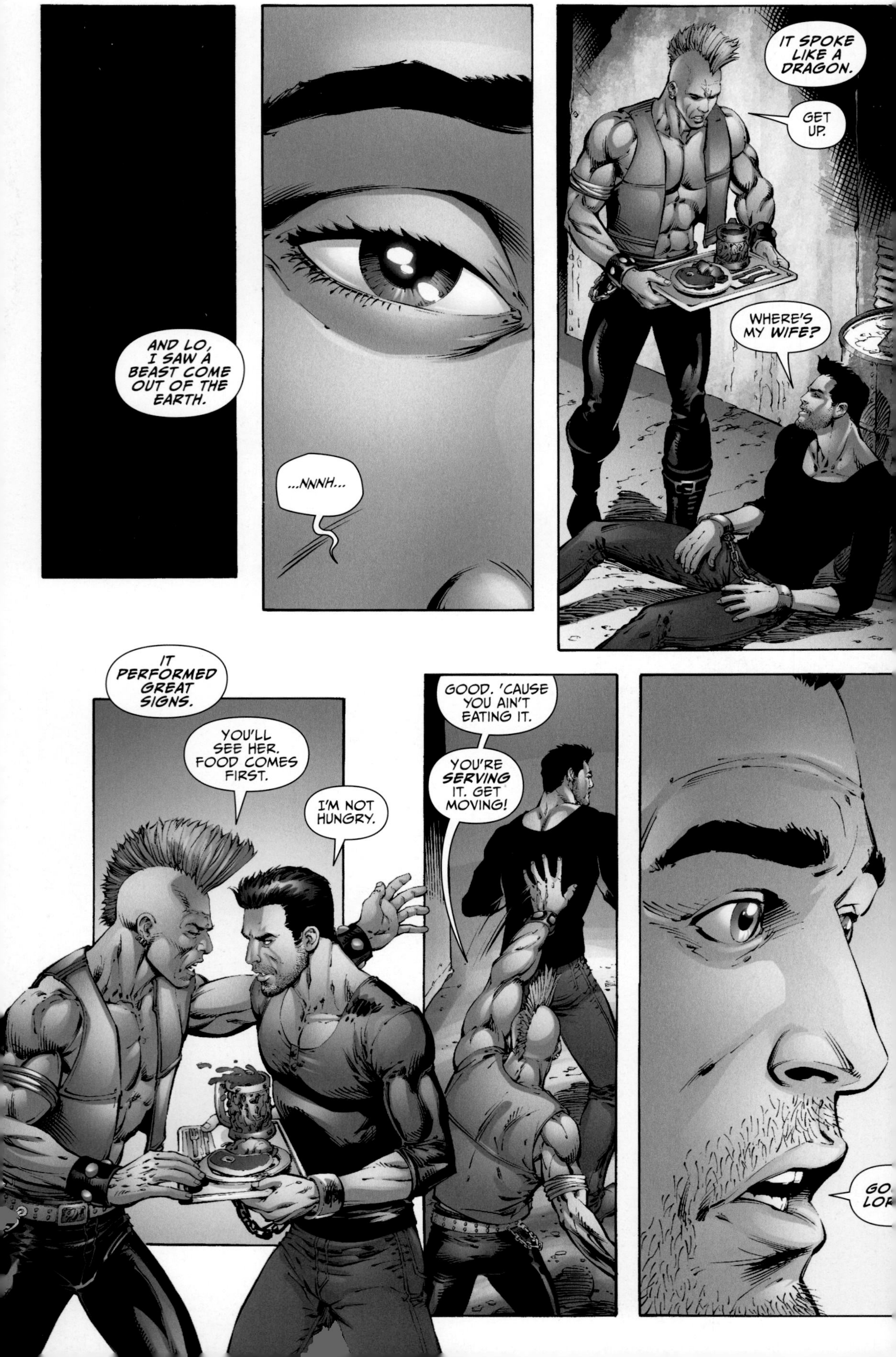
AND LO, I SAW A BEAST COME OUT OF THE EARTH.
...NNNH...
IT SPOKE LIKE A DRAGON.
GET UP.
WHERE'S MY *WIFE?*
IT PERFORMED GREAT SIGNS.
YOU'LL SEE HER. FOOD COMES FIRST.
I'M NOT HUNGRY.
GOOD. 'CAUSE YOU AIN'T EATING IT.
YOU'RE *SERVING* IT. GET MOVING!

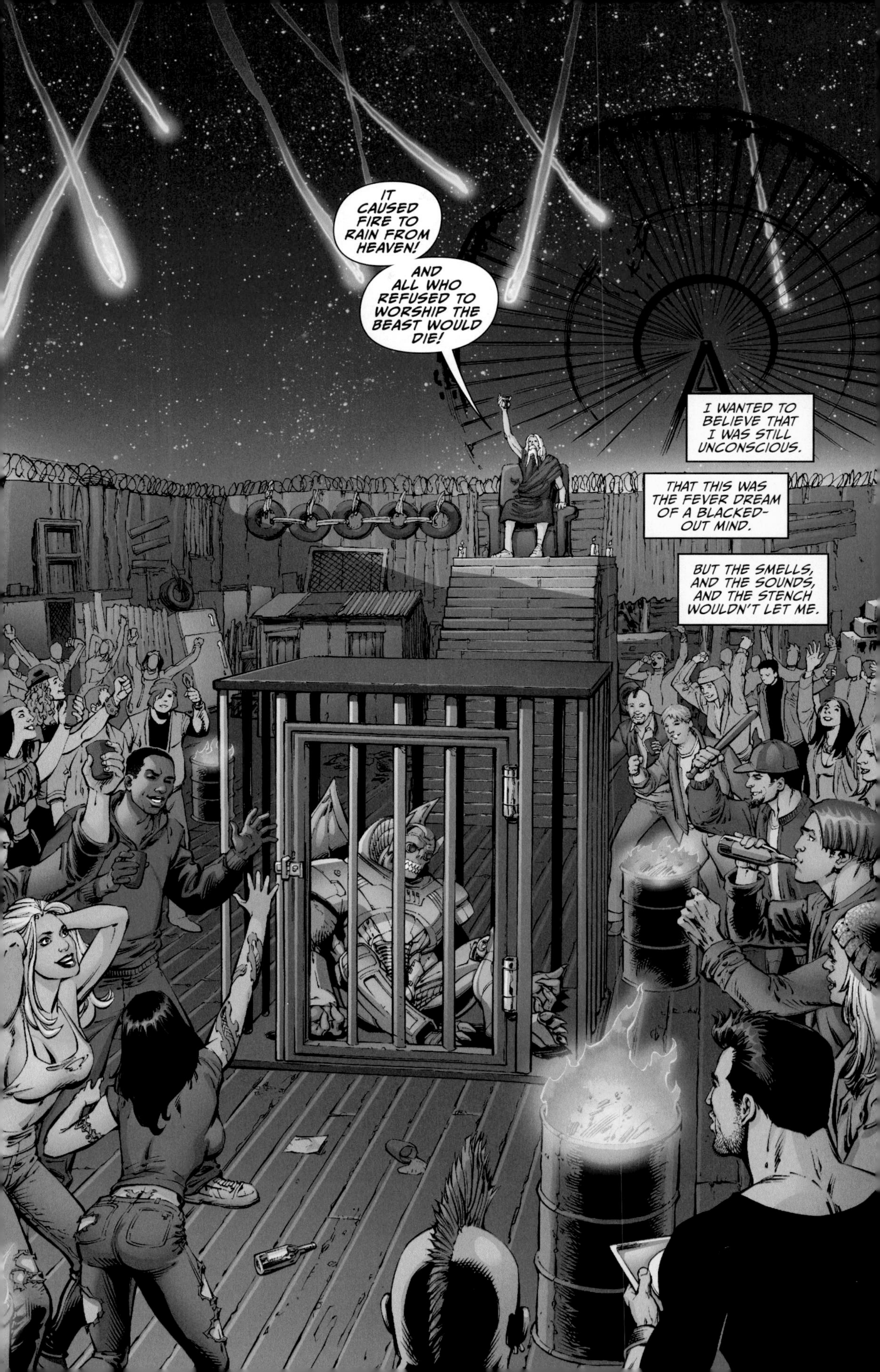
IT CAUSED FIRE TO RAIN FROM HEAVEN!
AND ALL WHO REFUSED TO WORSHIP THE BEAST WOULD DIE!
I WANTED TO BELIEVE THAT I WAS STILL UNCONSCIOUS.
THAT THIS WAS THE FEVER DREAM OF A BLACKED-OUT MIND.
BUT THE SMELLS, AND THE SOUNDS, AND THE STENCH WOULDN'T LET ME.

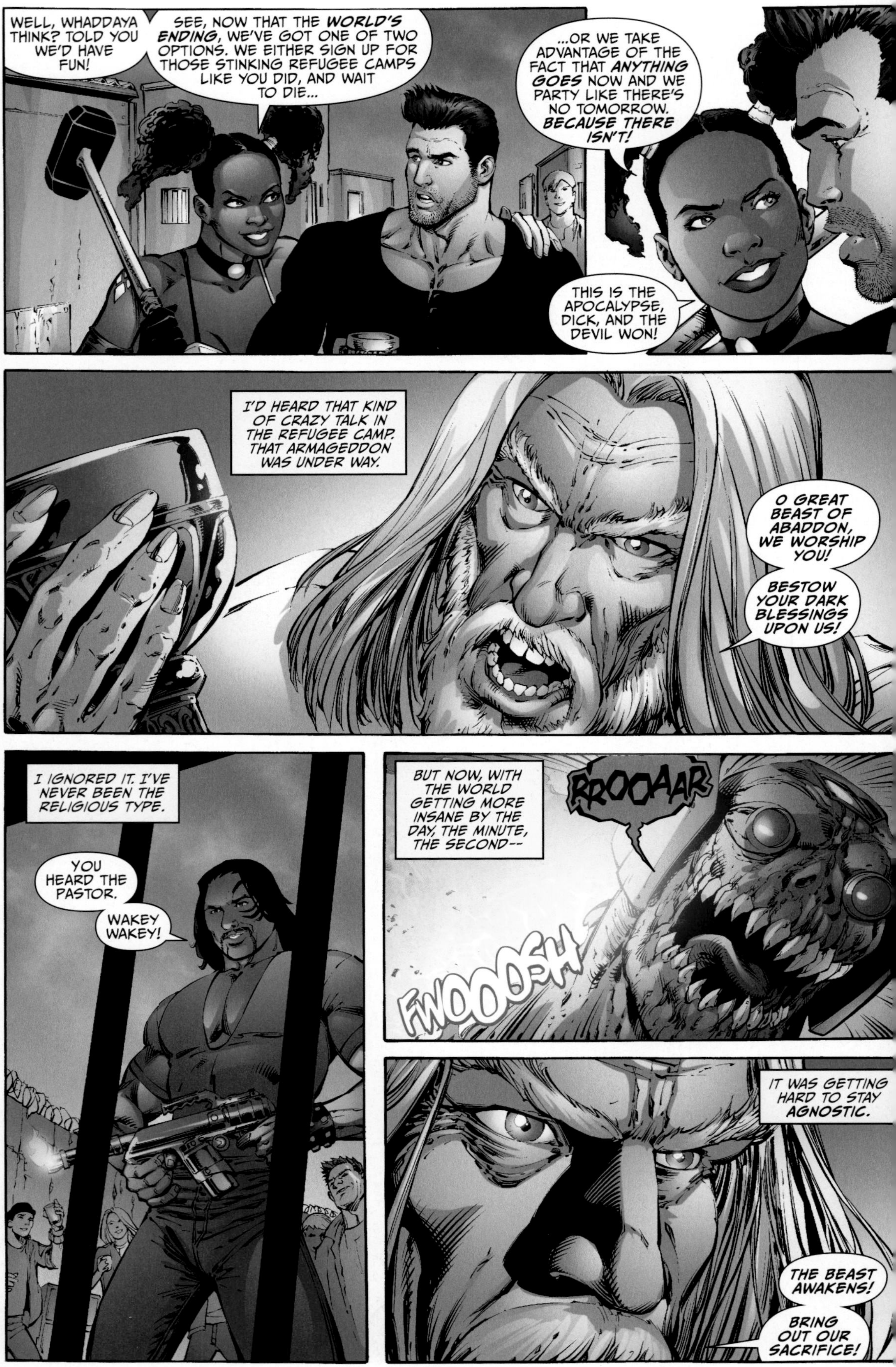
WELL, WHADDAYA THINK? TOLD YOU WE'D HAVE FUN!
SEE, NOW THAT THE WORLD'S ENDING, WE'VE GOT ONE OF TWO OPTIONS. WE EITHER SIGN UP FOR THOSE STINKING REFUGEE CAMPS LIKE YOU DID, AND WAIT TO DIE...
...OR WE TAKE ADVANTAGE OF THE FACT THAT ANYTHING GOES NOW AND WE PARTY LIKE THERE'S NO TOMORROW. BECAUSE THERE ISN'T!
THIS IS THE APOCALYPSE, DICK, AND THE DEVIL WON!
I'D HEARD THAT KIND OF CRAZY TALK IN THE REFUGEE CAMP. THAT ARMAGEDDON WAS UNDER WAY.
O GREAT BEAST OF ABADDON, WE WORSHIP YOU!
BESTOW YOUR DARK BLESSINGS UPON US!
I IGNORED IT. I'VE NEVER BEEN THE RELIGIOUS TYPE.
YOU HEARD THE PASTOR.
WAKEY WAKEY!
BUT NOW, WITH THE WORLD GETTING MORE INSANE BY THE DAY, THE MINUTE, THE SECOND--
RROOAAR
FWOOOSH
IT WAS GETTING HARD TO STAY AGNOSTIC.
THE BEAST AWAKENS!
BRING OUT OUR SACRIFICE!

BEAST! BEAST! BEAST!
BEAST! BEAST! BEAST!
BEAST!

LET--

GO--!

BARBARA!

UH-UH. YOU JUST GET TO WATCH.

RWOOOAR

I OPEN. YOU THROW.

YOU OPEN. I THROW.

GET-- OFF ME--!

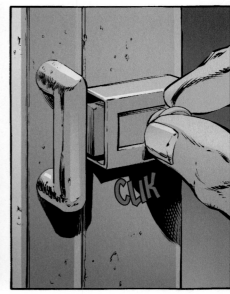

CLIK

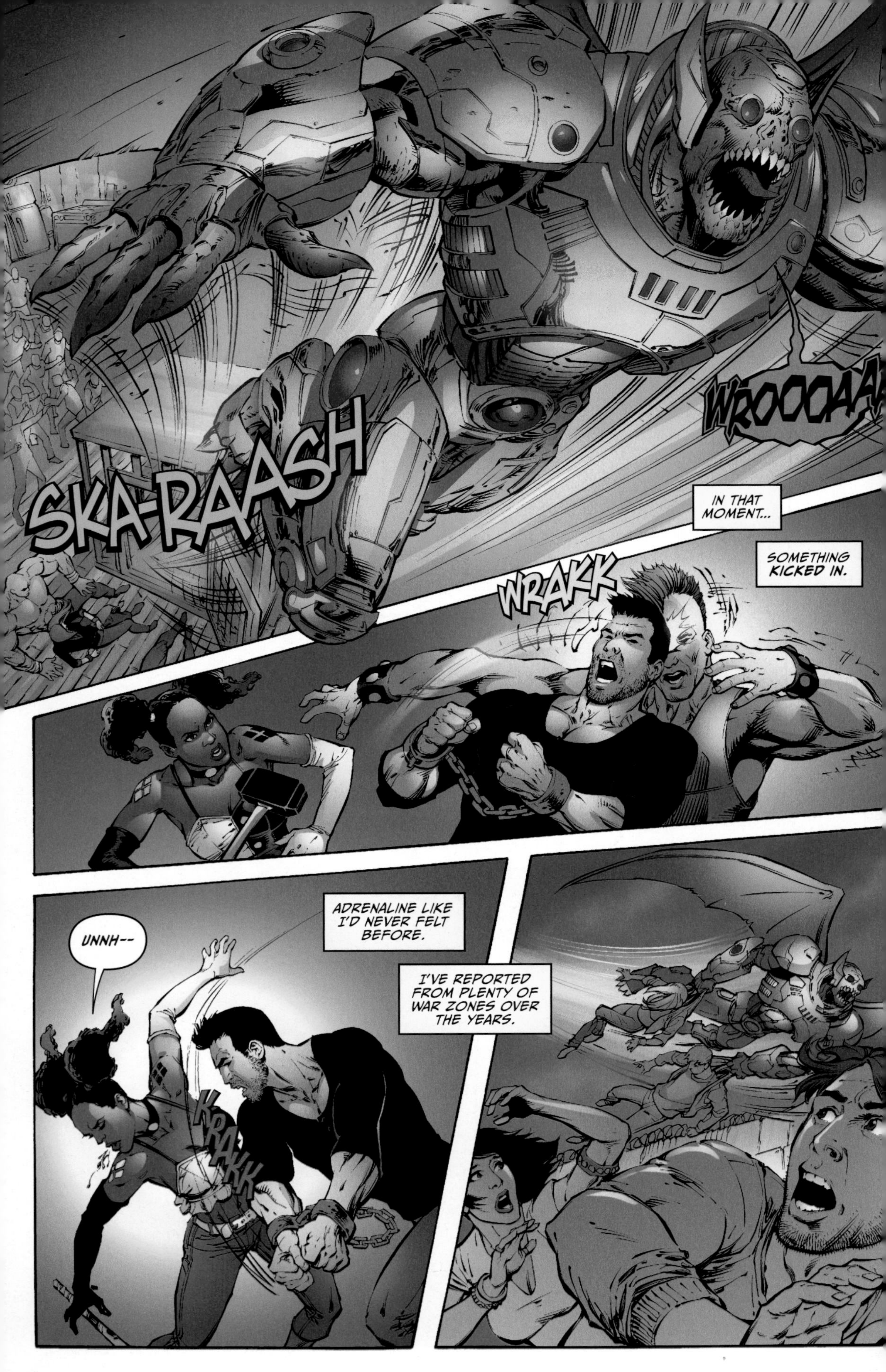
WROOOAA
SKA-RAASH
IN THAT MOMENT...
SOMETHING KICKED IN.
WRAKK
UNNH--
ADRENALINE LIKE I'D NEVER FELT BEFORE.
KRAKK
I'VE REPORTED FROM PLENTY OF WAR ZONES OVER THE YEARS.

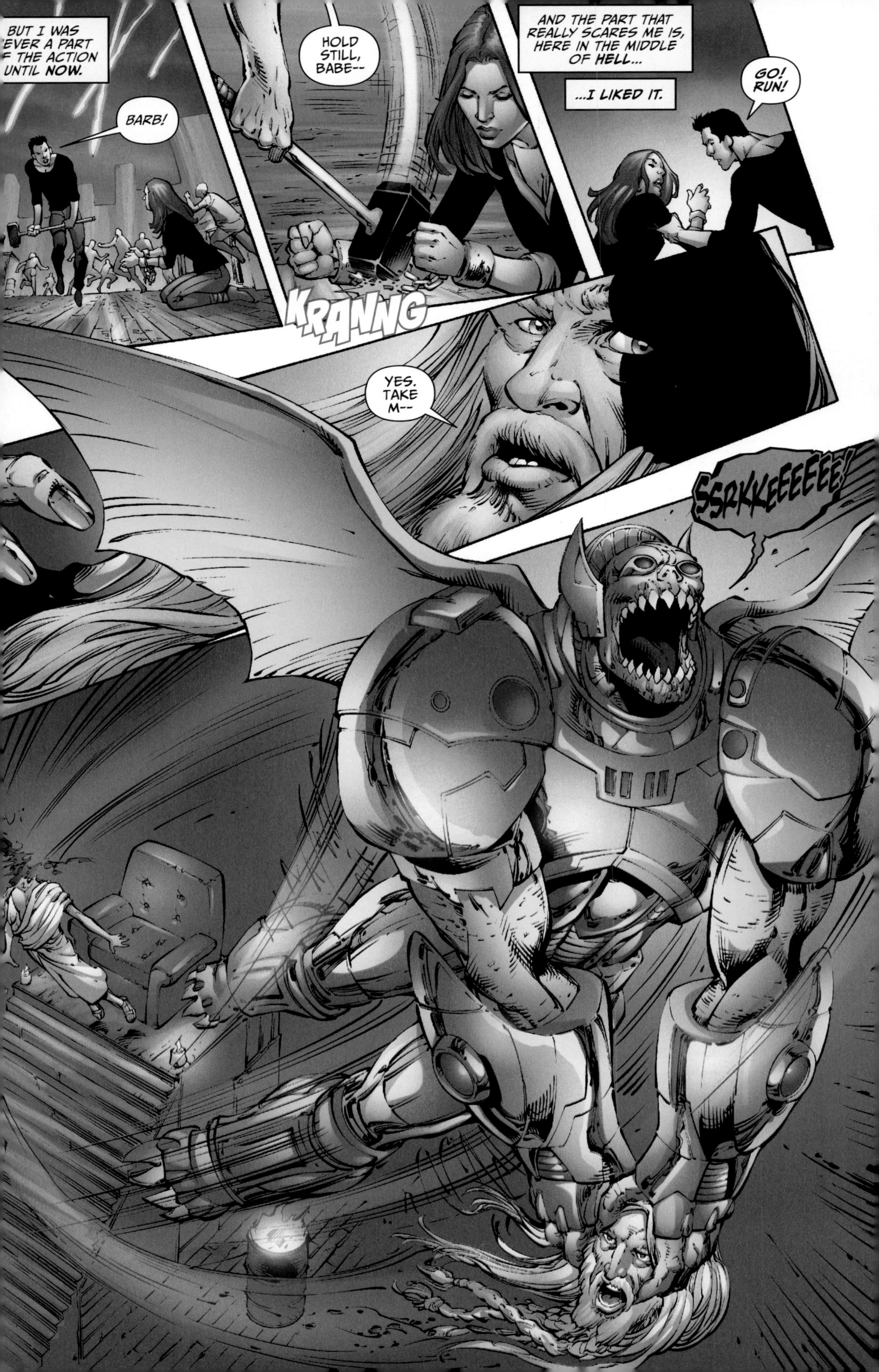

BUT I WAS
EVER A PART
F THE ACTION
UNTIL NOW.
BARB!
HOLD STILL, BABE--
AND THE PART THAT REALLY SCARES ME IS, HERE IN THE MIDDLE OF HELL...
...I LIKED IT.
GO! RUN!
KRANNG
YES. TAKE M--
SSRKKEEEEEE!

JUST SO WE'RE CLEAR--

--I WAS TOTALLY ABOUT TO ESCAPE BEFORE YOU RESCUED ME.

WRROOOM

NO DOUBT.

I HAVE TO ADMIT, THOUGH, IT WAS KIND OF *SEXY* SEEING MY HUSBAND IN ACTION.

YEAH, WELL, LET'S HOPE IT'S THE LAST TIME.

LET'S JUST GET BACK TO JOHNNY AND HOPE THOSE *REFUGEE TRAINS* ARE FINALLY ROLLING OUT OF THE CITY.

WE'LL FIND A NEW HOME. A SAFE PLACE TO START OVER.

I HEAR MYSELF SAY THE WORDS.

EVERYTHING'S GOING TO BE ALL RIGHT.

I JUST WISH I BELIEVED THEM.

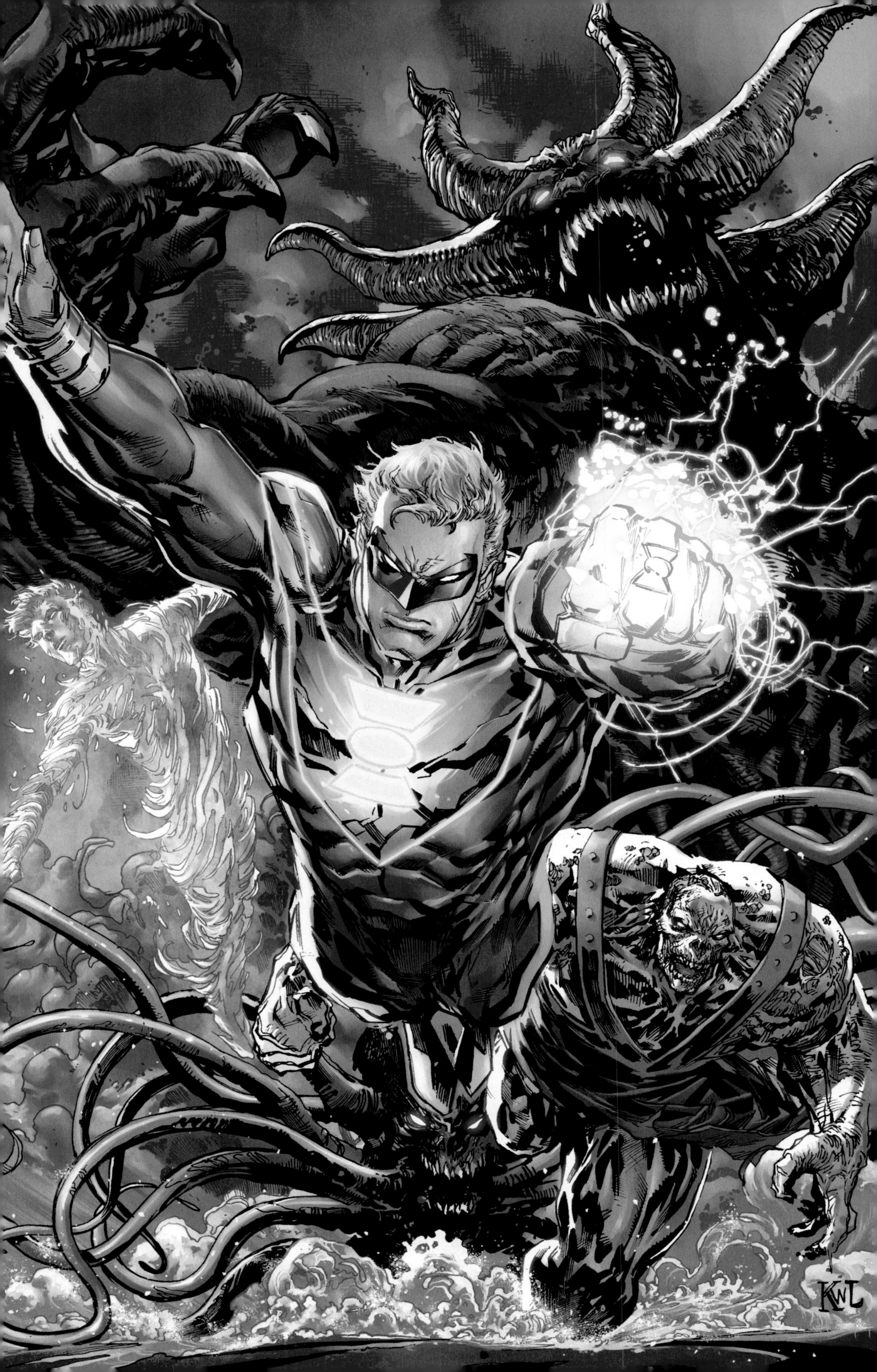
KWL

AVATARS

MARGUERITE BENNETT, MIKE JOHNSON writers **ANDY SMITH, TREVOR SCOTT, TYLER KIRKHAM, CLIFF RICHARDS, THONY SILAS** artists **PETER PANTAZIS** colorist **DEZI SIENTY** letterer cover by **KEN LASHLEY** and **TOMEU MOREY**

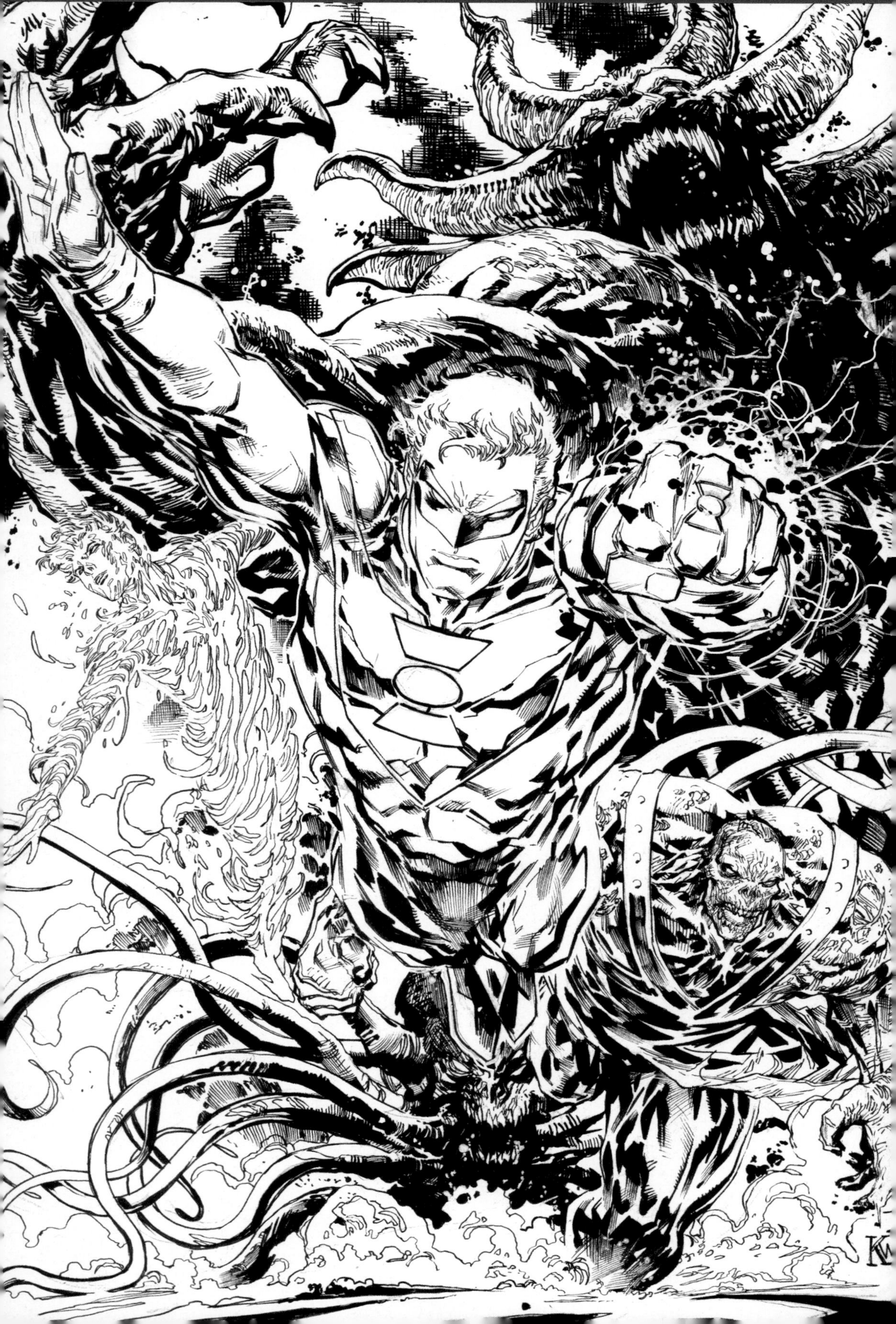

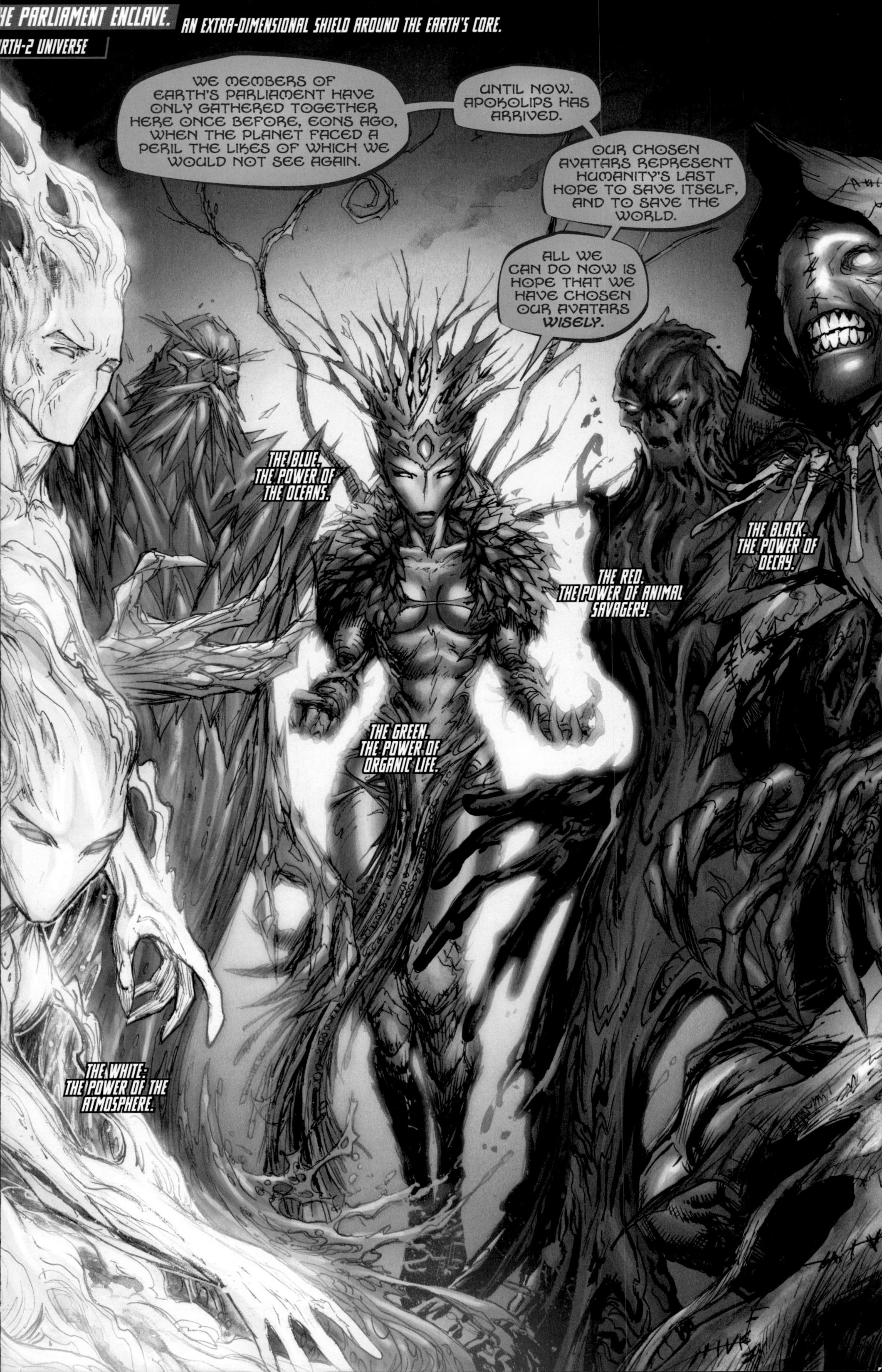
HE PARLIAMENT ENCLAVE.
AN EXTRA-DIMENSIONAL SHIELD AROUND THE EARTH'S CORE.
RTH-2 UNIVERSE
WE MEMBERS OF EARTH'S PARLIAMENT HAVE ONLY GATHERED TOGETHER HERE ONCE BEFORE, EONS AGO, WHEN THE PLANET FACED A PERIL THE LIKES OF WHICH WE WOULD NOT SEE AGAIN.
UNTIL NOW. APOKOLIPS HAS ARRIVED.
OUR CHOSEN AVATARS REPRESENT HUMANITY'S LAST HOPE TO SAVE ITSELF, AND TO SAVE THE WORLD.
ALL WE CAN DO NOW IS HOPE THAT WE HAVE CHOSEN OUR AVATARS WISELY.
THE BLUE. THE POWER OF THE OCEANS.
THE BLACK. THE POWER OF DECAY.
THE RED. THE POWER OF ANIMAL SAVAGERY.
THE GREEN. THE POWER OF ORGANIC LIFE.
THE WHITE: THE POWER OF THE ATMOSPHERE.

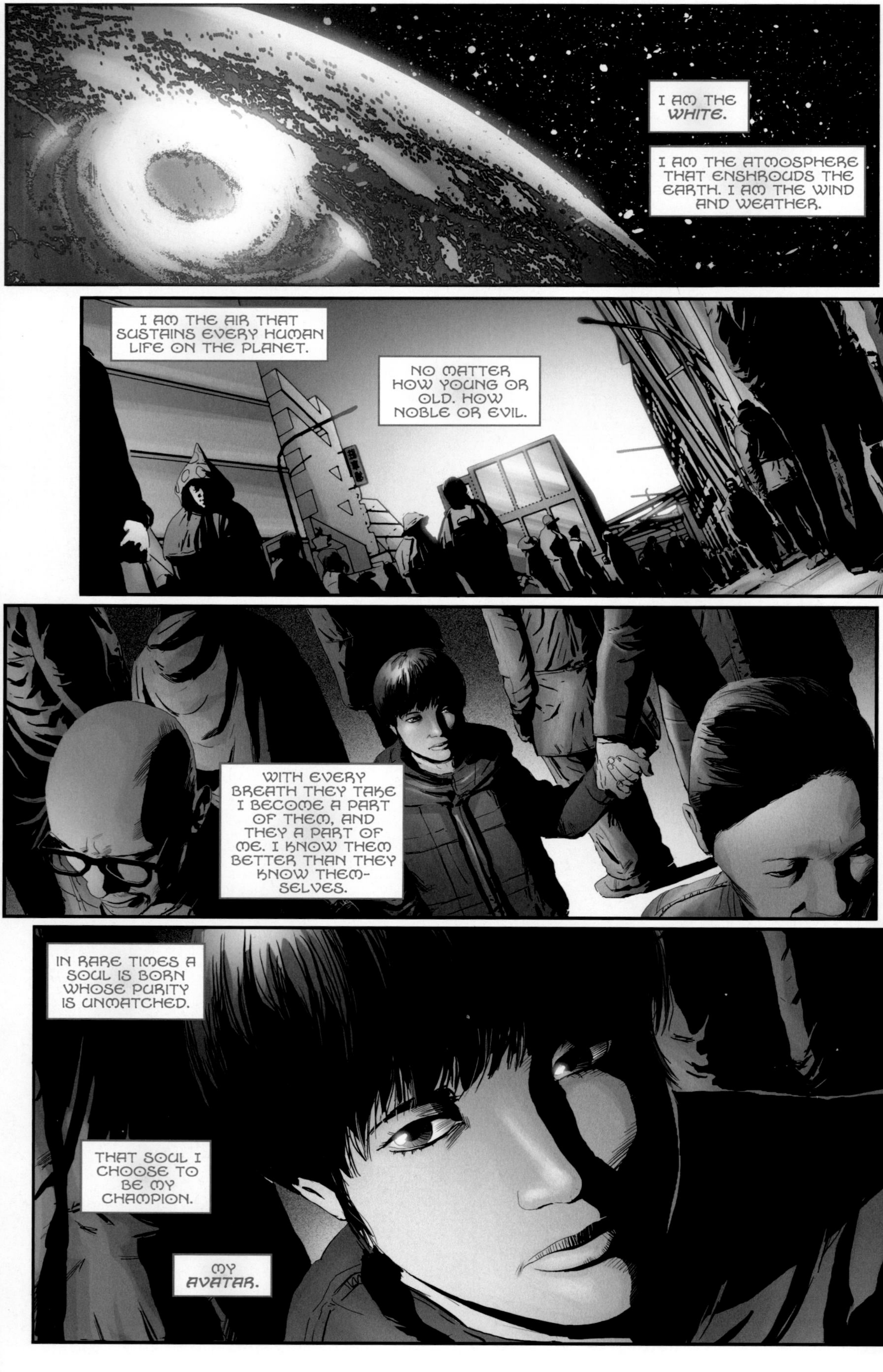
I AM THE WHITE.
I AM THE ATMOSPHERE THAT ENSHROUDS THE EARTH. I AM THE WIND AND WEATHER.
I AM THE AIR THAT SUSTAINS EVERY HUMAN LIFE ON THE PLANET.
NO MATTER HOW YOUNG OR OLD. HOW NOBLE OR EVIL.
WITH EVERY BREATH THEY TAKE I BECOME A PART OF THEM, AND THEY A PART OF ME. I KNOW THEM BETTER THAN THEY KNOW THEM-SELVES.
IN RARE TIMES A SOUL IS BORN WHOSE PURITY IS UNMATCHED.
THAT SOUL I CHOOSE TO BE MY CHAMPION.
MY AVATAR.

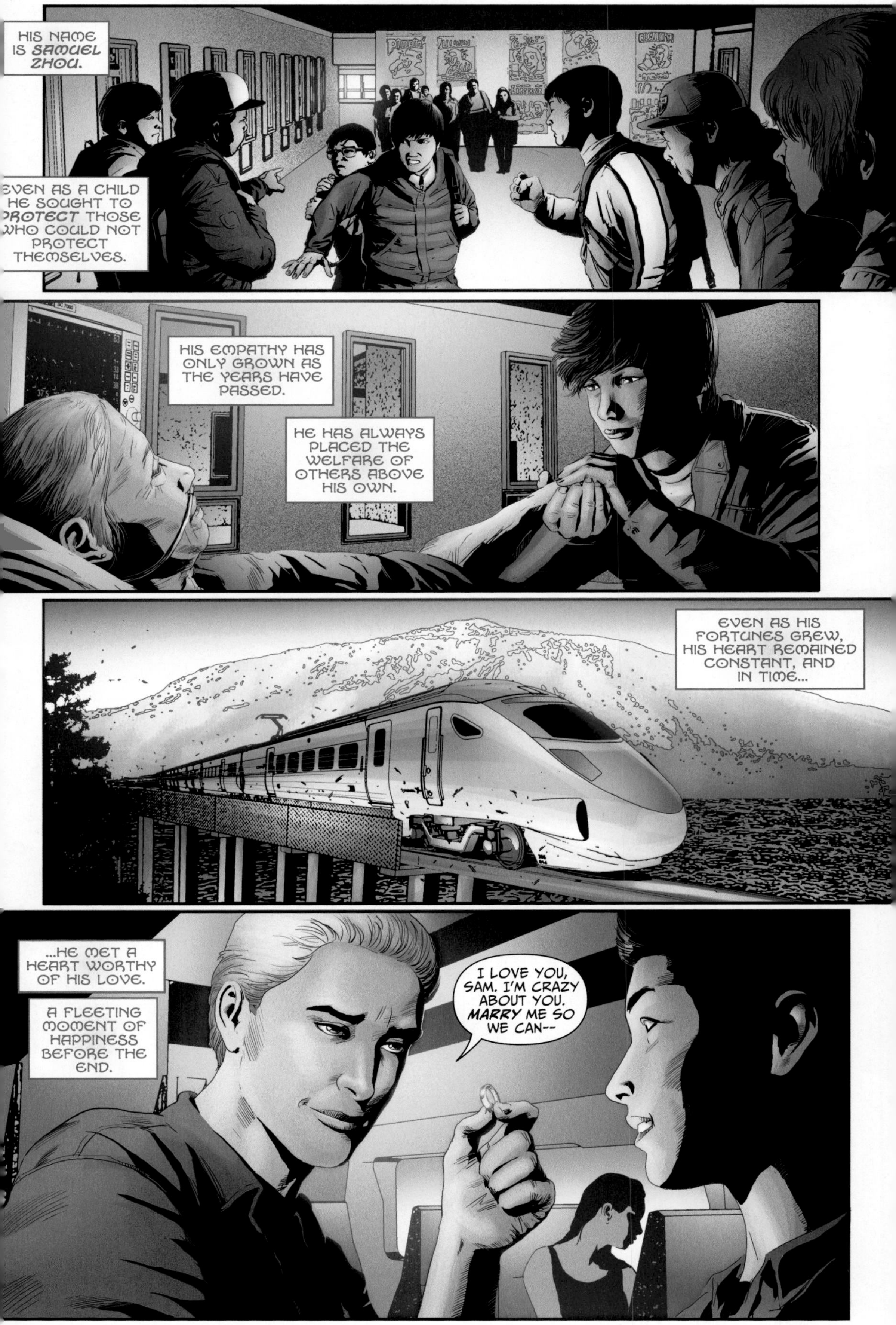
HIS NAME IS SAMUEL ZHOU.
EVEN AS A CHILD HE SOUGHT TO PROTECT THOSE WHO COULD NOT PROTECT THEMSELVES.
HIS EMPATHY HAS ONLY GROWN AS THE YEARS HAVE PASSED.
HE HAS ALWAYS PLACED THE WELFARE OF OTHERS ABOVE HIS OWN.
EVEN AS HIS FORTUNES GREW, HIS HEART REMAINED CONSTANT, AND IN TIME...
...HE MET A HEART WORTHY OF HIS LOVE.
A FLEETING MOMENT OF HAPPINESS BEFORE THE END.
I LOVE YOU, SAM. I'M CRAZY ABOUT YOU. MARRY ME SO WE CAN--

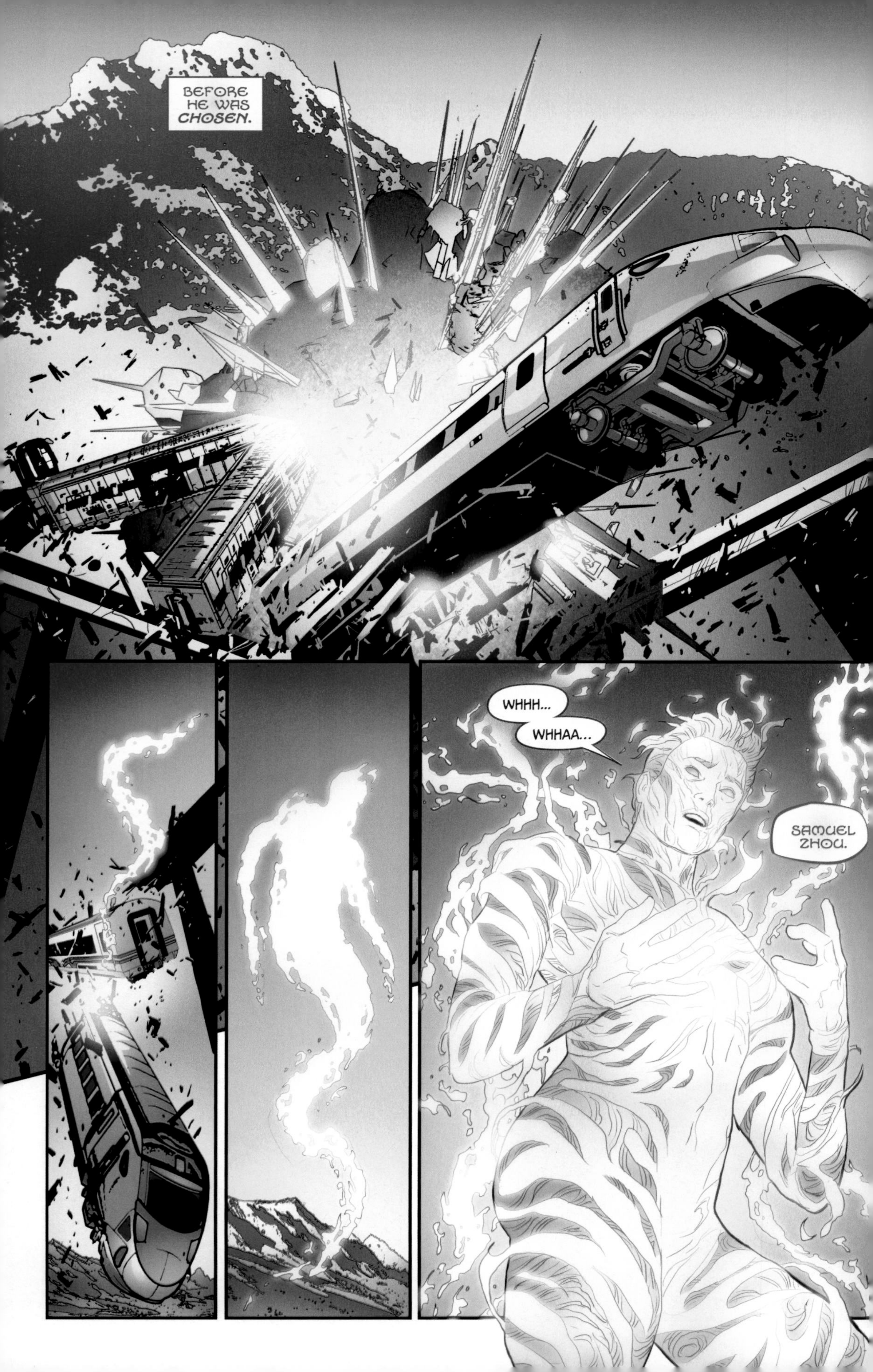
BEFORE HE WAS CHOSEN.
WHHH...
WHHAA...
SAMUEL ZHOU.

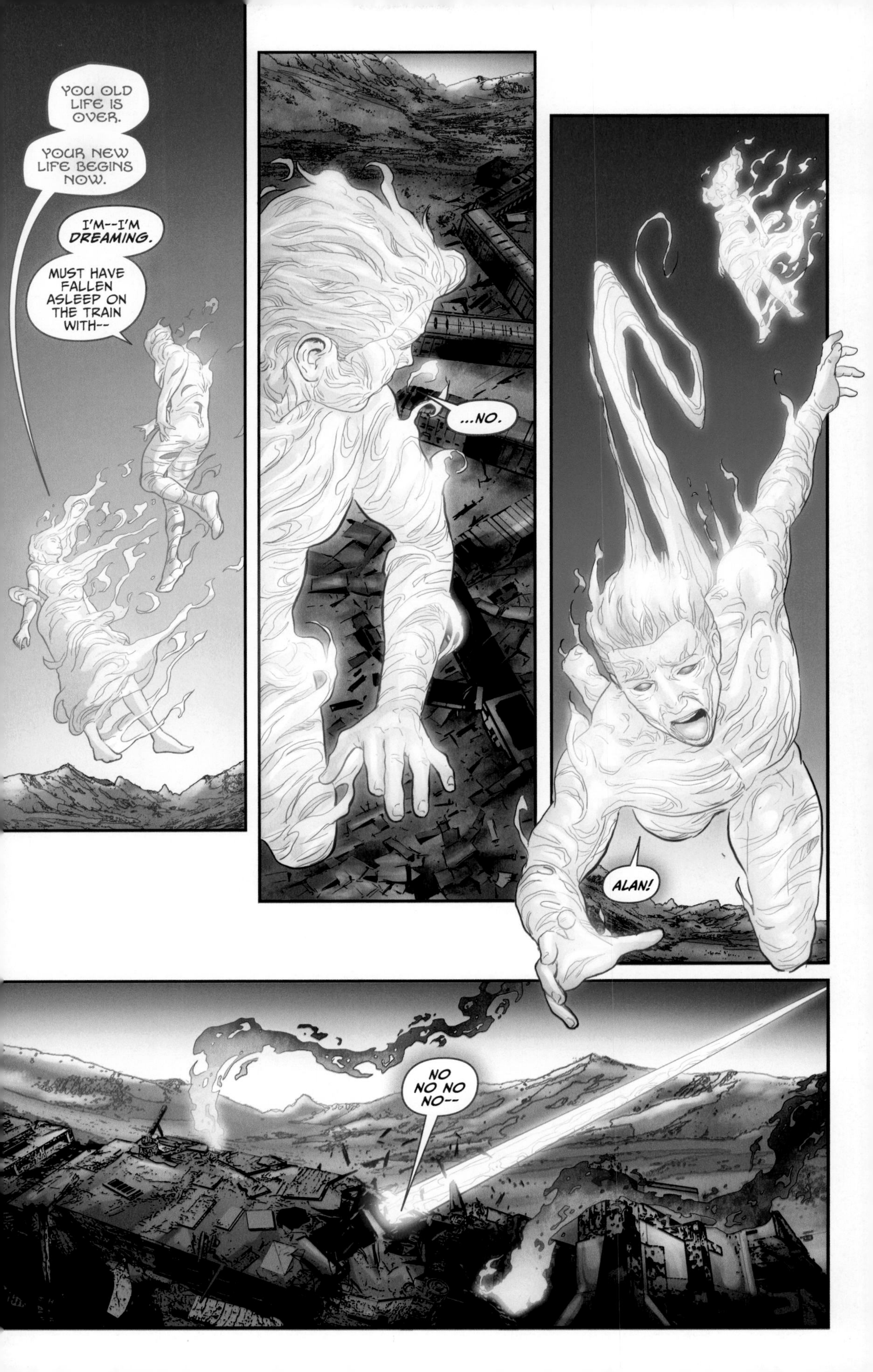
YOU OLD LIFE IS OVER.
YOUR NEW LIFE BEGINS NOW.
I'M--I'M DREAMING.
MUST HAVE FALLEN ASLEEP ON THE TRAIN WITH--
...NO.
ALAN!
NO NO NO NO--

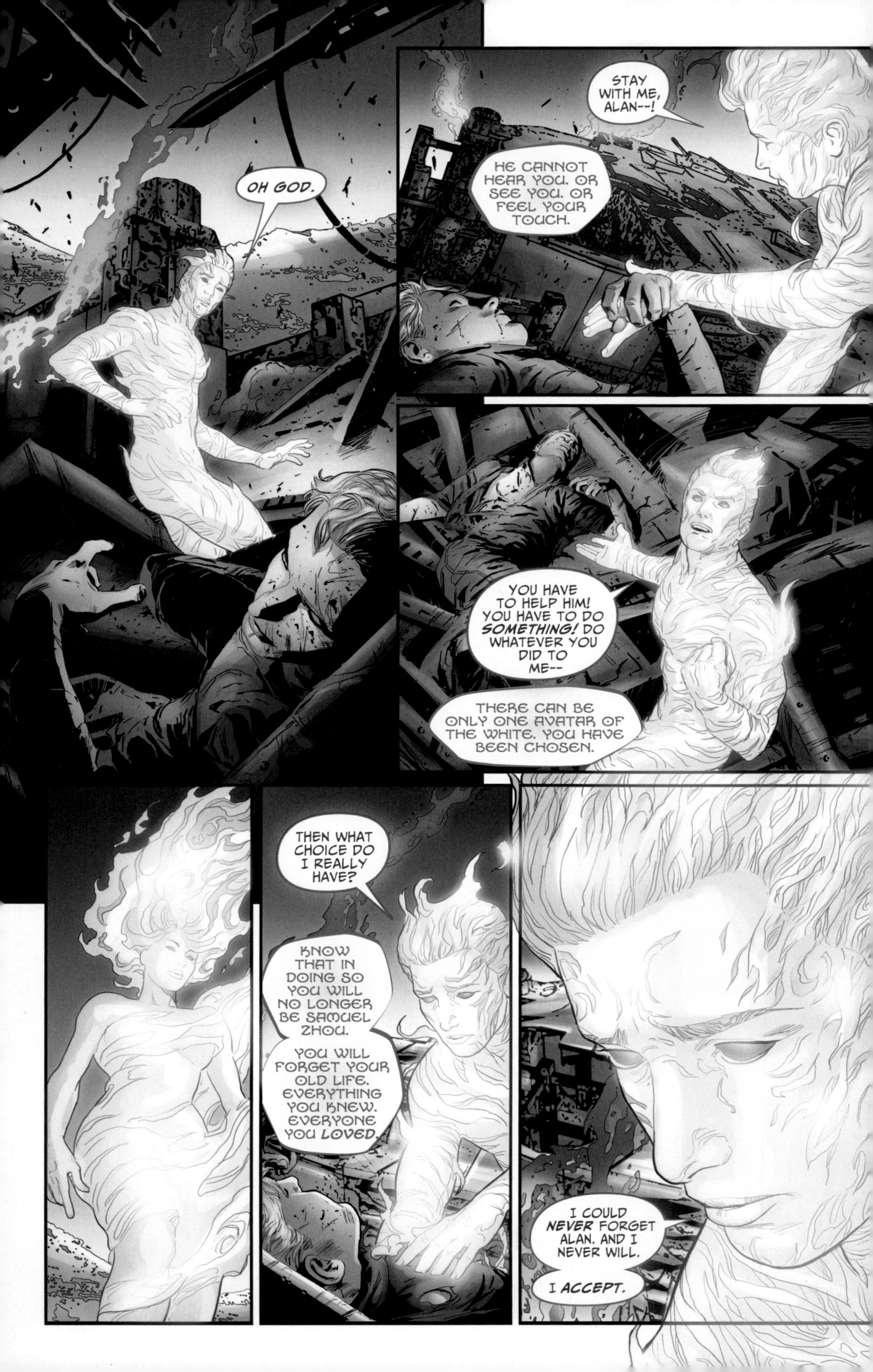
OH GOD.
STAY WITH ME, ALAN--!
HE CANNOT HEAR YOU. OR SEE YOU. OR FEEL YOUR TOUCH.
YOU HAVE TO HELP HIM! YOU HAVE TO DO SOMETHING! DO WHATEVER YOU DID TO ME--
THERE CAN BE ONLY ONE AVATAR OF THE WHITE. YOU HAVE BEEN CHOSEN.
THEN WHAT CHOICE DO I REALLY HAVE?
KNOW THAT IN DOING SO YOU WILL NO LONGER BE SAMUEL ZHOU.
YOU WILL FORGET YOUR OLD LIFE. EVERYTHING YOU KNEW. EVERYONE YOU LOVED.
I COULD NEVER FORGET ALAN. AND I NEVER WILL.
I ACCEPT.

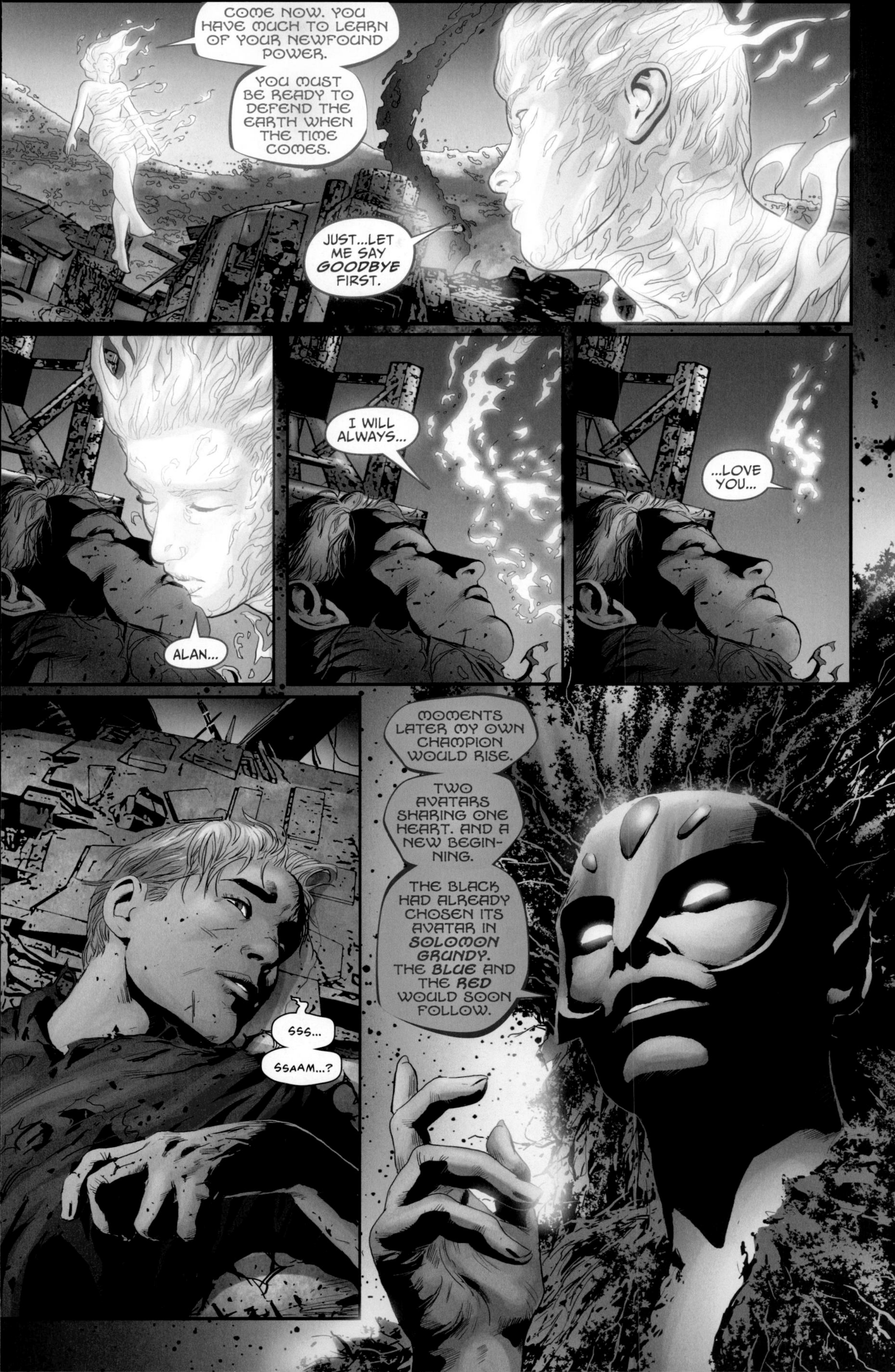
COME NOW. YOU HAVE MUCH TO LEARN OF YOUR NEWFOUND POWER.
YOU MUST BE READY TO DEFEND THE EARTH WHEN THE TIME COMES.
JUST...LET ME SAY GOODBYE FIRST.
ALAN...
I WILL ALWAYS...
...LOVE YOU...
MOMENTS LATER MY OWN CHAMPION WOULD RISE.
TWO AVATARS SHARING ONE HEART. AND A NEW BEGIN-NING.
THE BLACK HAD ALREADY CHOSEN ITS AVATAR IN SOLOMON GRUNDY. THE BLUE AND THE RED WOULD SOON FOLLOW.
SSS...
SSAAM...?

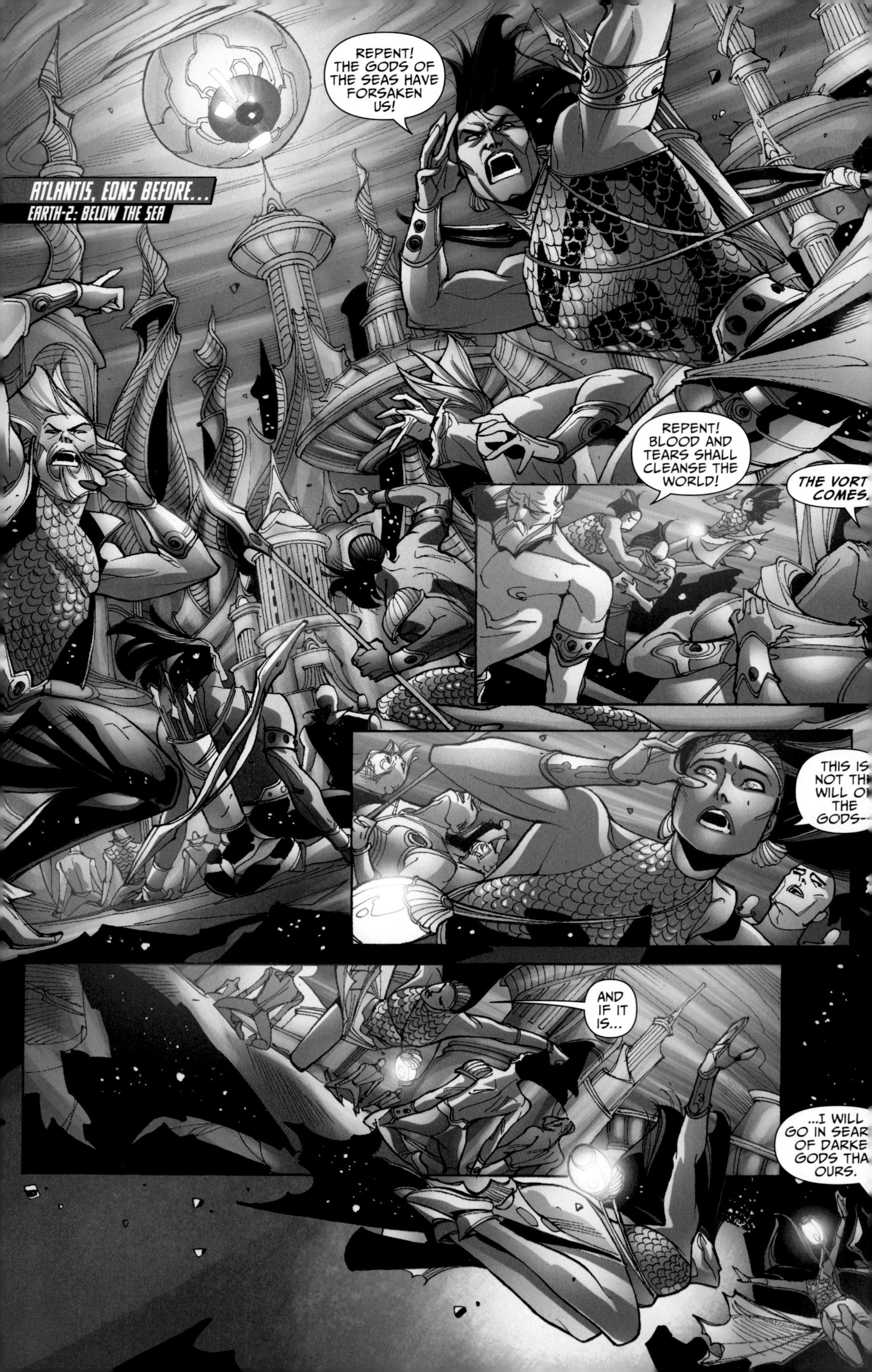

ATLANTIS, EONS BEFORE...
EARTH-2: BELOW THE SEA
REPENT! THE GODS OF THE SEAS HAVE FORSAKEN US!
REPENT! BLOOD AND TEARS SHALL CLEANSE THE WORLD!
THE VORT COMES.
THIS IS NOT TH WILL O THE GODS--
AND IF IT IS...
...I WILL GO IN SEAR OF DARKE GODS THA OURS.

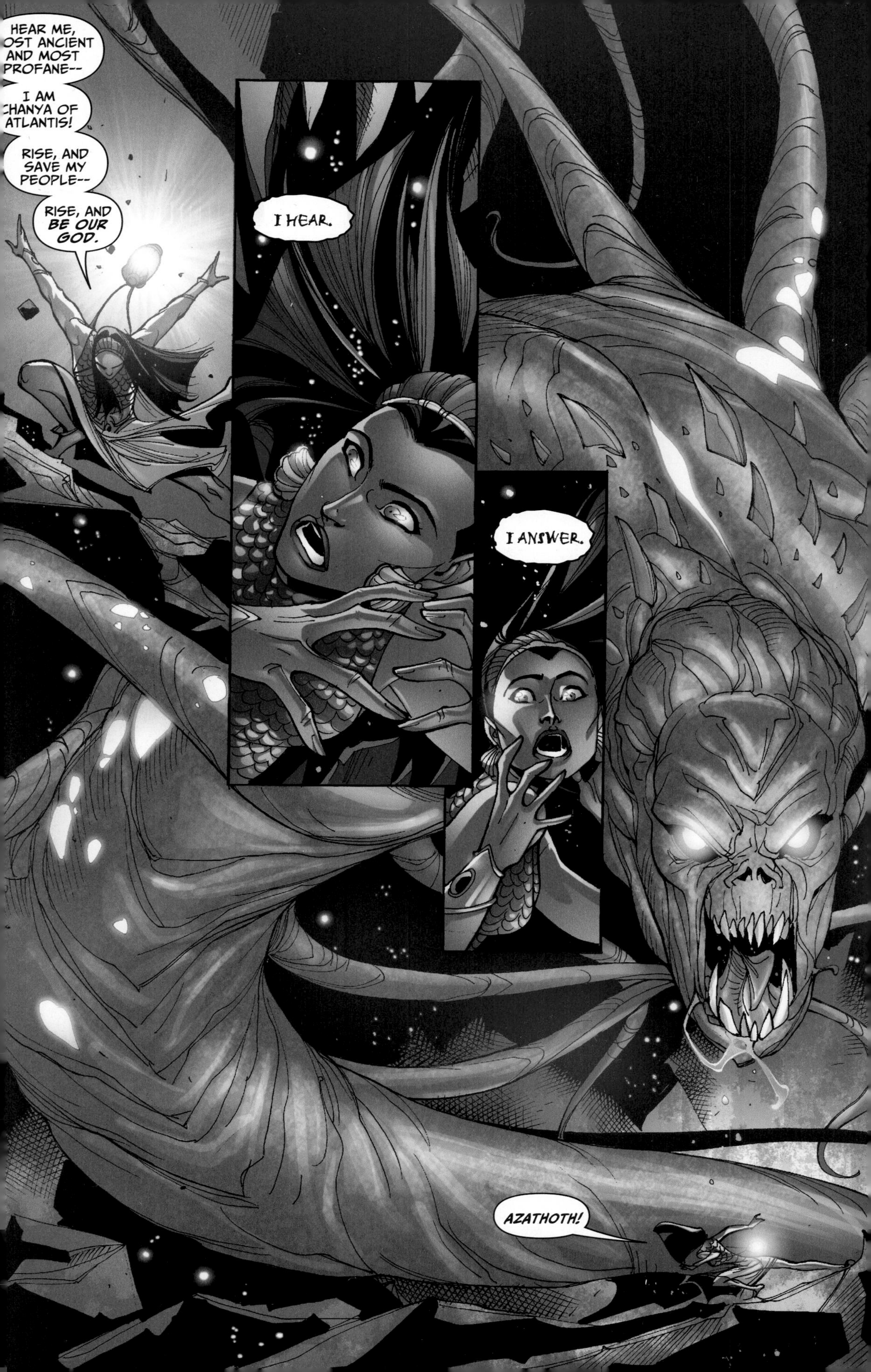
HEAR ME, OST ANCIENT AND MOST PROFANE--
I AM CHANYA OF ATLANTIS!
RISE, AND SAVE MY PEOPLE--
RISE, AND *BE OUR GOD.*
I HEAR.
I ANSWER.
AZATHOTH!

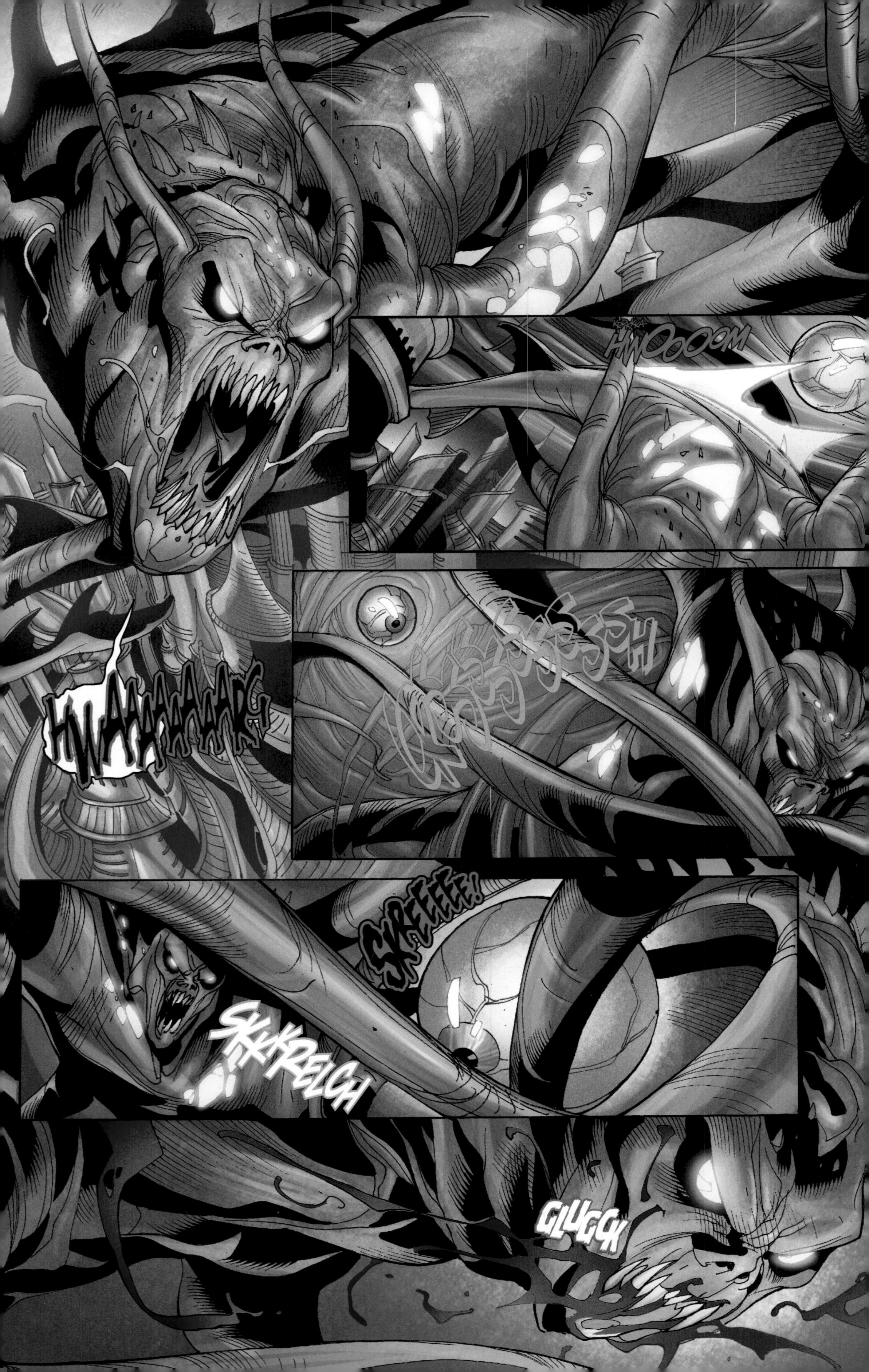
KRAKA-
HWOOOOM
HWAAAAAAARG!
SKREEEEE!
SKKKRELCH
GLUGGK

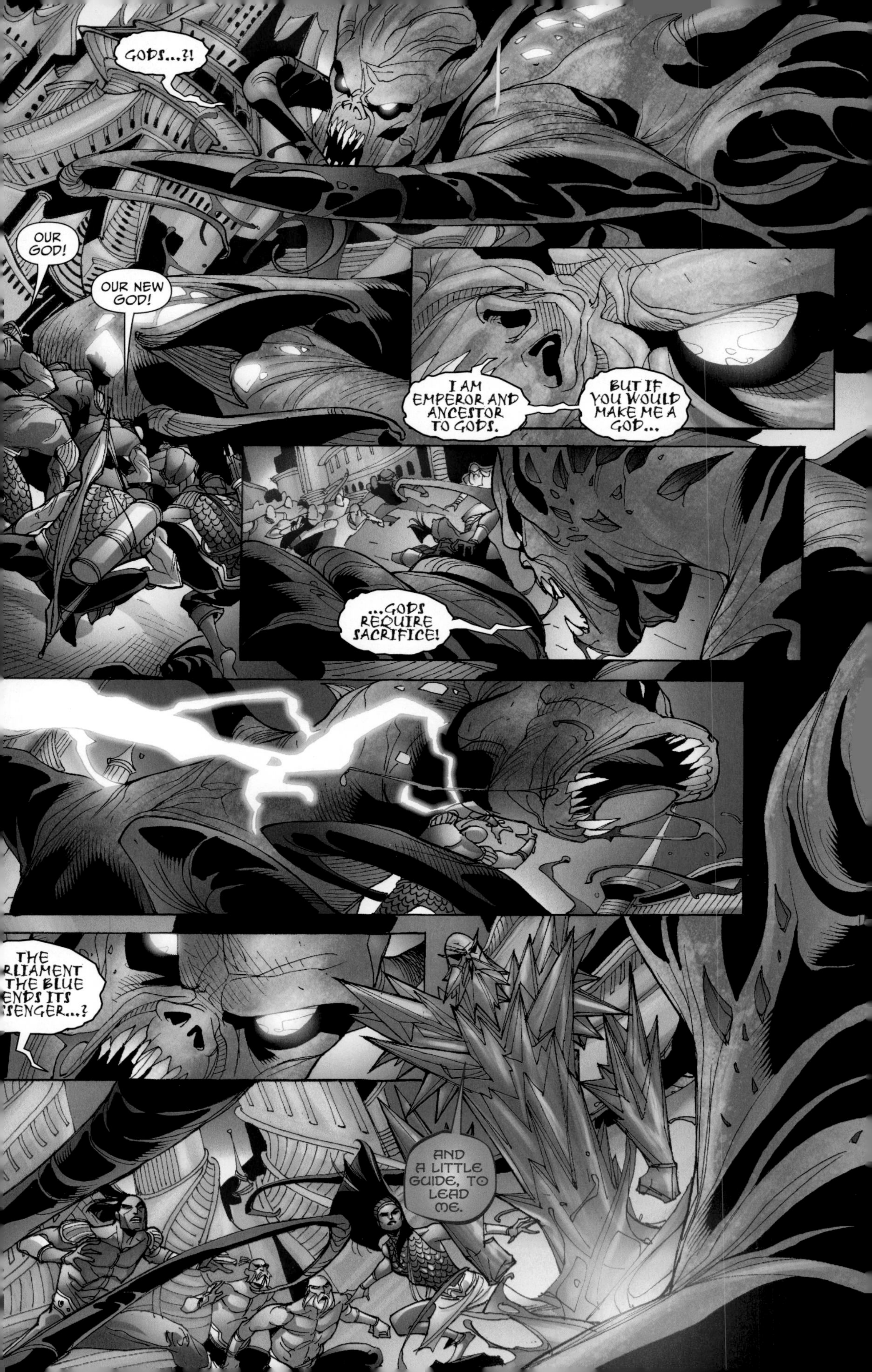
GODS...?!
OUR GOD!
OUR NEW GOD!
I AM EMPEROR AND ANCESTOR TO GODS.
BUT IF YOU WOULD MAKE ME A GOD...
...GODS REQUIRE SACRIFICE!
AND A LITTLE GUIDE, TO LEAD ME.

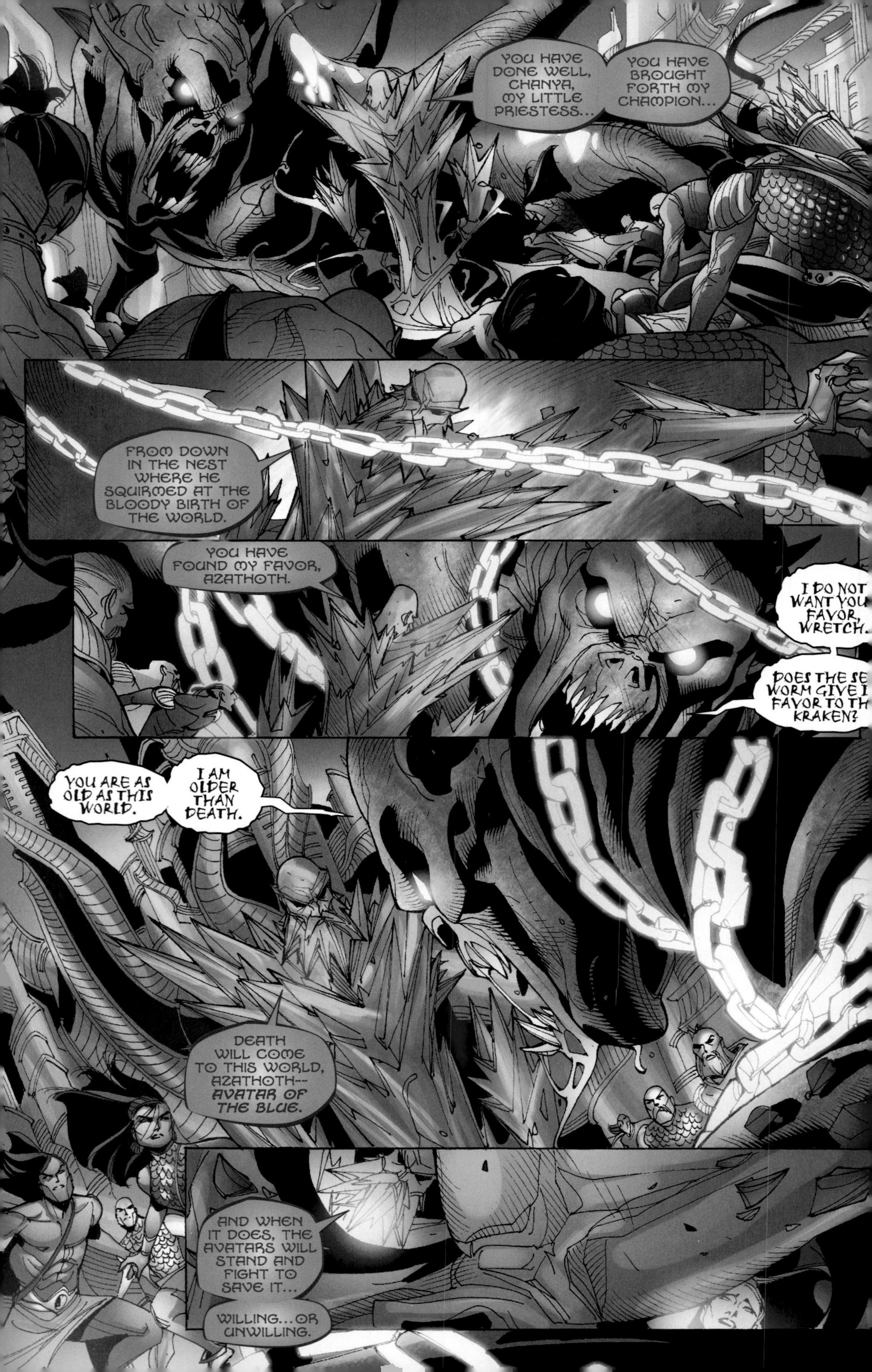
YOU HAVE DONE WELL, CHANYA, MY LITTLE PRIESTESS...
YOU HAVE BROUGHT FORTH MY CHAMPION...
FROM DOWN IN THE NEST WHERE HE SQUIRMED AT THE BLOODY BIRTH OF THE WORLD.
YOU HAVE FOUND MY FAVOR, AZATHOTH.
I DO NOT WANT YOU FAVOR, WRETCH.
DOES THE SE WORM GIVE I FAVOR TO TH KRAKEN?
YOU ARE AS OLD AS THIS WORLD.
I AM OLDER THAN DEATH.
DEATH WILL COME TO THIS WORLD, AZATHOTH-- AVATAR OF THE BLUE.
AND WHEN IT DOES, THE AVATARS WILL STAND AND FIGHT TO SAVE IT...
WILLING...OR UNWILLING.

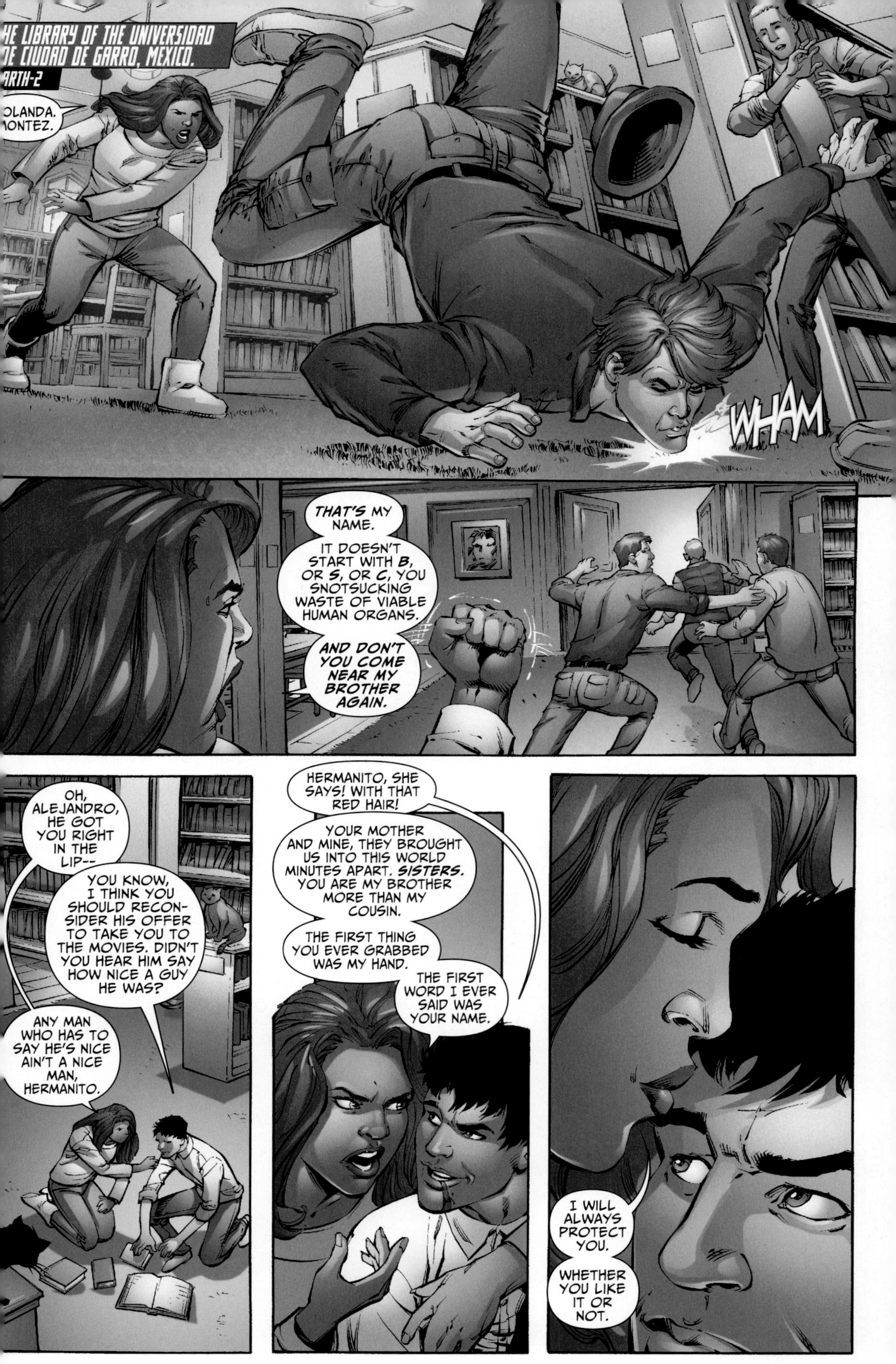

HE LIBRARY OF THE UNIVERSIDAD DE CIUDAD DE GARRO, MEXICO.
ARTH-2
OLANDA. MONTEZ.
WHAM
THAT'S MY NAME.
IT DOESN'T START WITH B, OR S, OR C, YOU SNOTSUCKING WASTE OF VIABLE HUMAN ORGANS.
AND DON'T YOU COME NEAR MY BROTHER AGAIN.
OH, ALEJANDRO, HE GOT YOU RIGHT IN THE LIP--
YOU KNOW, I THINK YOU SHOULD RECON-SIDER HIS OFFER TO TAKE YOU TO THE MOVIES. DIDN'T YOU HEAR HIM SAY HOW NICE A GUY HE WAS?
ANY MAN WHO HAS TO SAY HE'S NICE AIN'T A NICE MAN, HERMANITO.
HERMANITO, SHE SAYS! WITH THAT RED HAIR!
YOUR MOTHER AND MINE, THEY BROUGHT US INTO THIS WORLD MINUTES APART. SISTERS. YOU ARE MY BROTHER MORE THAN MY COUSIN.
THE FIRST THING YOU EVER GRABBED WAS MY HAND.
THE FIRST WORD I EVER SAID WAS YOUR NAME.
I WILL ALWAYS PROTECT YOU.
WHETHER YOU LIKE IT OR NOT.

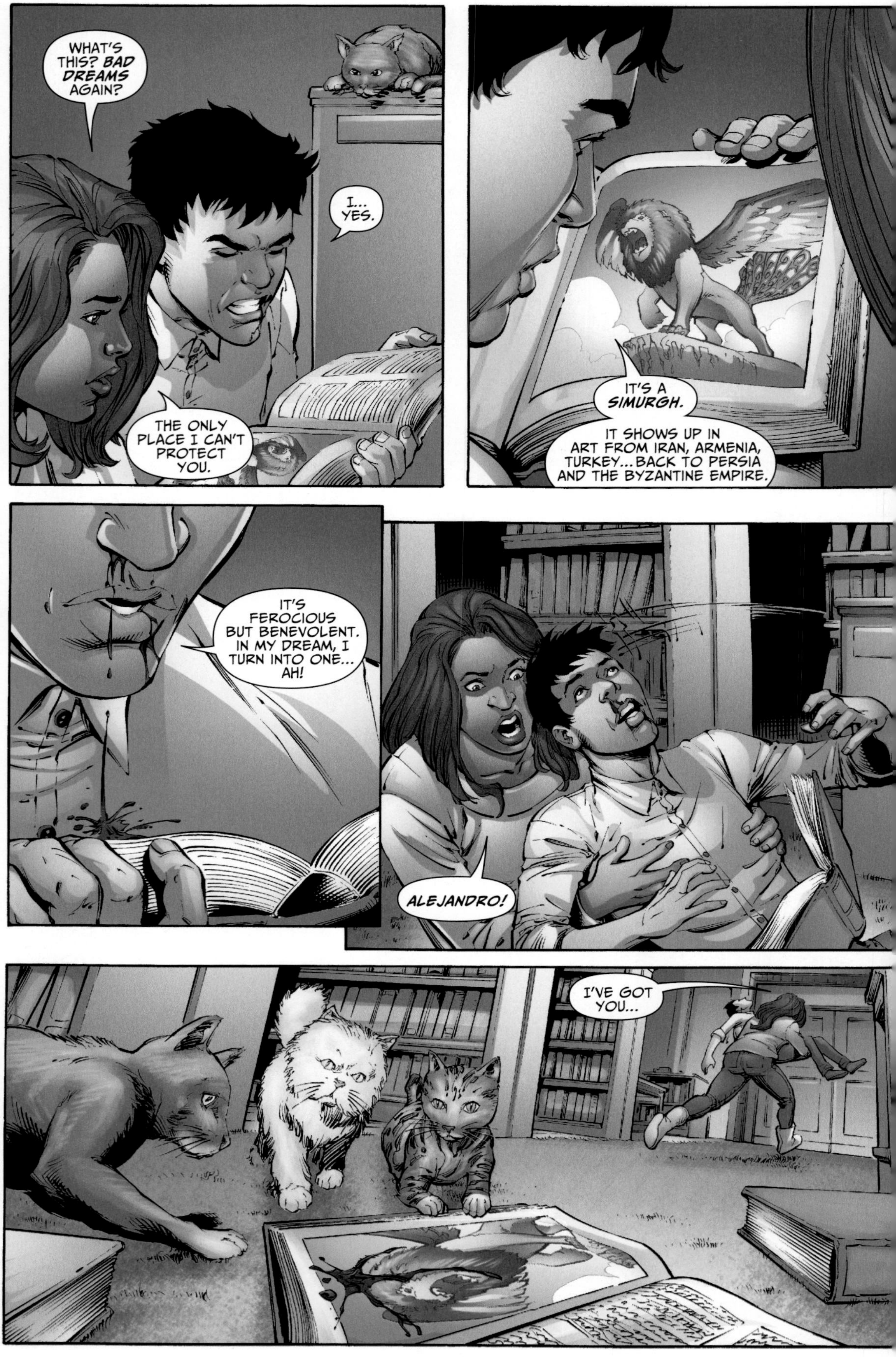
WHAT'S THIS? BAD DREAMS AGAIN?
I... YES.
THE ONLY PLACE I CAN'T PROTECT YOU.
IT'S A SIMURGH.
IT SHOWS UP IN ART FROM IRAN, ARMENIA, TURKEY...BACK TO PERSIA AND THE BYZANTINE EMPIRE.
IT'S FEROCIOUS BUT BENEVOLENT. IN MY DREAM, I TURN INTO ONE... AH!
ALEJANDRO!
I'VE GOT YOU...

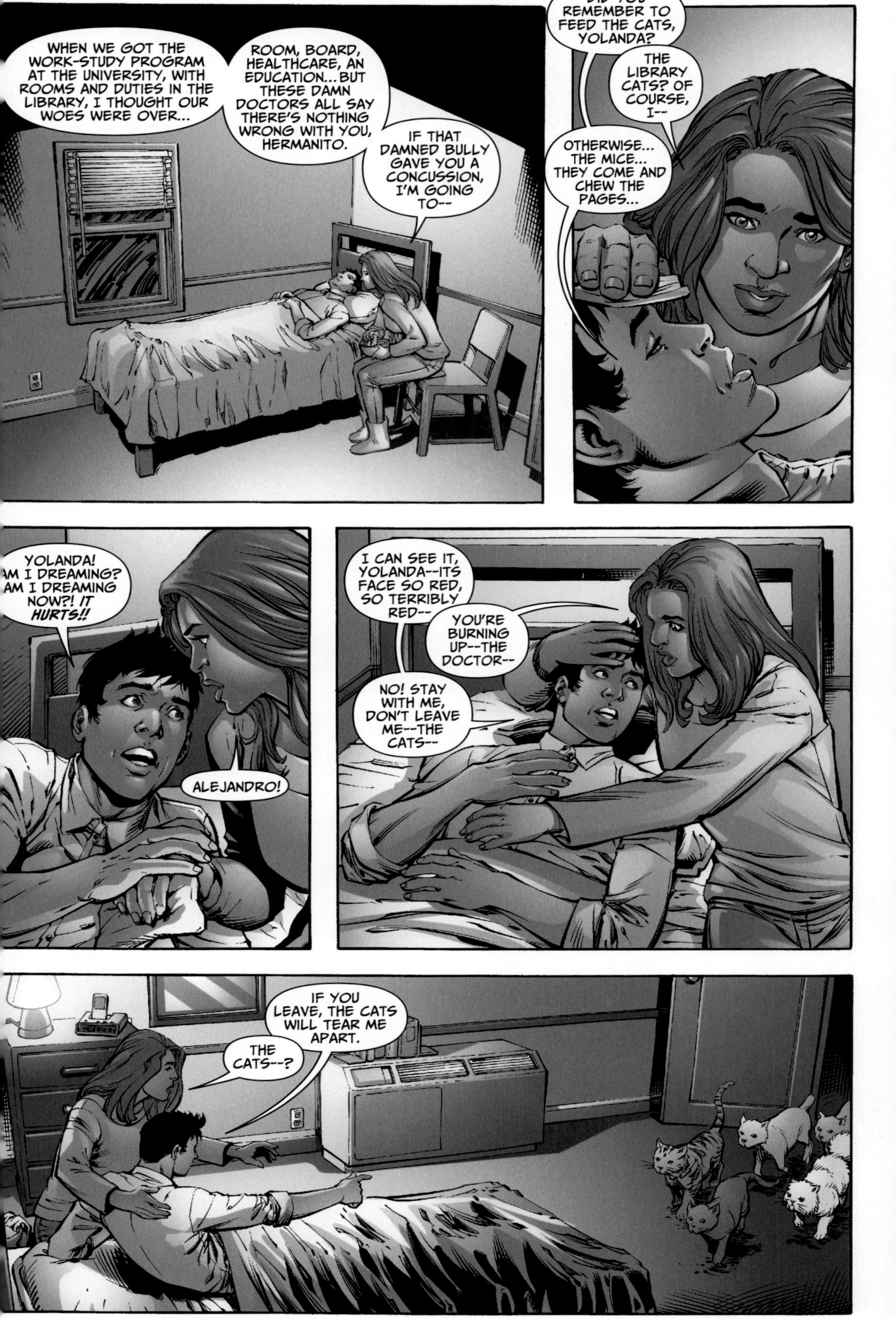
WHEN WE GOT THE WORK-STUDY PROGRAM AT THE UNIVERSITY, WITH ROOMS AND DUTIES IN THE LIBRARY, I THOUGHT OUR WOES WERE OVER...
ROOM, BOARD, HEALTHCARE, AN EDUCATION... BUT THESE DAMN DOCTORS ALL SAY THERE'S NOTHING WRONG WITH YOU, HERMANITO.
IF THAT DAMNED BULLY GAVE YOU A CONCUSSION, I'M GOING TO--
DID YOU REMEMBER TO FEED THE CATS, YOLANDA?
THE LIBRARY CATS? OF COURSE, I--
OTHERWISE... THE MICE... THEY COME AND CHEW THE PAGES...
YOLANDA! AM I DREAMING? AM I DREAMING NOW?! *IT HURTS!!*
ALEJANDRO!
I CAN SEE IT, YOLANDA--ITS FACE SO RED, SO TERRIBLY RED--
YOU'RE BURNING UP--THE DOCTOR--
NO! STAY WITH ME, DON'T LEAVE ME--THE CATS--
IF YOU LEAVE, THE CATS WILL TEAR ME APART.
THE CATS--?

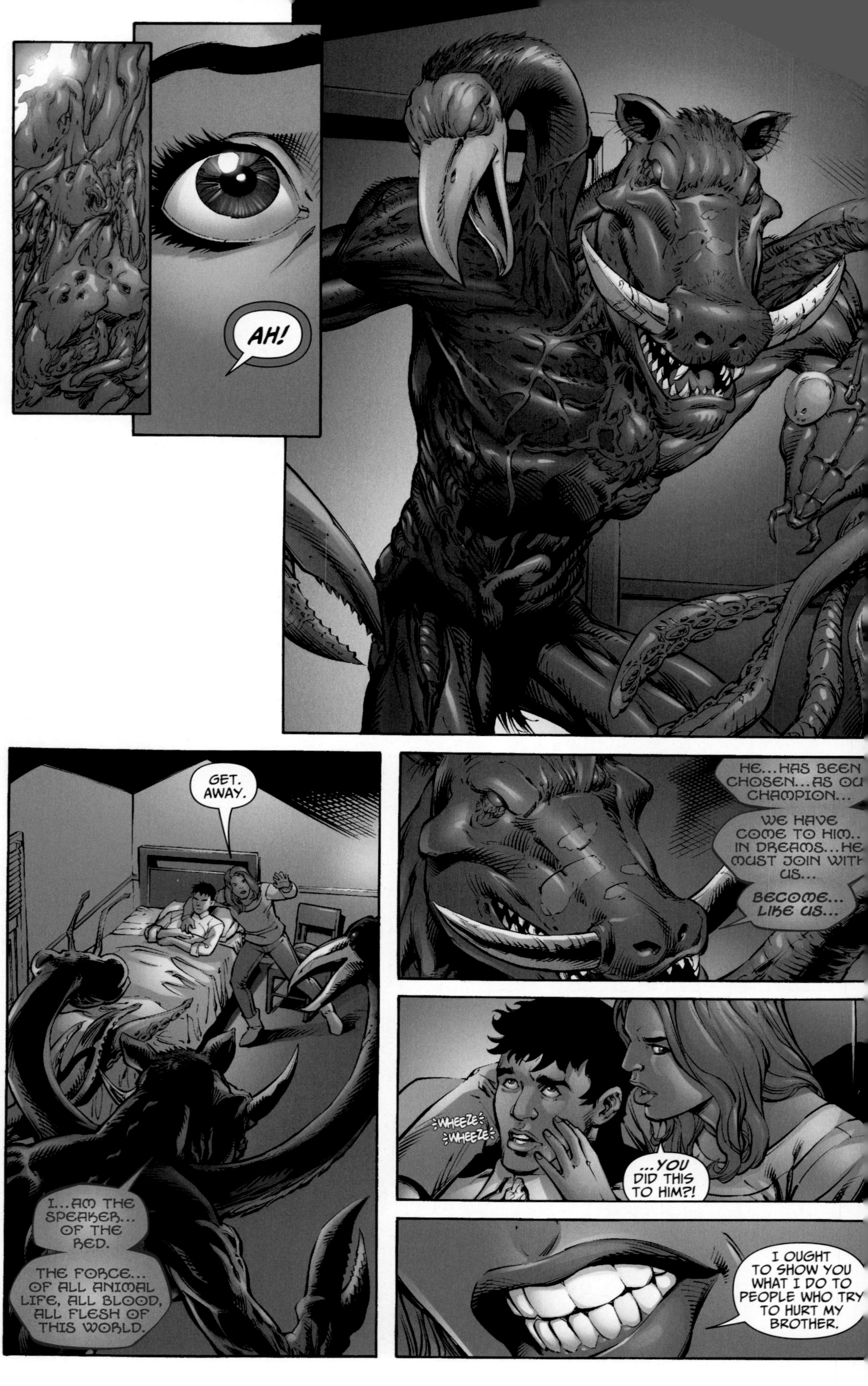
AH!
GET. AWAY.
I...AM THE SPEAKER... OF THE RED.
THE FORCE... OF ALL ANIMAL LIFE, ALL BLOOD, ALL FLESH OF THIS WORLD.
HE...HAS BEEN CHOSEN...AS OU CHAMPION...
WE HAVE COME TO HIM... IN DREAMS...HE MUST JOIN WITH US...
BECOME... LIKE US...
WHEEZE WHEEZE
...YOU DID THIS TO HIM?!
I OUGHT TO SHOW YOU WHAT I DO TO PEOPLE WHO TRY TO HURT MY BROTHER.

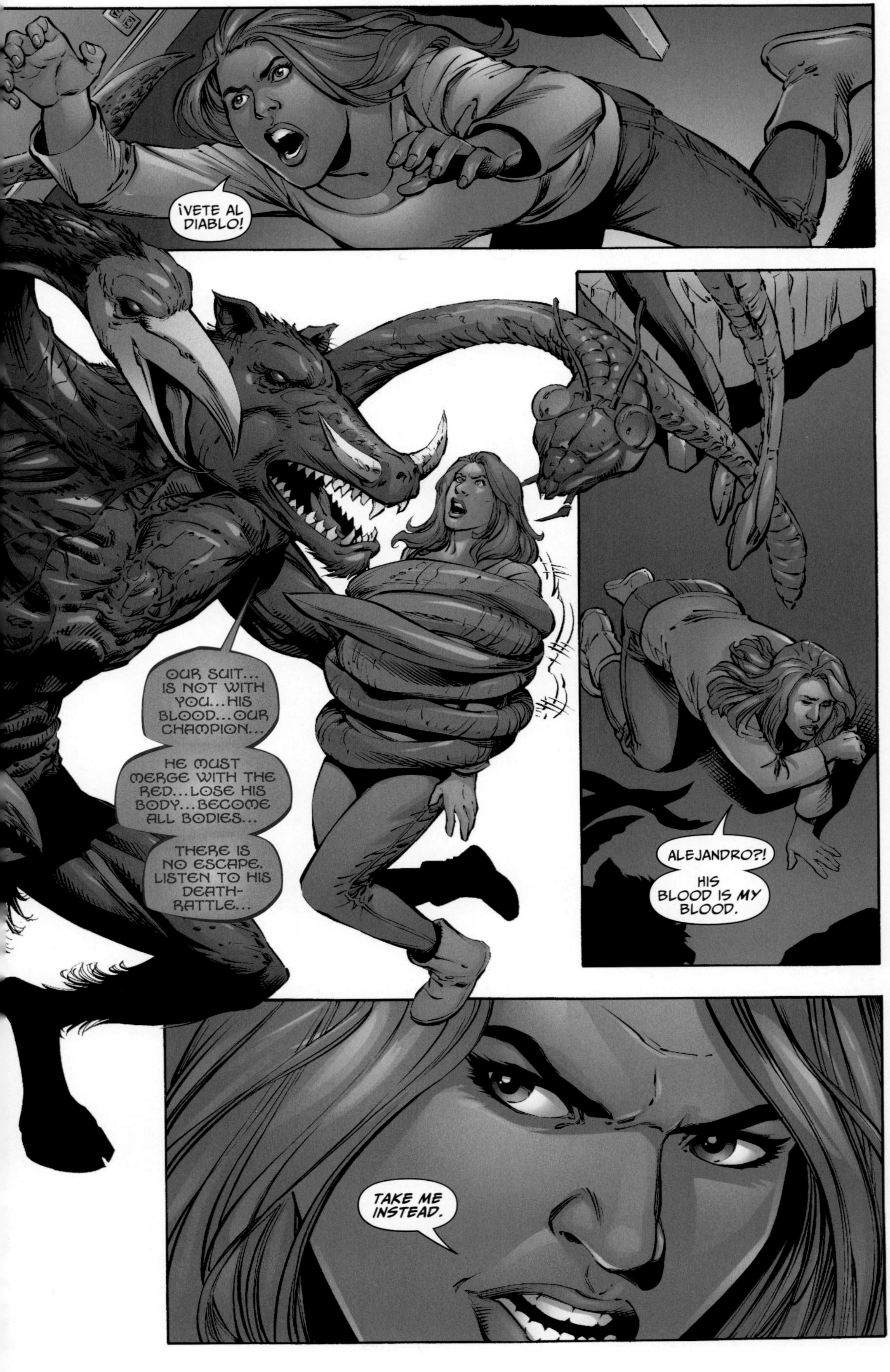
¡VETE AL DIABLO!
OUR SUIT... IS NOT WITH YOU...HIS BLOOD...OUR CHAMPION...
HE MUST MERGE WITH THE RED...LOSE HIS BODY...BECOME ALL BODIES...
THERE IS NO ESCAPE. LISTEN TO HIS DEATH-RATTLE...
ALEJANDRO?!
HIS BLOOD IS MY BLOOD.
TAKE ME INSTEAD.

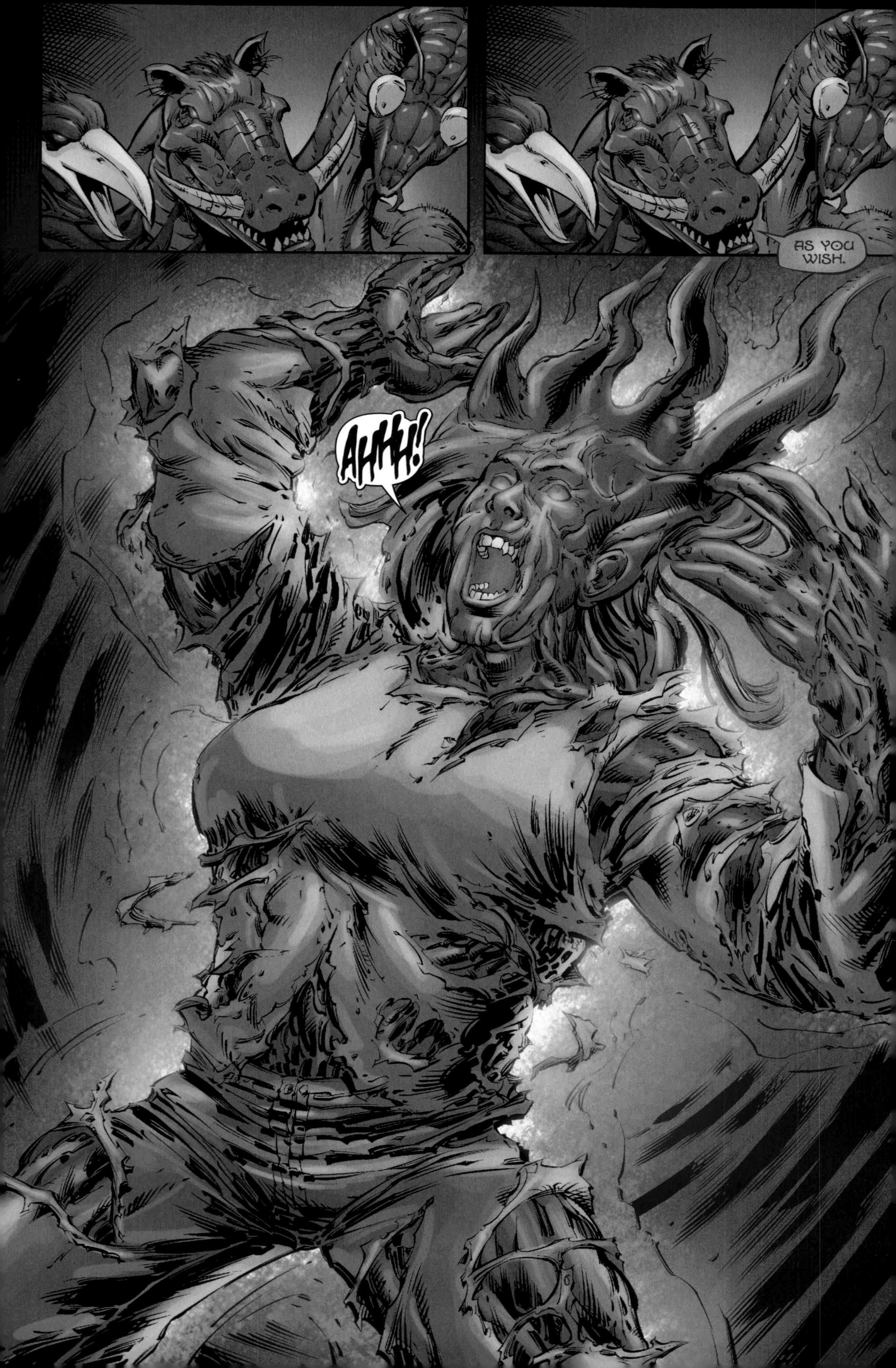
AS YOU WISH.
AHHH!

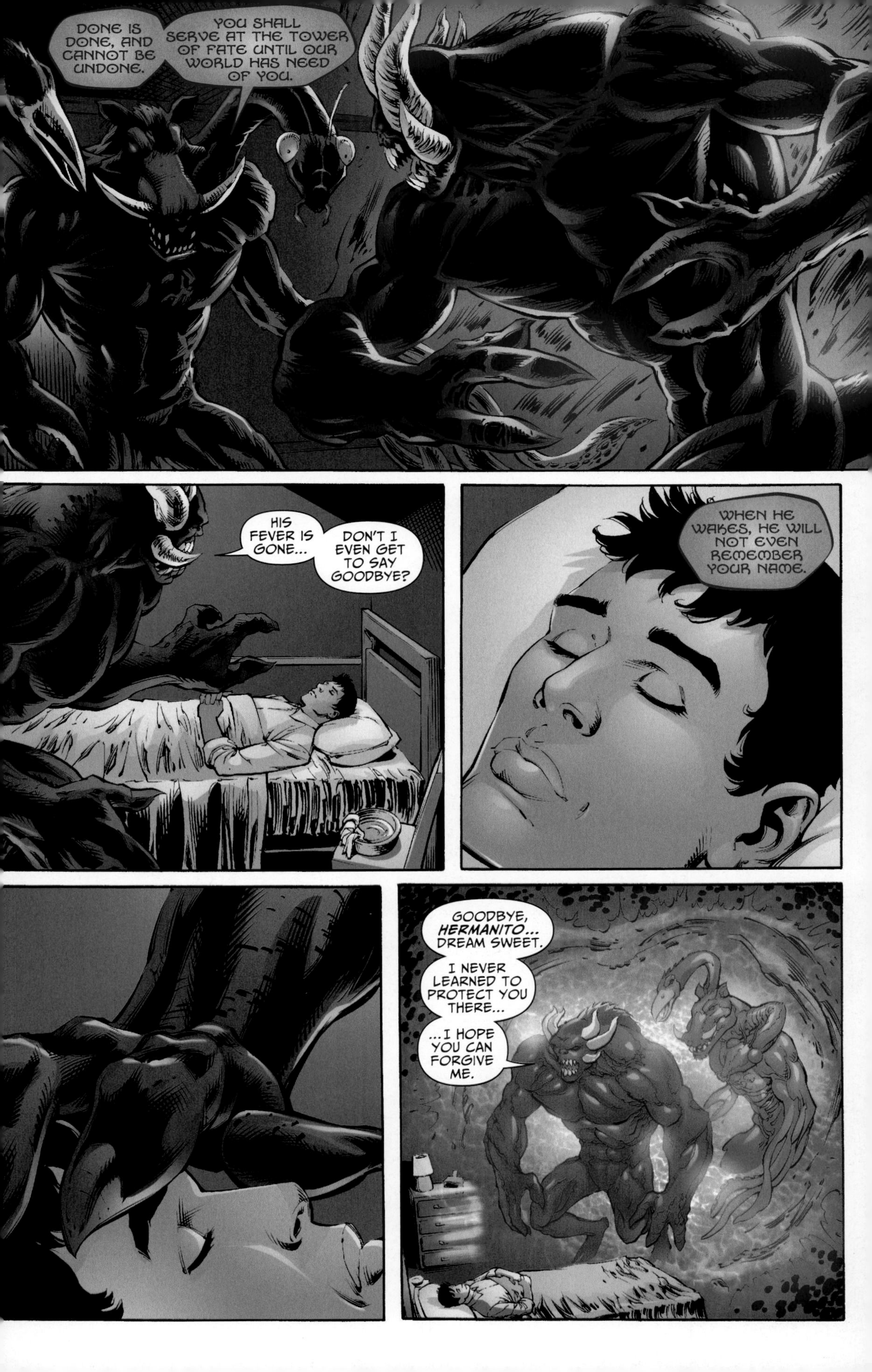
DONE IS DONE, AND CANNOT BE UNDONE.
YOU SHALL SERVE AT THE TOWER OF FATE UNTIL OUR WORLD HAS NEED OF YOU.
HIS FEVER IS GONE...
DON'T I EVEN GET TO SAY GOODBYE?
WHEN HE WAKES, HE WILL NOT EVEN REMEMBER YOUR NAME.
GOODBYE, HERMANITO... DREAM SWEET.
I NEVER LEARNED TO PROTECT YOU THERE...
...I HOPE YOU CAN FORGIVE ME.

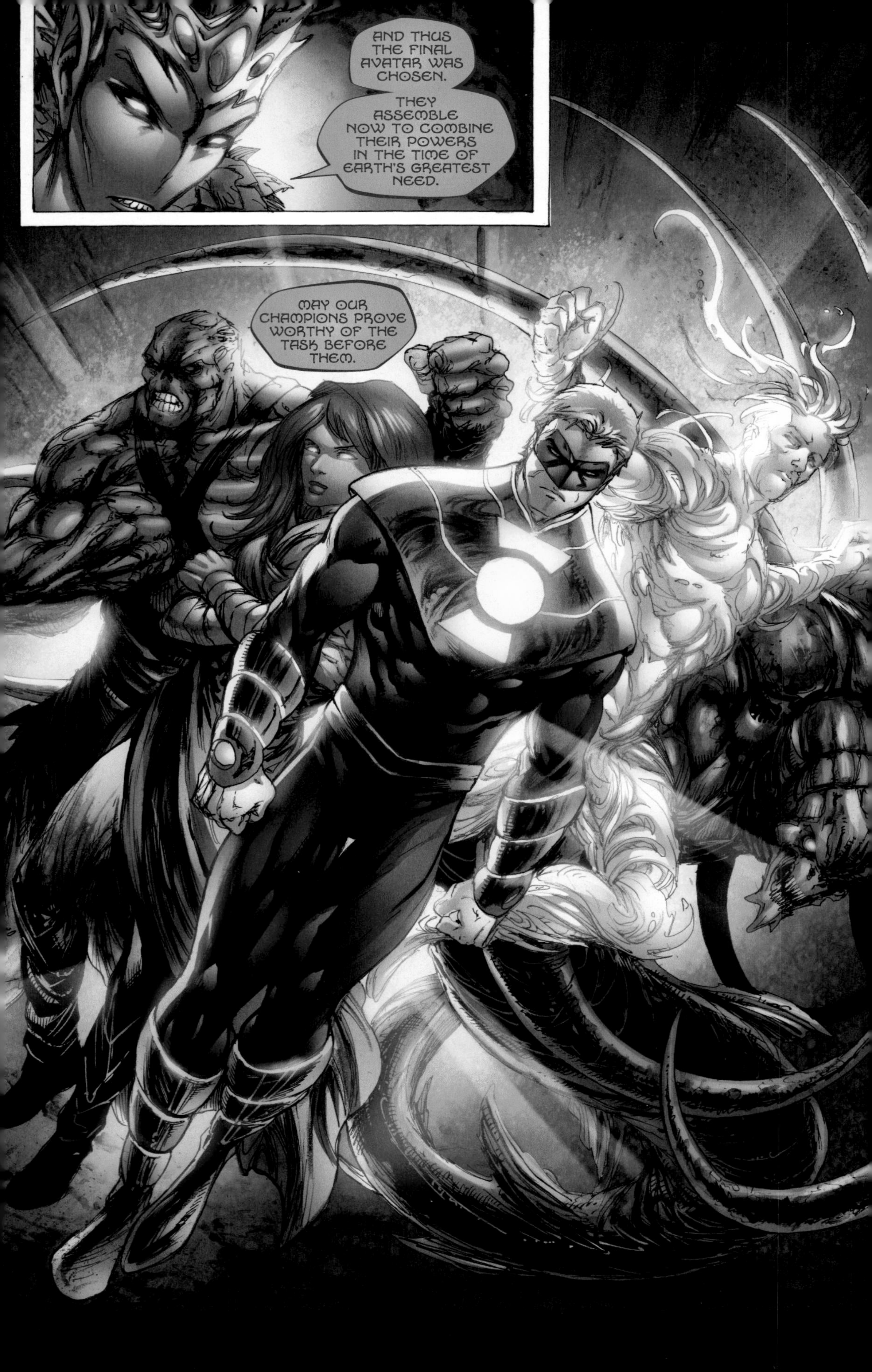
AND THUS THE FINAL AVATAR WAS CHOSEN.
THEY ASSEMBLE NOW TO COMBINE THEIR POWERS IN THE TIME OF EARTH'S GREATEST NEED.
MAY OUR CHAMPIONS PROVE WORTHY OF THE TASK BEFORE THEM.

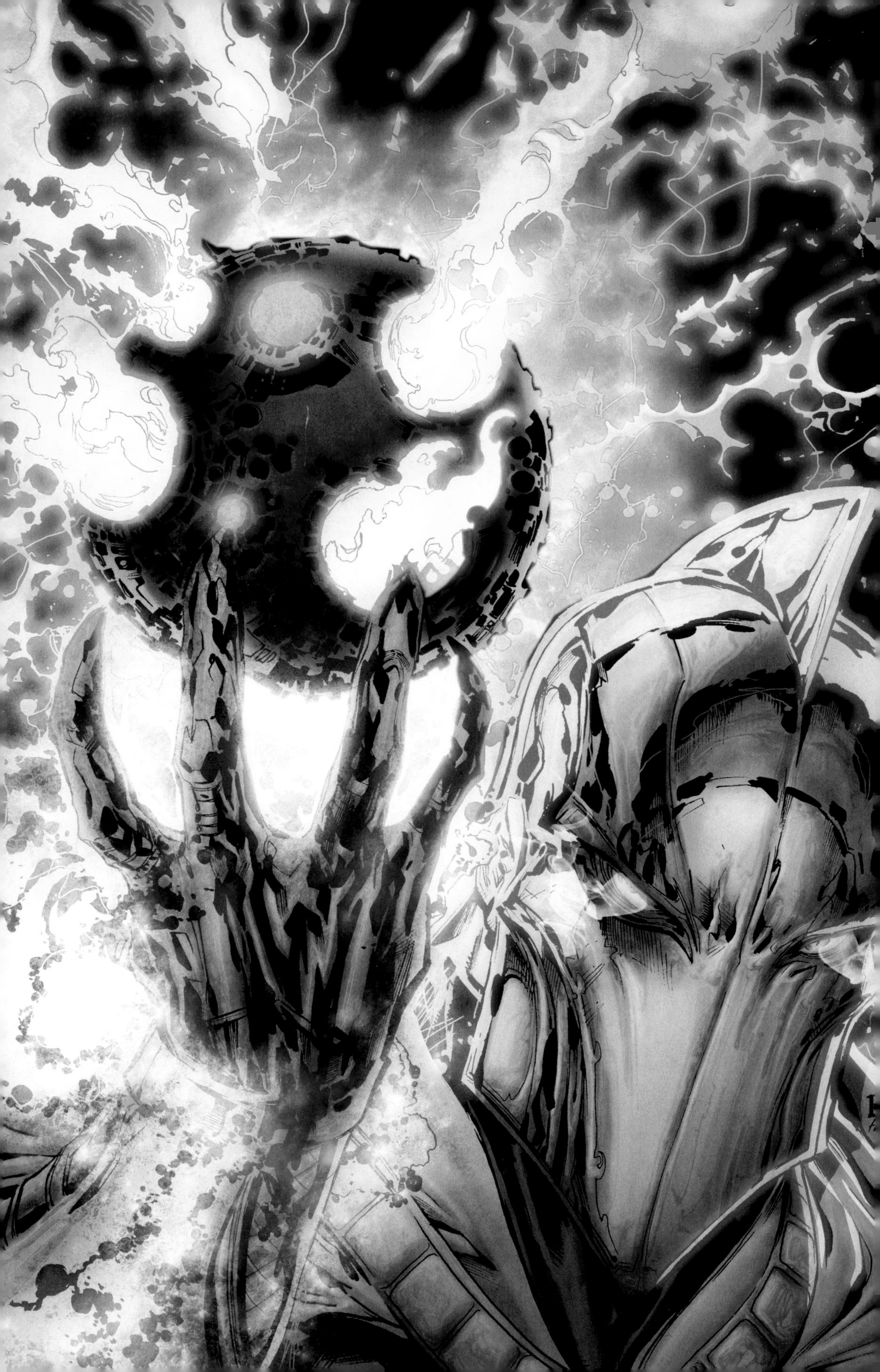

FATE & FURY

DANIEL H. WILSON, MARGUERITE BENNETT, MIKE JOHNSON writers ANDY SMITH, CLIFF RICHARDS pencillers TREVOR SCOTT, CLIFF RICHARDS inker
PETER PANTAZIS colorist TRAVIS LANHAM letterer cover by KEN LASHLEY and ANDREW DALHOUSE

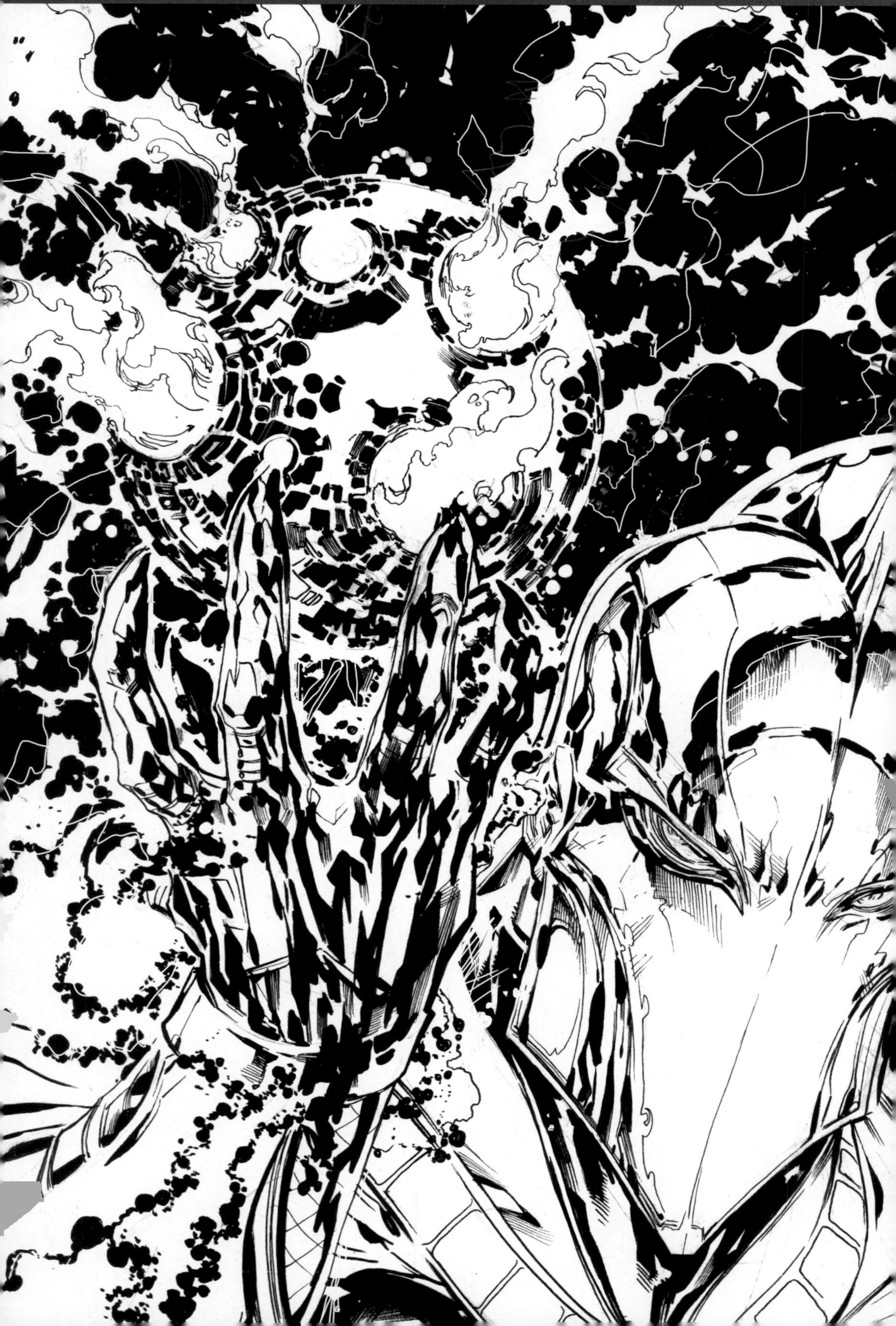

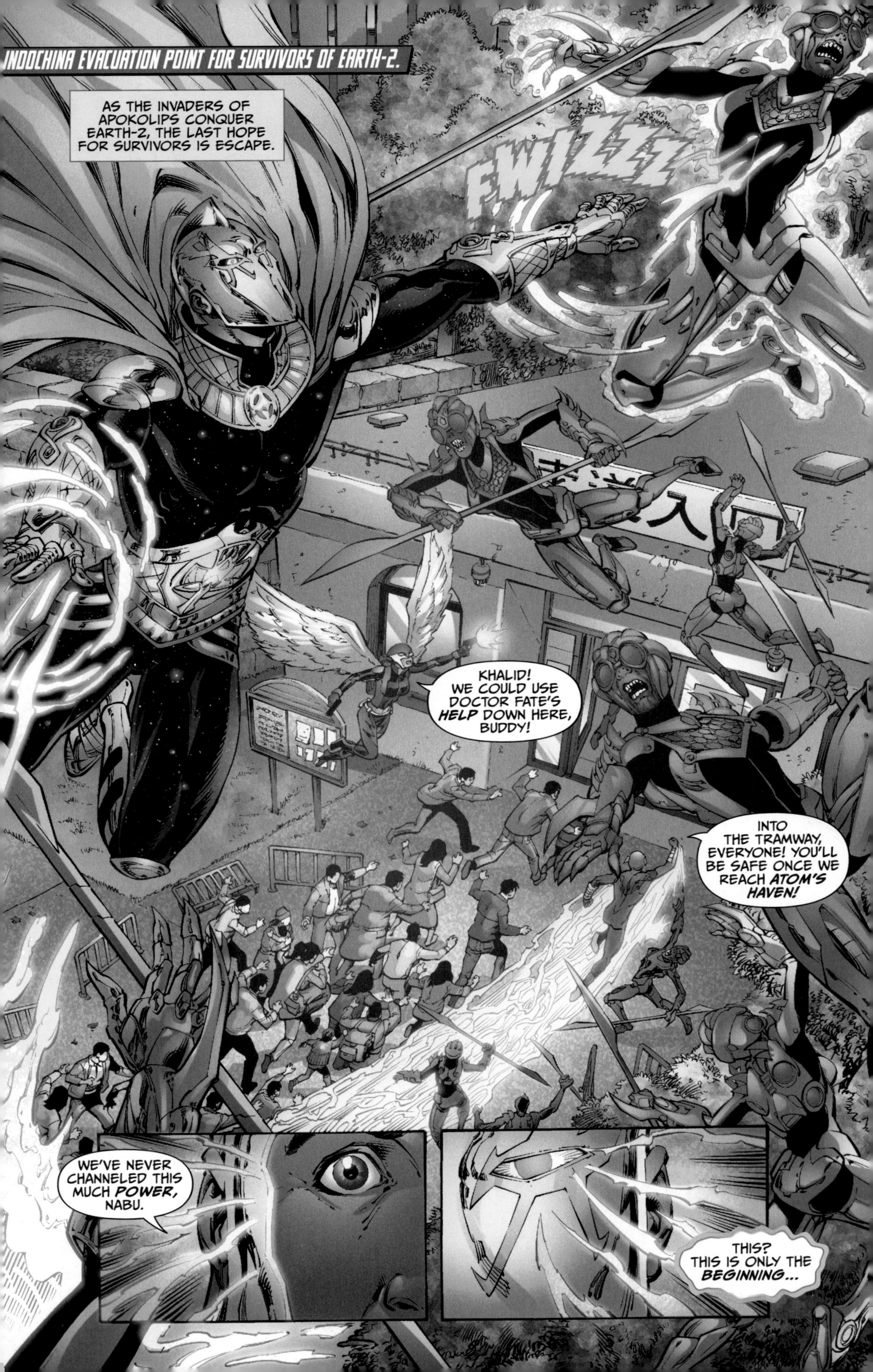
INDOCHINA EVACUATION POINT FOR SURVIVORS OF EARTH-2.
AS THE INVADERS OF APOKOLIPS CONQUER EARTH-2, THE LAST HOPE FOR SURVIVORS IS ESCAPE.
FWIZZZ
KHALID! WE COULD USE DOCTOR FATE'S HELP DOWN HERE, BUDDY!
INTO THE TRAMWAY, EVERYONE! YOU'LL BE SAFE ONCE WE REACH ATOM'S HAVEN!
WE'VE NEVER CHANNELED THIS MUCH POWER, NABU.
THIS? THIS IS ONLY THE BEGINNING...

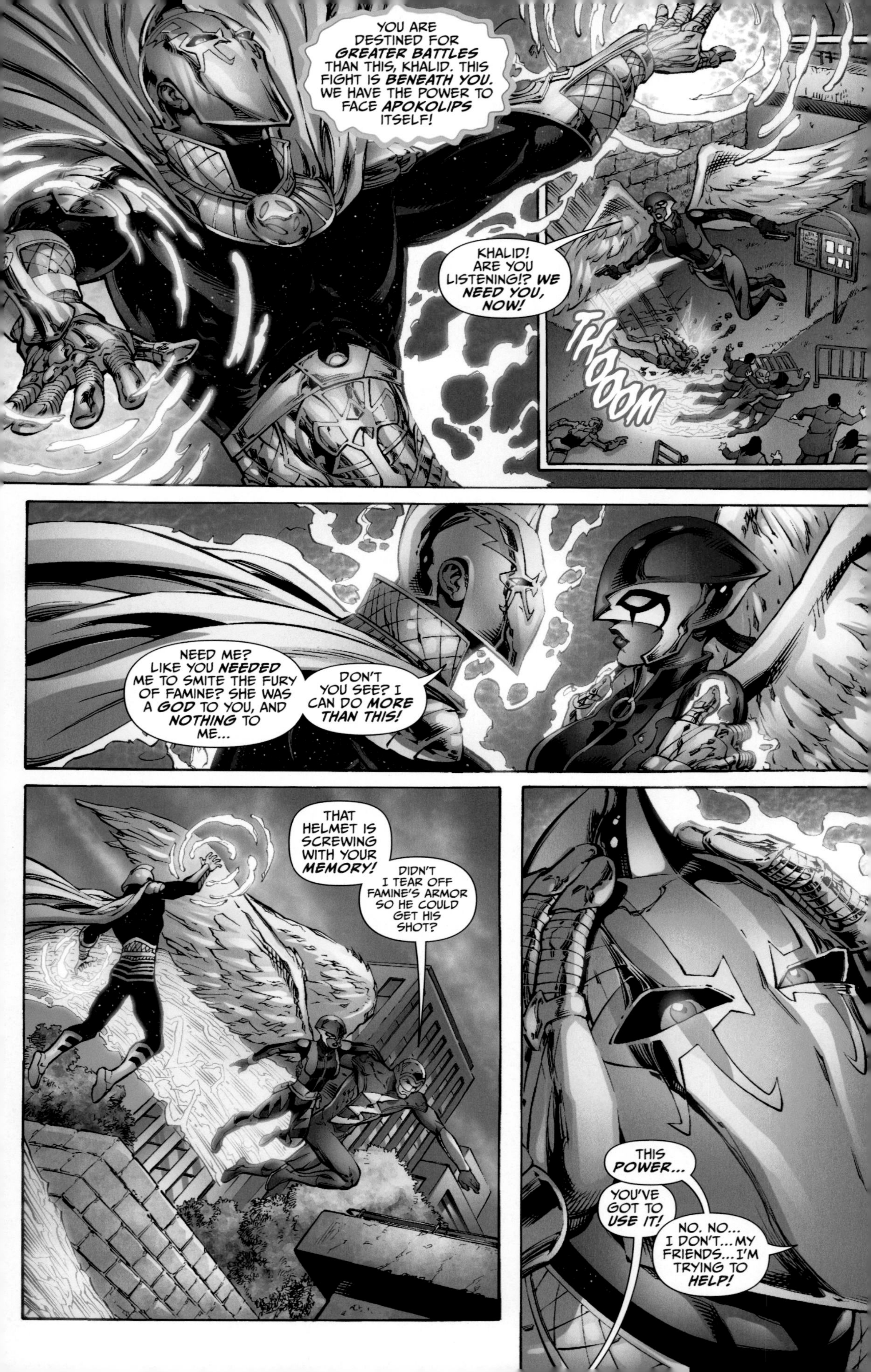
YOU ARE DESTINED FOR GREATER BATTLES THAN THIS, KHALID. THIS FIGHT IS BENEATH YOU. WE HAVE THE POWER TO FACE APOKOLIPS ITSELF!
KHALID! ARE YOU LISTENING!? WE NEED YOU, NOW!
THOOOM
NEED ME? LIKE YOU NEEDED ME TO SMITE THE FURY OF FAMINE? SHE WAS A GOD TO YOU, AND NOTHING TO ME...
DON'T YOU SEE? I CAN DO MORE THAN THIS!
THAT HELMET IS SCREWING WITH YOUR MEMORY!
DIDN'T I TEAR OFF FAMINE'S ARMOR SO HE COULD GET HIS SHOT?
THIS POWER...
YOU'VE GOT TO USE IT!
NO. NO... I DON'T... MY FRIENDS... I'M TRYING TO HELP!

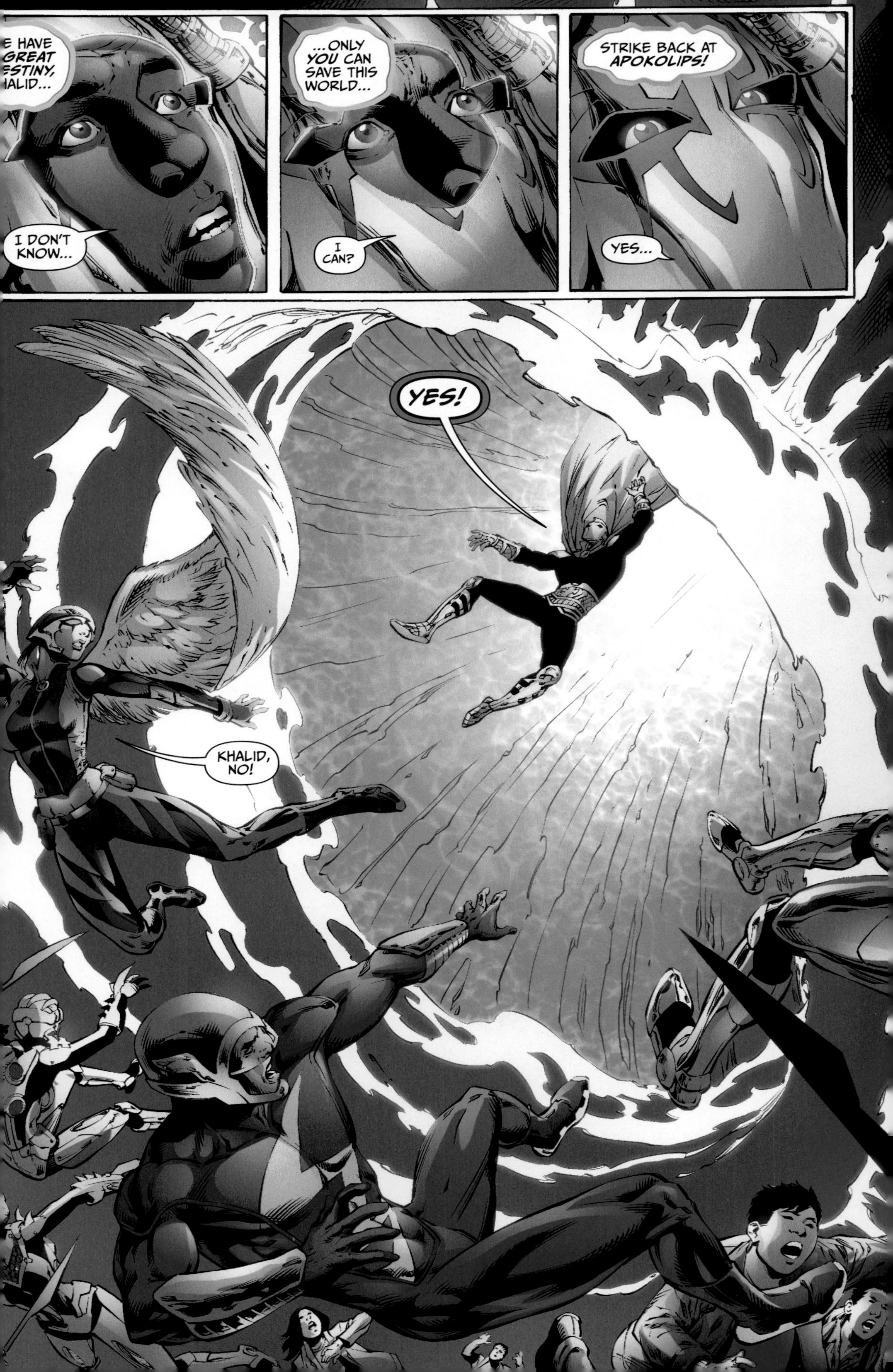
E HAVE GREAT ESTINY, HALID...
I DON'T KNOW...
...ONLY YOU CAN SAVE THIS WORLD...
I CAN?
STRIKE BACK AT APOKOLIPS!
YES...
YES!
KHALID, NO!

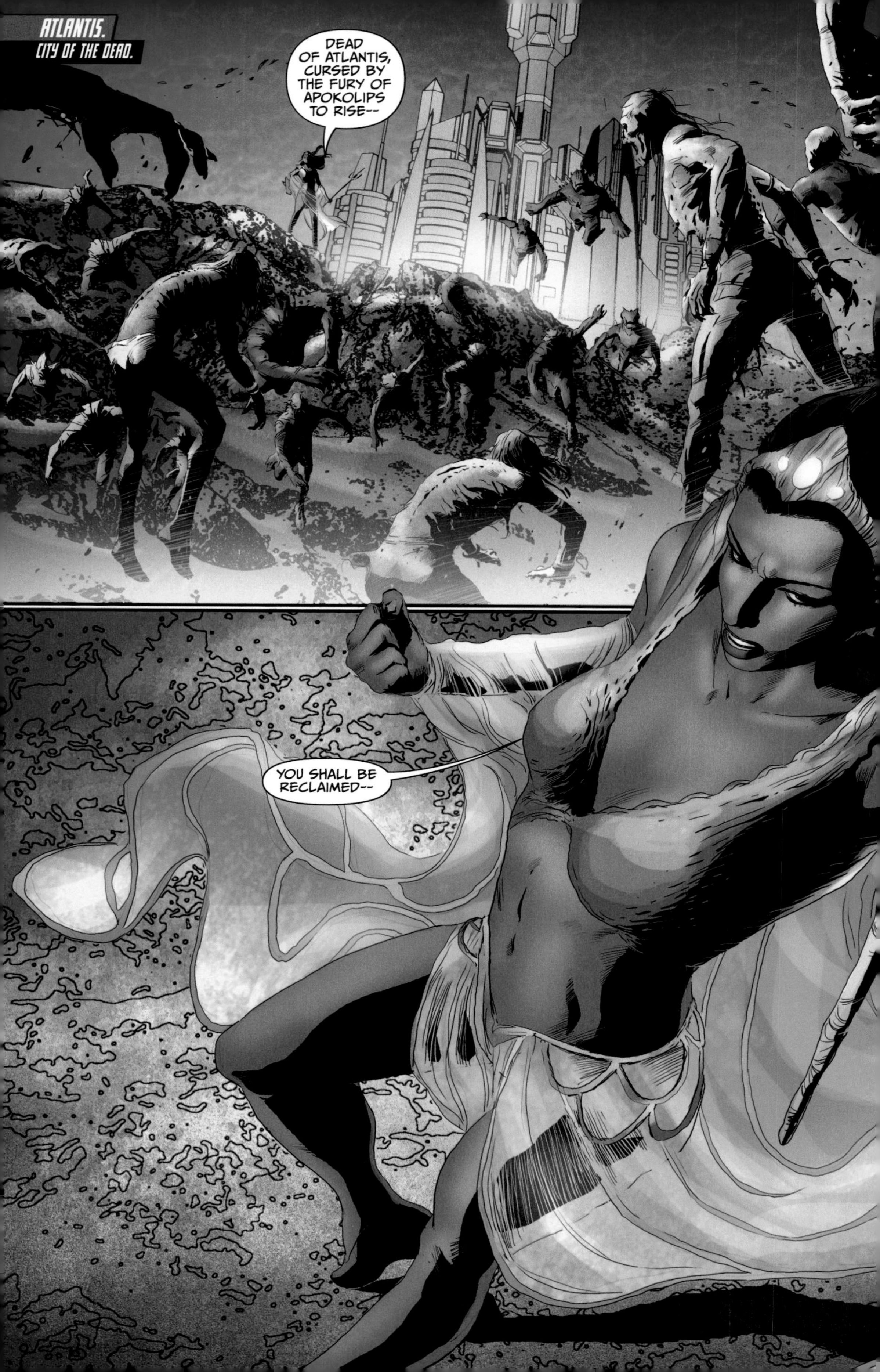
ATLANTIS.
CITY OF THE DEAD.
DEAD OF ATLANTIS, CURSED BY THE FURY OF APOKOLIPS TO RISE--
YOU SHALL BE RECLAIMED--

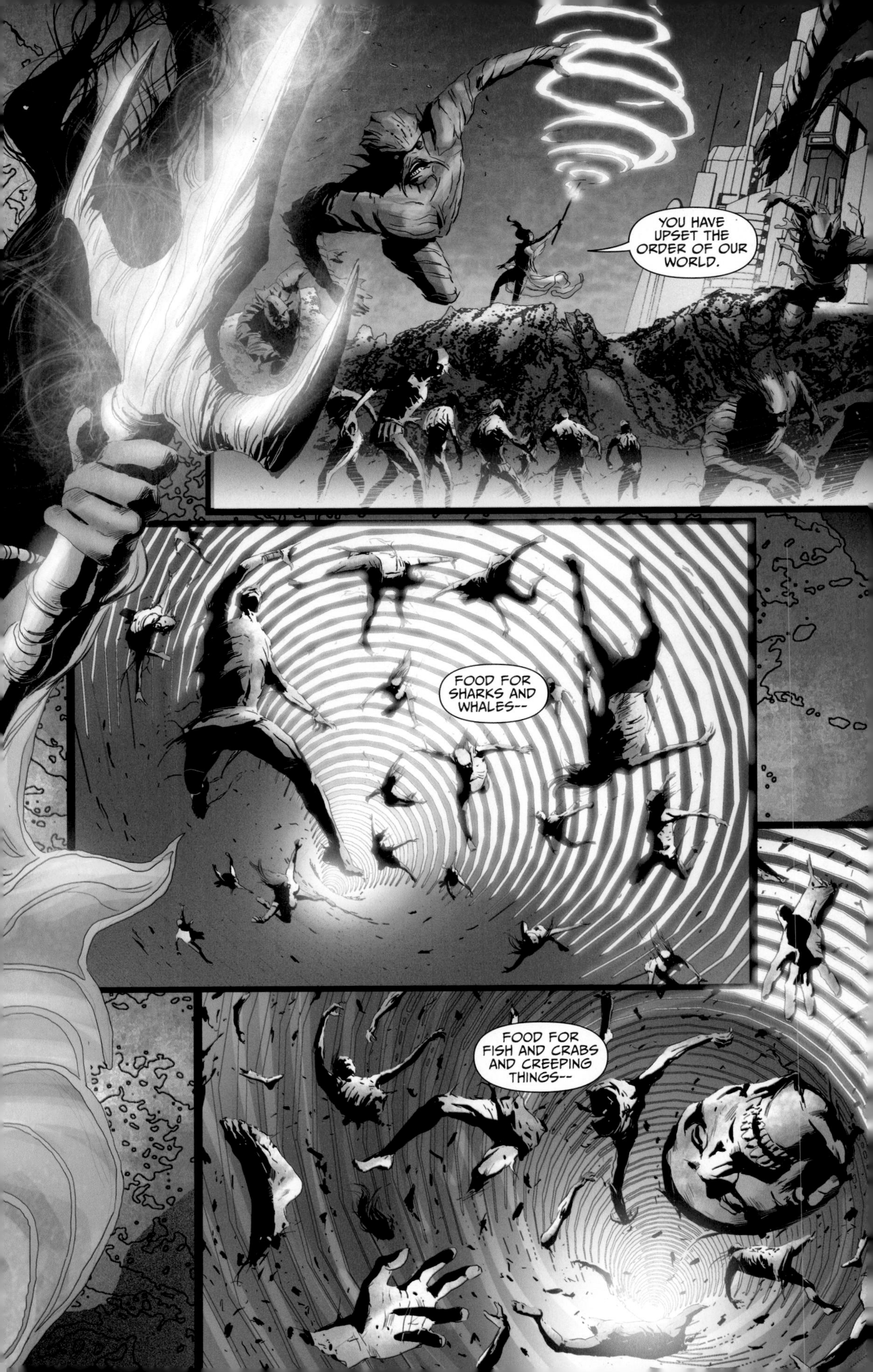
YOU HAVE UPSET THE ORDER OF OUR WORLD.
FOOD FOR SHARKS AND WHALES--
FOOD FOR FISH AND CRABS AND CREEPING THINGS--

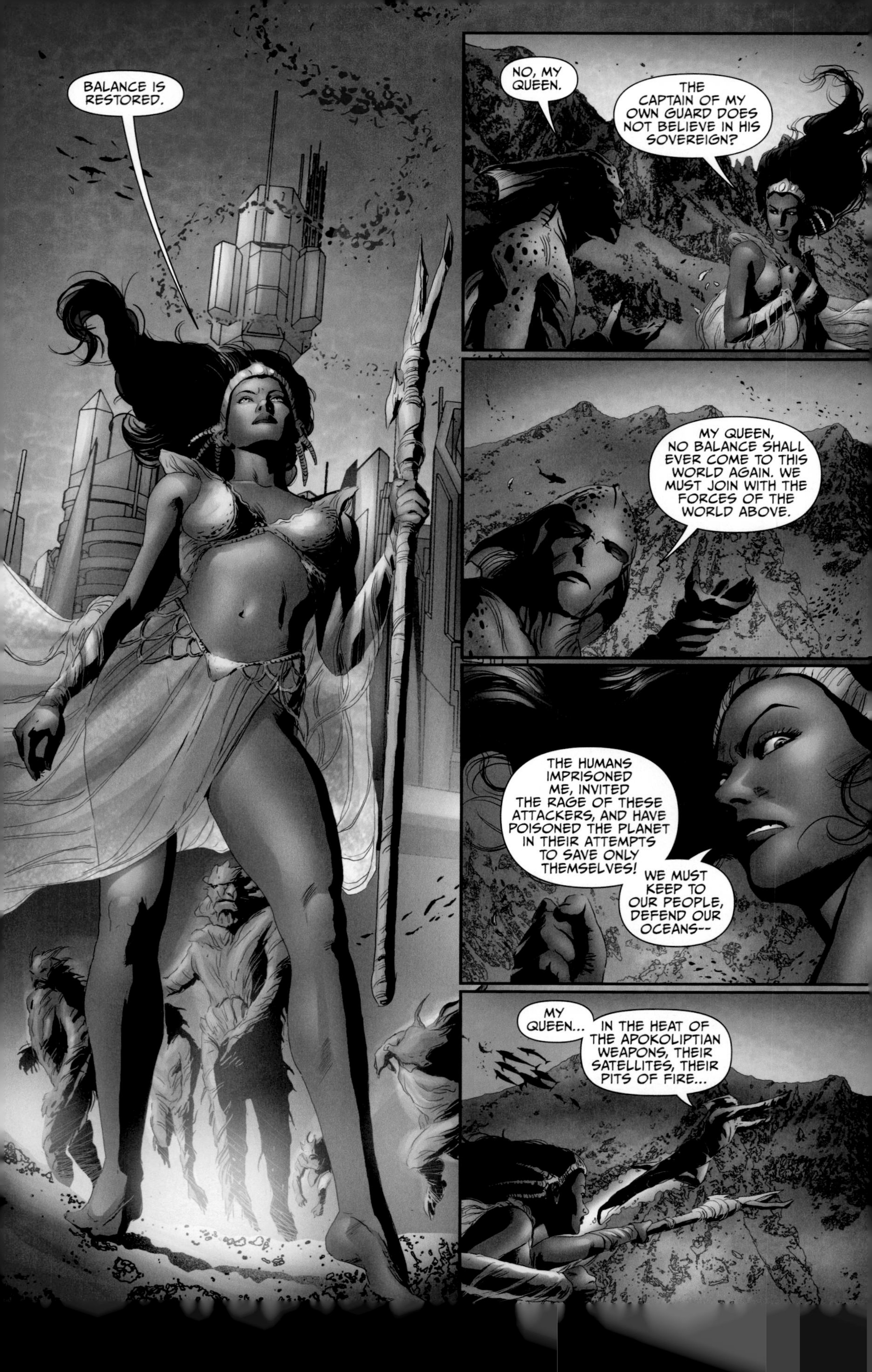
BALANCE IS RESTORED.
NO, MY QUEEN.
THE CAPTAIN OF MY OWN GUARD DOES NOT BELIEVE IN HIS SOVEREIGN?
MY QUEEN, NO BALANCE SHALL EVER COME TO THIS WORLD AGAIN. WE MUST JOIN WITH THE FORCES OF THE WORLD ABOVE.
THE HUMANS IMPRISONED ME, INVITED THE RAGE OF THESE ATTACKERS, AND HAVE POISONED THE PLANET IN THEIR ATTEMPTS TO SAVE ONLY THEMSELVES!
WE MUST KEEP TO OUR PEOPLE, DEFEND OUR OCEANS--
MY QUEEN...
IN THE HEAT OF THE APOKOLIPTIAN WEAPONS, THEIR SATELLITES, THEIR PITS OF FIRE...

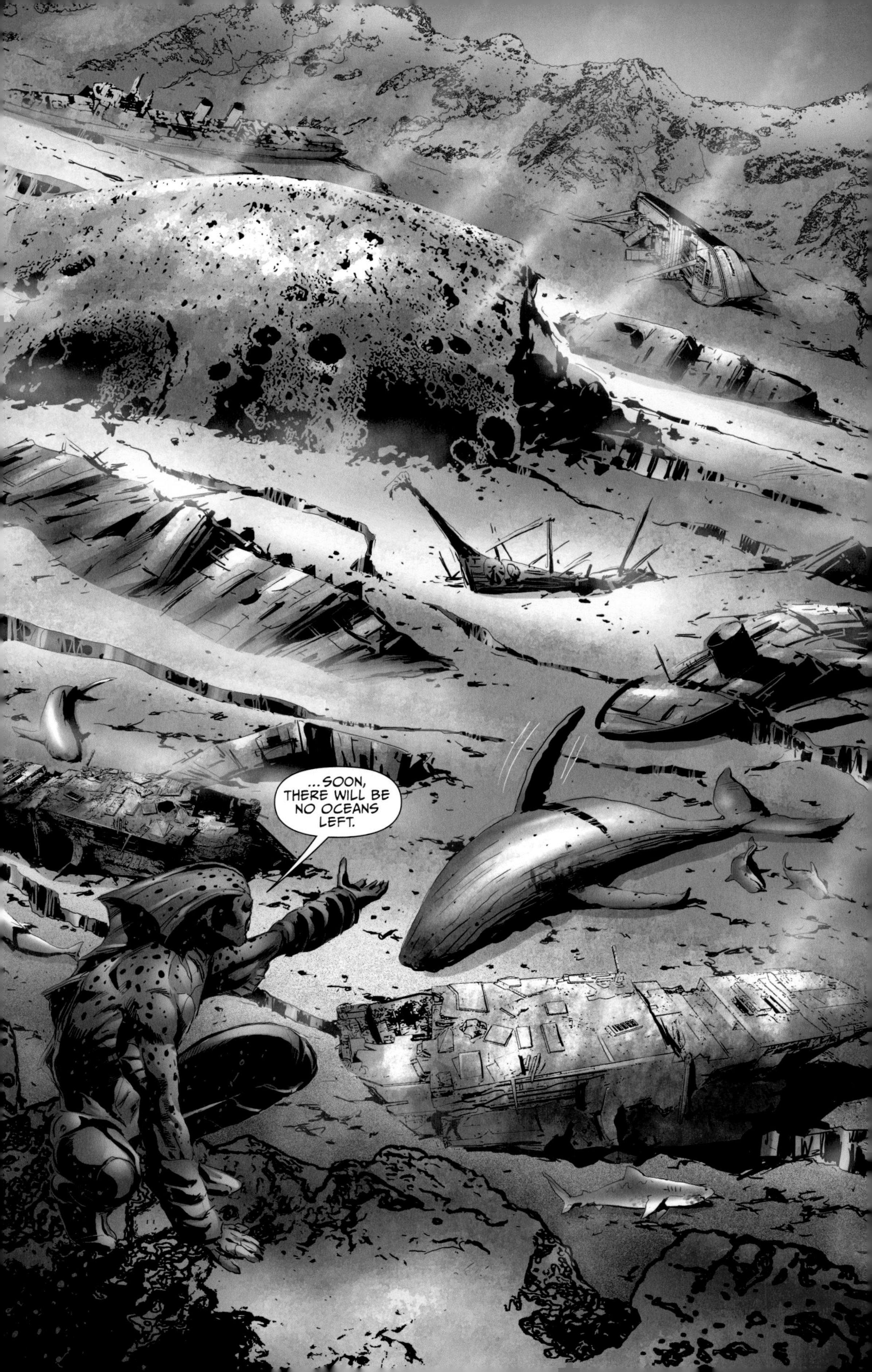
...SOON, THERE WILL BE NO OCEANS LEFT.

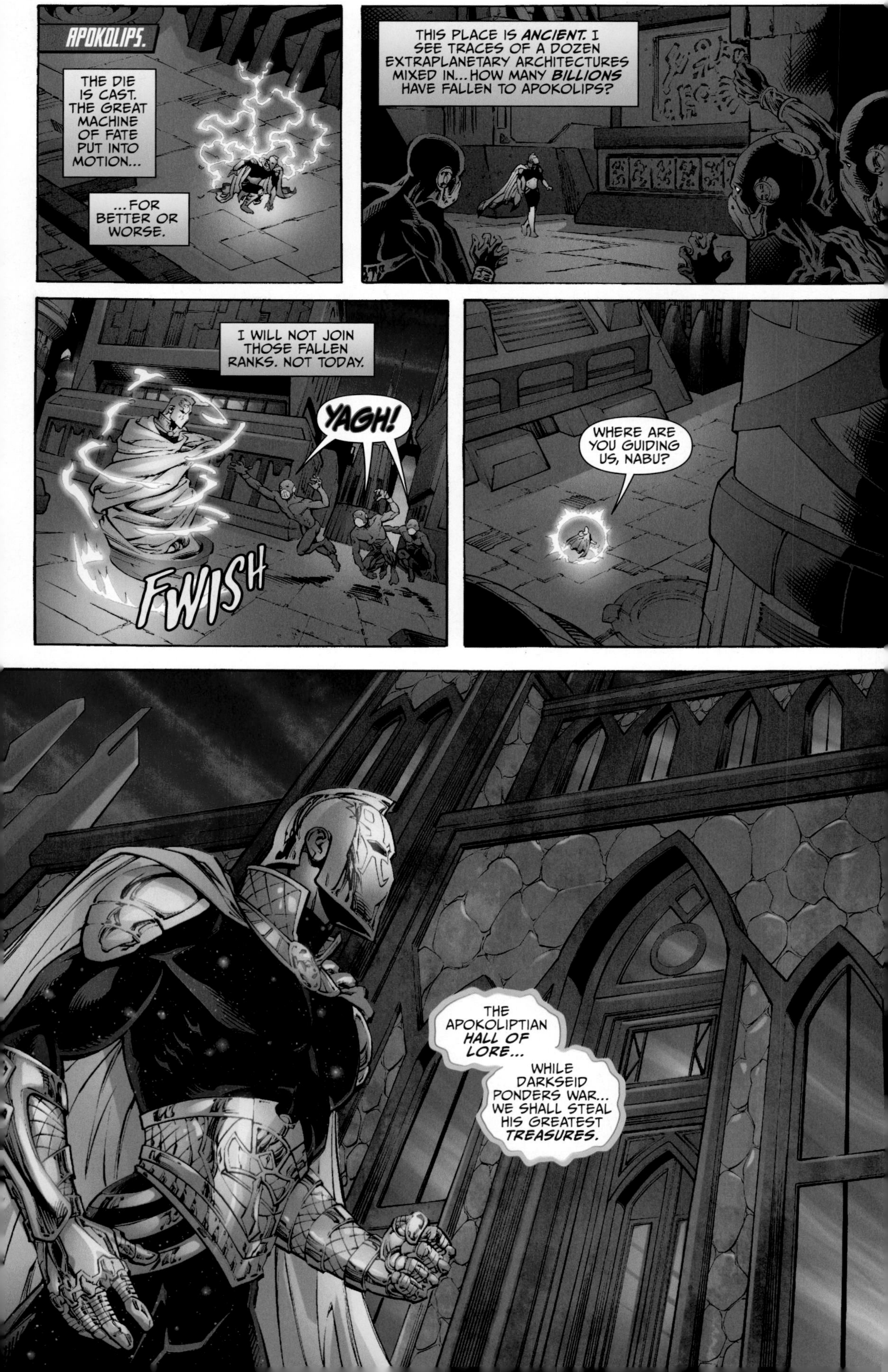
APOKOLIPS.
THE DIE IS CAST. THE GREAT MACHINE OF FATE PUT INTO MOTION...
...FOR BETTER OR WORSE.
THIS PLACE IS ANCIENT. I SEE TRACES OF A DOZEN EXTRAPLANETARY ARCHITECTURES MIXED IN... HOW MANY BILLIONS HAVE FALLEN TO APOKOLIPS?
I WILL NOT JOIN THOSE FALLEN RANKS. NOT TODAY.
YAGH!
FWISH
WHERE ARE YOU GUIDING US, NABU?
THE APOKOLIPTIAN HALL OF LORE...
WHILE DARKSEID PONDERS WAR... WE SHALL STEAL HIS GREATEST TREASURES.

THE GREAT HALL OF LORE...FABLED REPOSITORY OF APOKOLIPS' MOST POWERFUL ARTIFACTS...

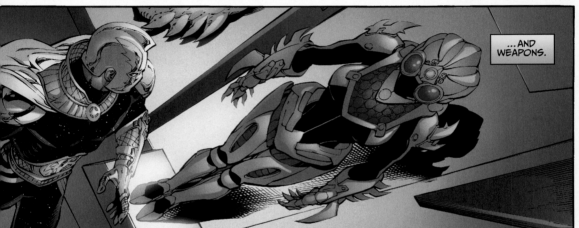

...AND WEAPONS.

THE SEAL OF A MOTHER BOX...

MANY OF THESE RELICS ARE OLDER THAN HISTORY... DESIGNED BY THOSE WHO LIVED BEFORE THE GODS THEMSELVES WERE BORN...

BUT WHAT FOUL MONSTERS OVERSEE THIS HOARD?

EMERGE, DEVIL!

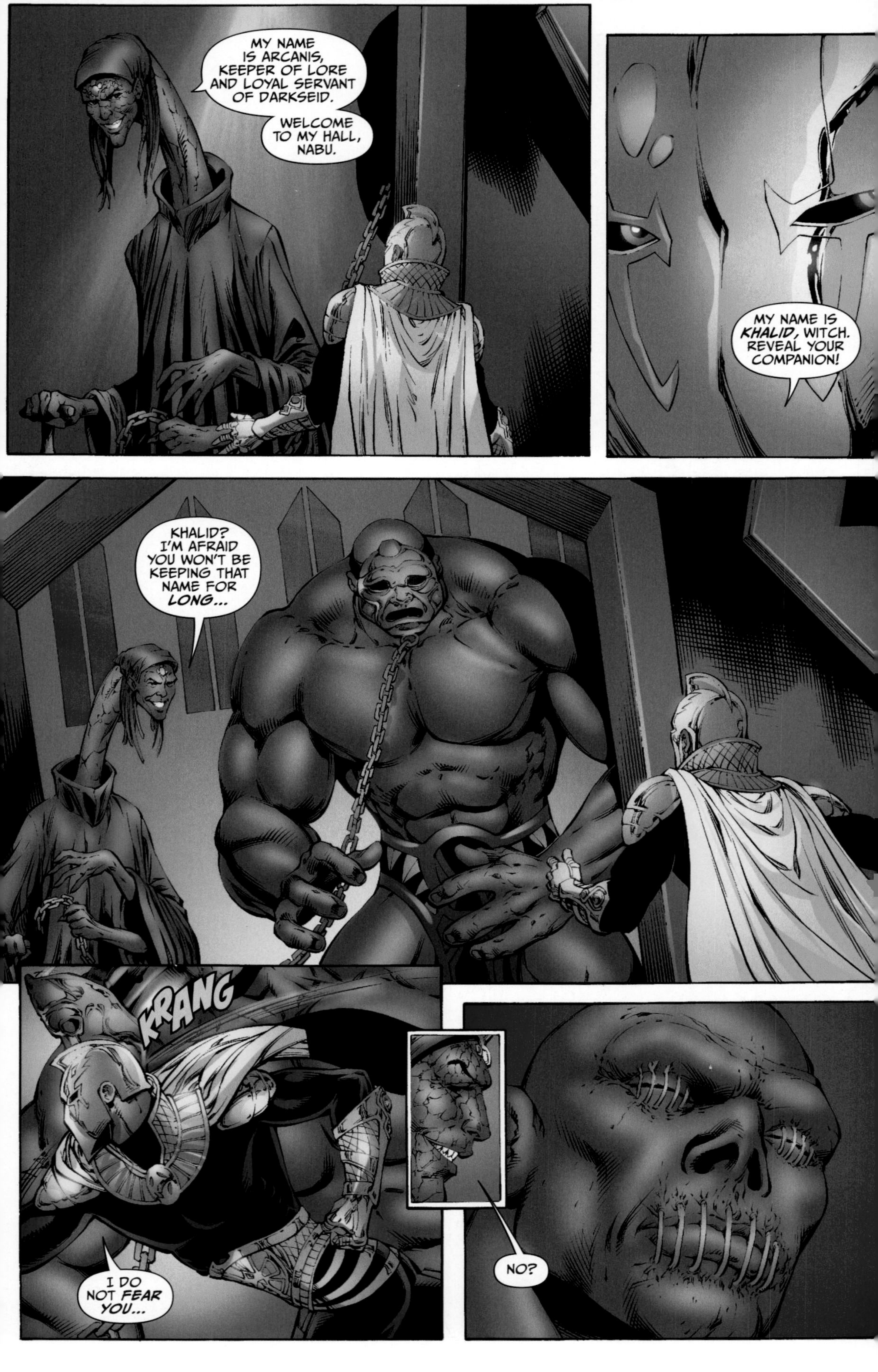
MY NAME IS ARCANIS, KEEPER OF LORE AND LOYAL SERVANT OF DARKSEID.
WELCOME TO MY HALL, NABU.
MY NAME IS *KHALID*, WITCH. REVEAL YOUR COMPANION!
KHALID? I'M AFRAID YOU WON'T BE KEEPING THAT NAME FOR *LONG*...
KRANG
I DO NOT *FEAR* YOU...
NO?

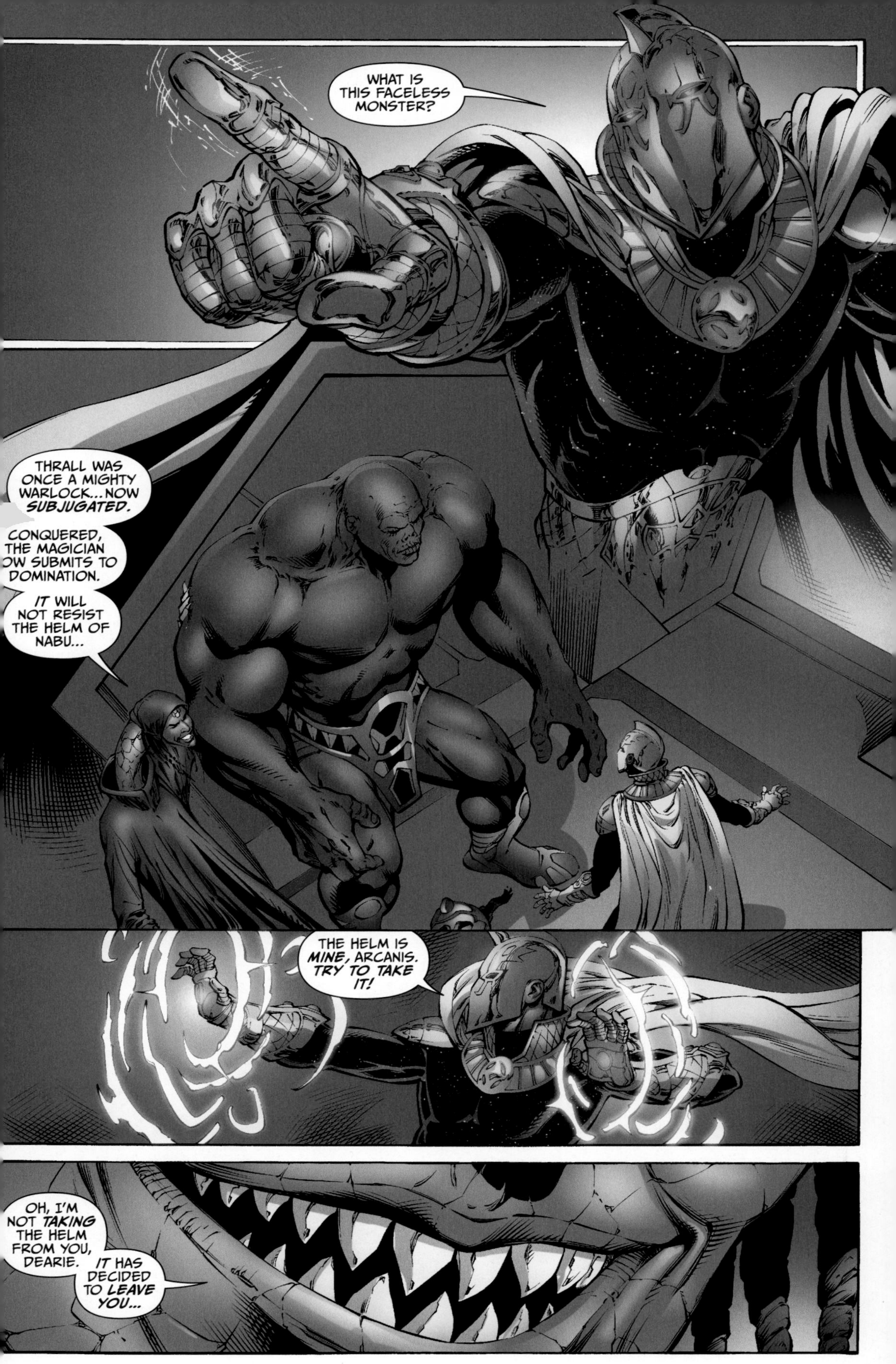
WHAT IS THIS FACELESS MONSTER?
THRALL WAS ONCE A MIGHTY WARLOCK...NOW *SUBJUGATED.*
CONQUERED, THE MAGICIAN NOW SUBMITS TO DOMINATION.
IT WILL NOT RESIST THE HELM OF NABU...
THE HELM IS *MINE*, ARCANIS. *TRY TO TAKE IT!*
OH, I'M NOT *TAKING* THE HELM FROM YOU, DEARIE.
IT HAS DECIDED TO *LEAVE YOU...*

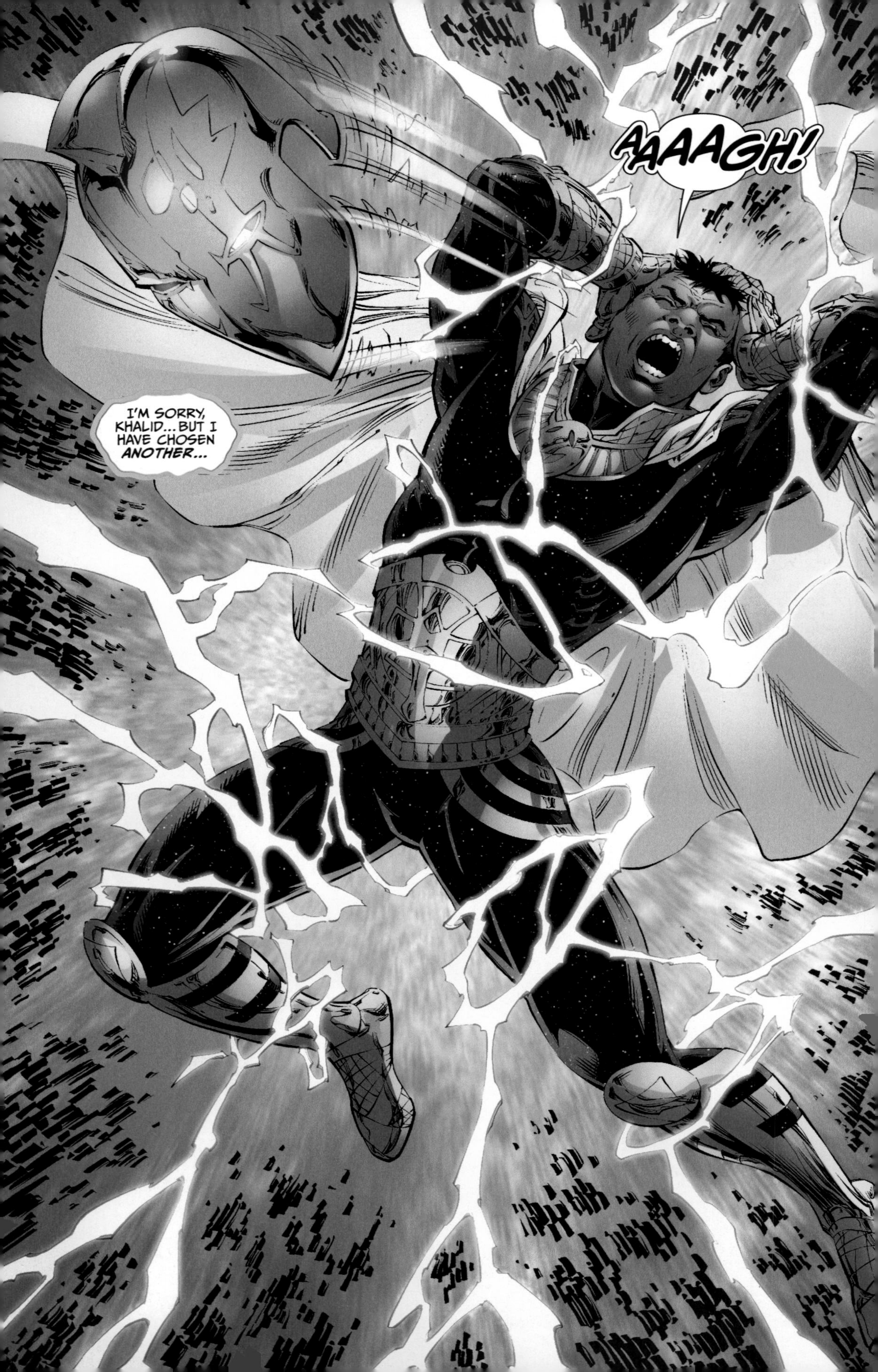
AAAAGH!
I'M SORRY, KHALID...BUT I HAVE CHOSEN ANOTHER...

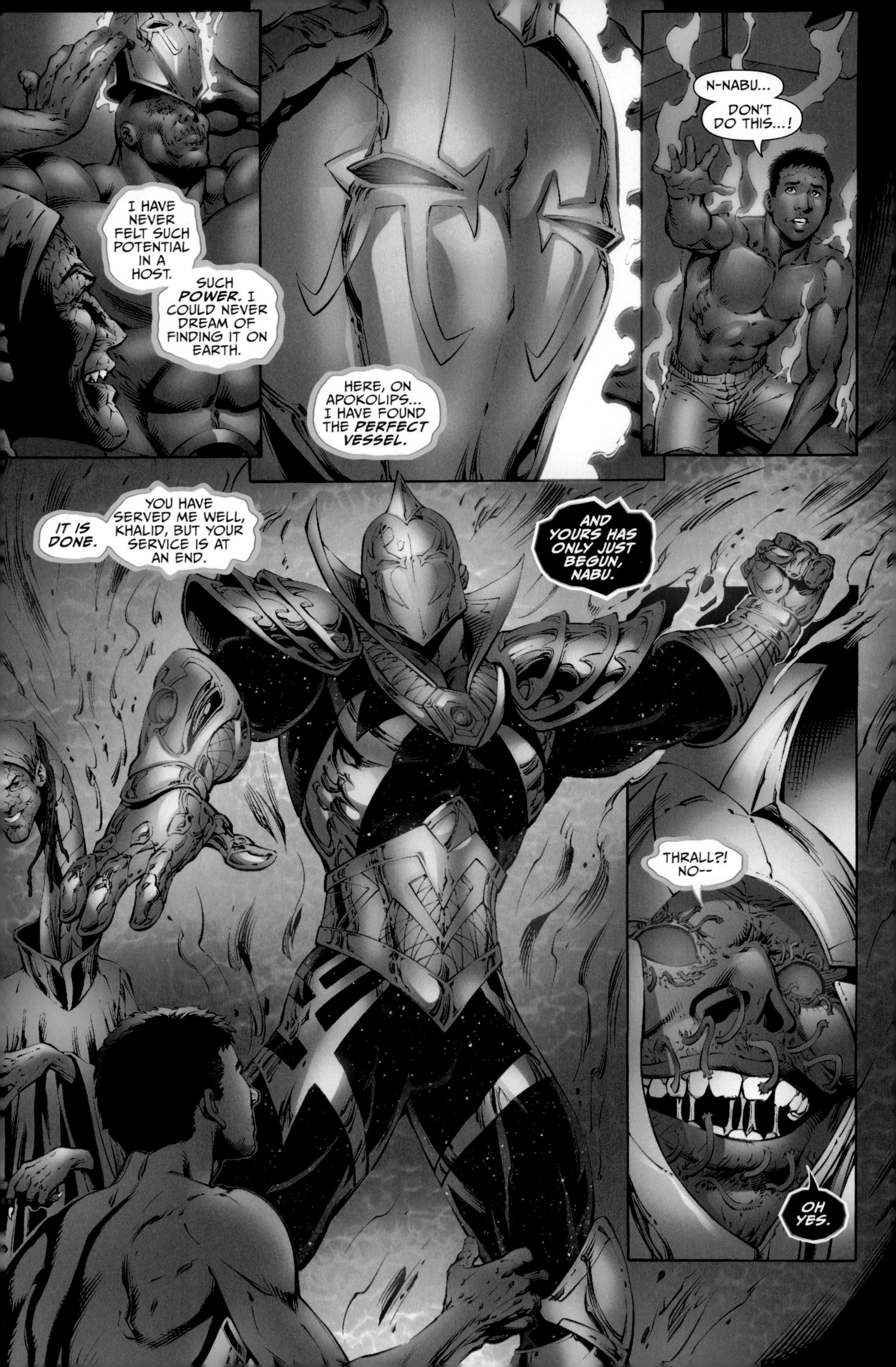
I HAVE NEVER FELT SUCH POTENTIAL IN A HOST.
SUCH *POWER.* I COULD NEVER DREAM OF FINDING IT ON EARTH.
HERE, ON APOKOLIPS... I HAVE FOUND THE *PERFECT VESSEL.*
N-NABU...
DON'T DO THIS...!
IT IS DONE.
YOU HAVE SERVED ME WELL, KHALID, BUT YOUR SERVICE IS AT AN END.
AND YOURS HAS ONLY JUST BEGUN, NABU.
THRALL?! NO--
OH YES.

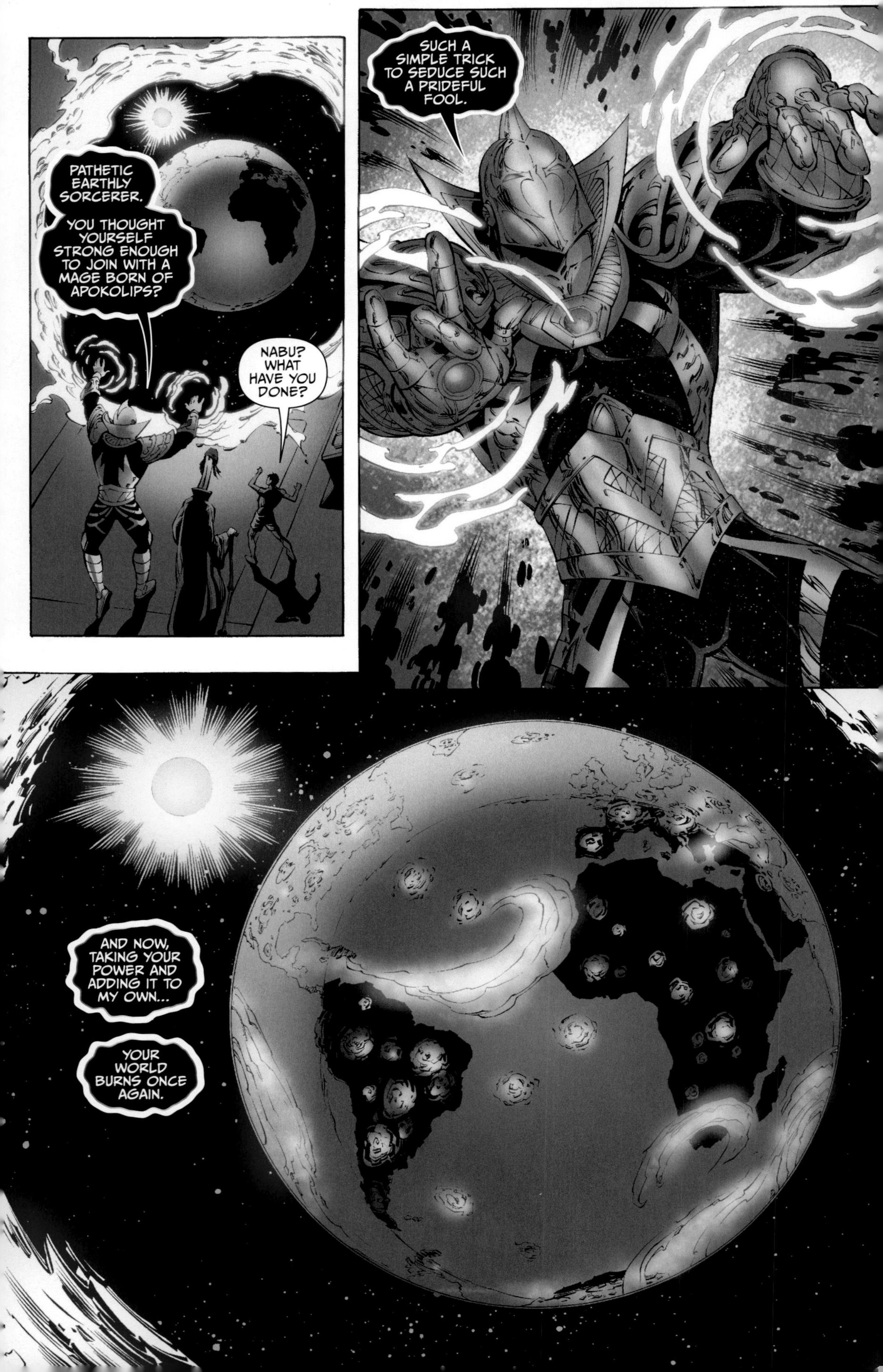
PATHETIC EARTHLY SORCERER.
YOU THOUGHT YOURSELF STRONG ENOUGH TO JOIN WITH A MAGE BORN OF APOKOLIPS?
NABU? WHAT HAVE YOU DONE?
SUCH A SIMPLE TRICK TO SEDUCE SUCH A PRIDEFUL FOOL.
AND NOW, TAKING YOUR POWER AND ADDING IT TO MY OWN...
YOUR WORLD BURNS ONCE AGAIN.

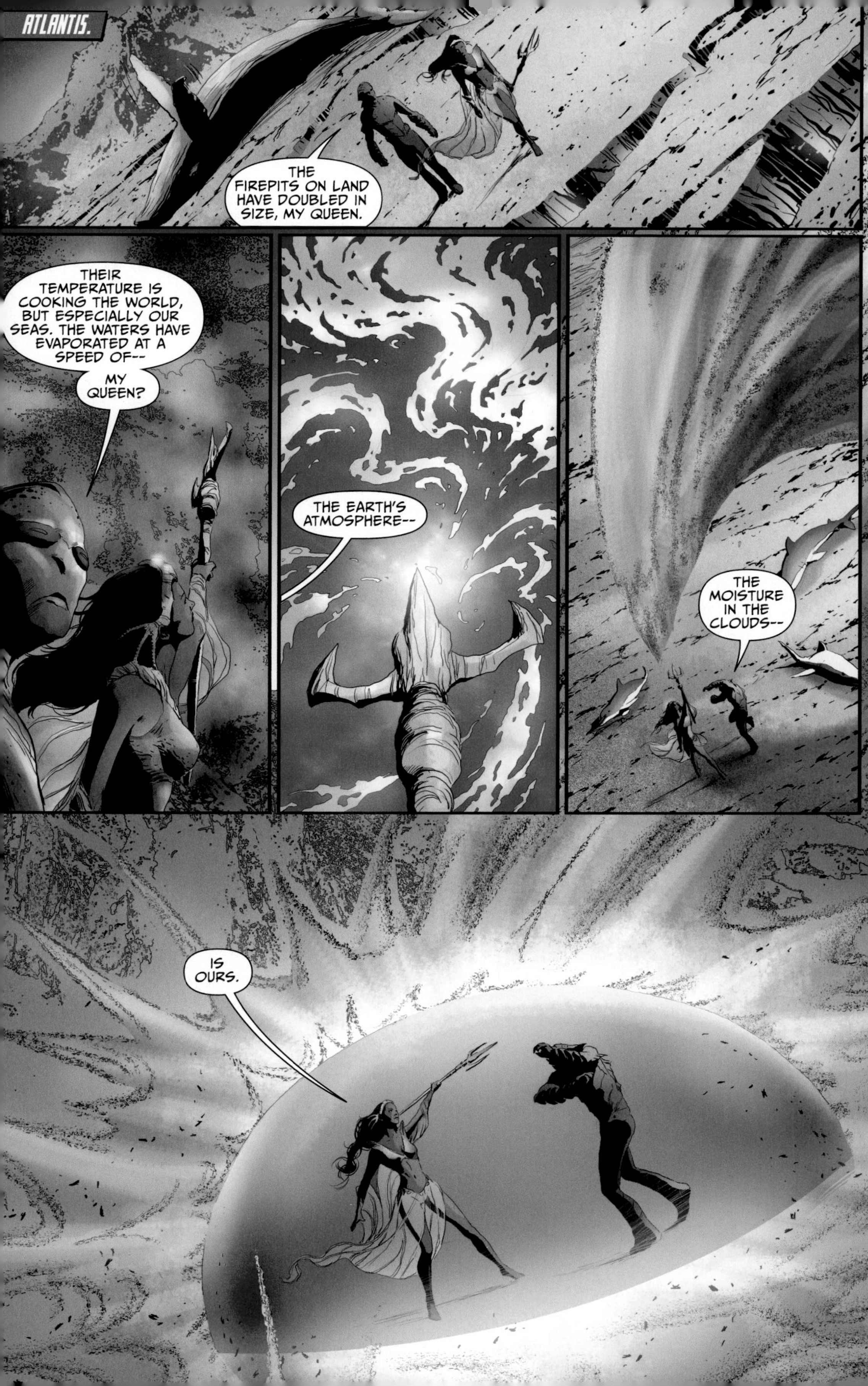
ATLANTIS.
THE FIREPITS ON LAND HAVE DOUBLED IN SIZE, MY QUEEN.
THEIR TEMPERATURE IS COOKING THE WORLD, BUT ESPECIALLY OUR SEAS. THE WATERS HAVE EVAPORATED AT A SPEED OF--
MY QUEEN?
THE EARTH'S ATMOSPHERE--
THE MOISTURE IN THE CLOUDS--
IS OURS.

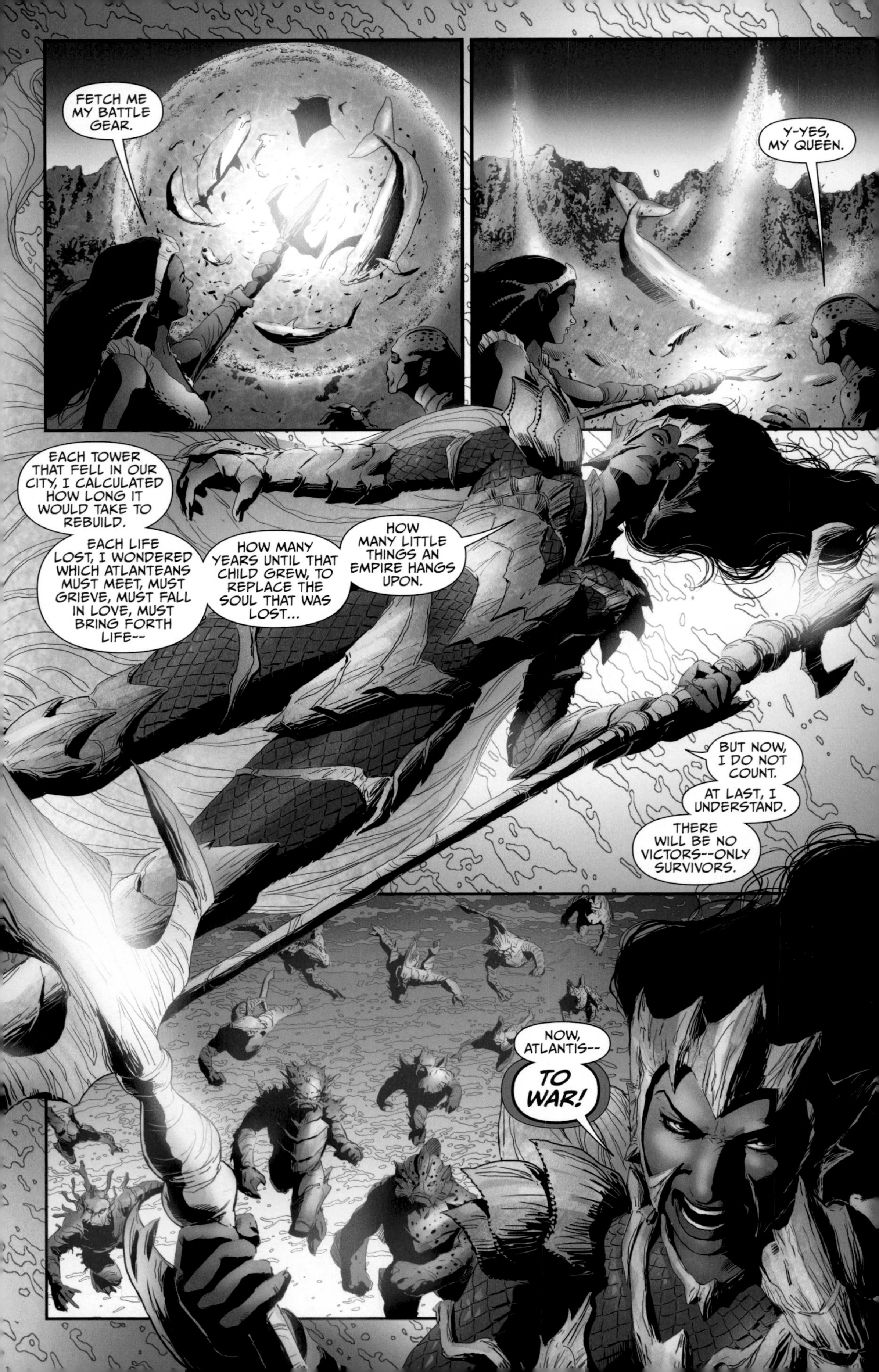
FETCH ME MY BATTLE GEAR.
Y-YES, MY QUEEN.
EACH TOWER THAT FELL IN OUR CITY, I CALCULATED HOW LONG IT WOULD TAKE TO REBUILD.
EACH LIFE LOST, I WONDERED WHICH ATLANTEANS MUST MEET, MUST GRIEVE, MUST FALL IN LOVE, MUST BRING FORTH LIFE--
HOW MANY YEARS UNTIL THAT CHILD GREW, TO REPLACE THE SOUL THAT WAS LOST...
HOW MANY LITTLE THINGS AN EMPIRE HANGS UPON.
BUT NOW, I DO NOT COUNT.
AT LAST, I UNDERSTAND.
THERE WILL BE NO VICTORS--ONLY SURVIVORS.
NOW, ATLANTIS--
TO WAR!

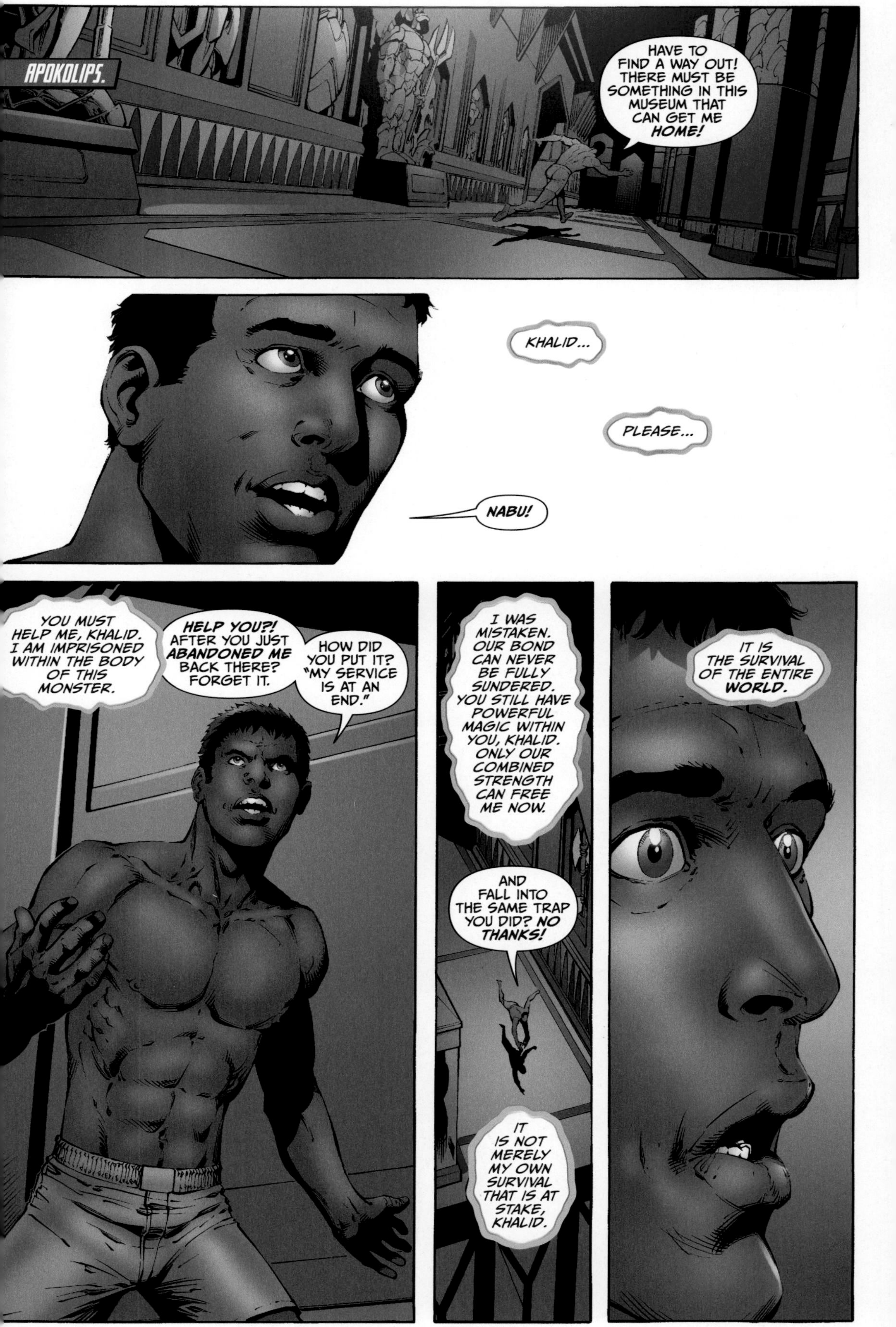
APOKOLIPS.
HAVE TO FIND A WAY OUT! THERE MUST BE SOMETHING IN THIS MUSEUM THAT CAN GET ME HOME!
KHALID...
PLEASE...
NABU!
YOU MUST HELP ME, KHALID. I AM IMPRISONED WITHIN THE BODY OF THIS MONSTER.
HELP YOU?! AFTER YOU JUST ABANDONED ME BACK THERE? FORGET IT.
HOW DID YOU PUT IT? "MY SERVICE IS AT AN END."
I WAS MISTAKEN. OUR BOND CAN NEVER BE FULLY SUNDERED. YOU STILL HAVE POWERFUL MAGIC WITHIN YOU, KHALID. ONLY OUR COMBINED STRENGTH CAN FREE ME NOW.
AND FALL INTO THE SAME TRAP YOU DID? NO THANKS!
IT IS NOT MERELY MY OWN SURVIVAL THAT IS AT STAKE, KHALID.
IT IS THE SURVIVAL OF THE ENTIRE WORLD.

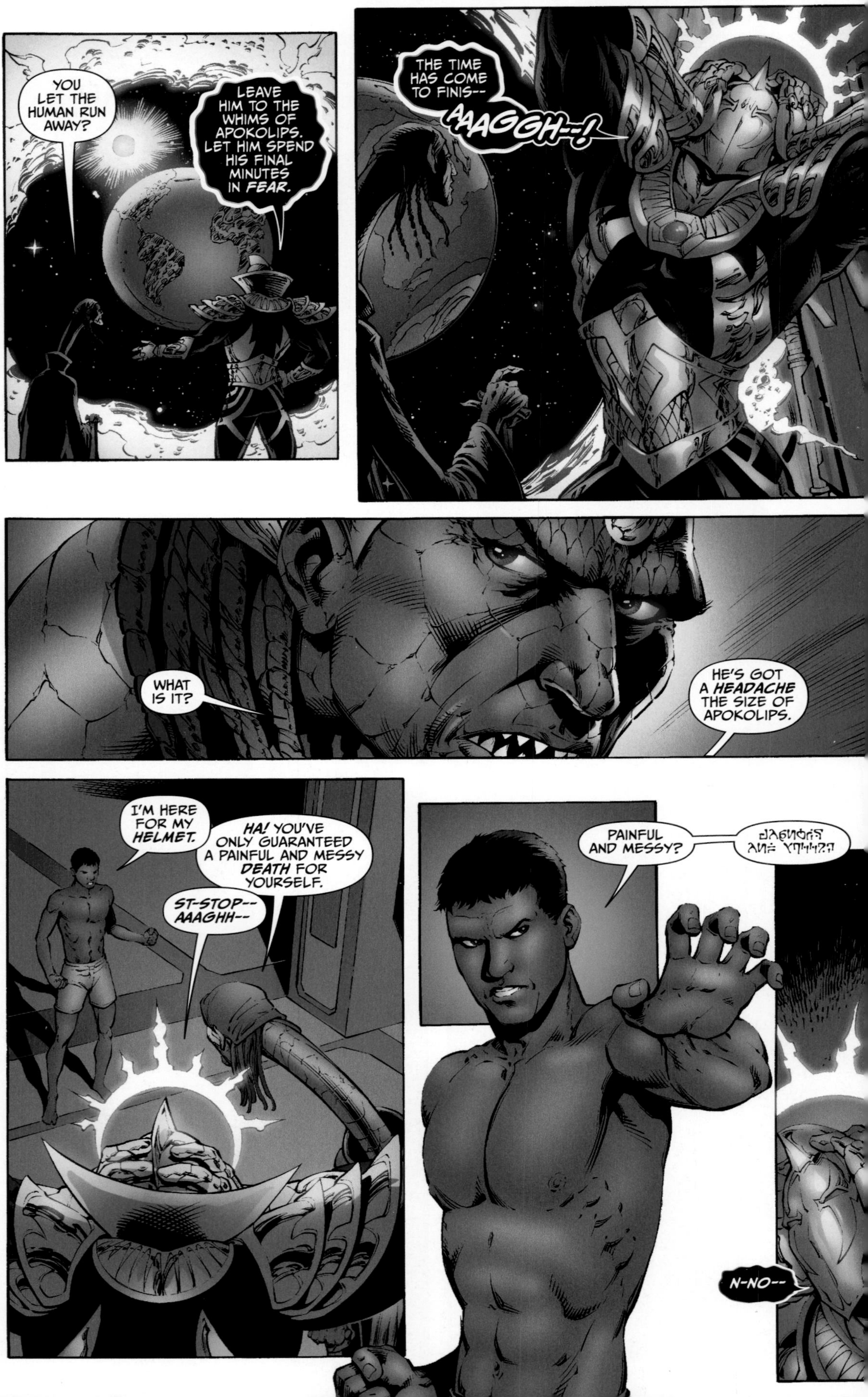
YOU LET THE HUMAN RUN AWAY?
LEAVE HIM TO THE WHIMS OF APOKOLIPS. LET HIM SPEND HIS FINAL MINUTES IN FEAR.
THE TIME HAS COME TO FINIS--
AAAGGH--!
WHAT IS IT?
HE'S GOT A HEADACHE THE SIZE OF APOKOLIPS.
I'M HERE FOR MY HELMET.
HA! YOU'VE ONLY GUARANTEED A PAINFUL AND MESSY DEATH FOR YOURSELF.
ST-STOP-- AAAGHH--
PAINFUL AND MESSY?
N-NO--

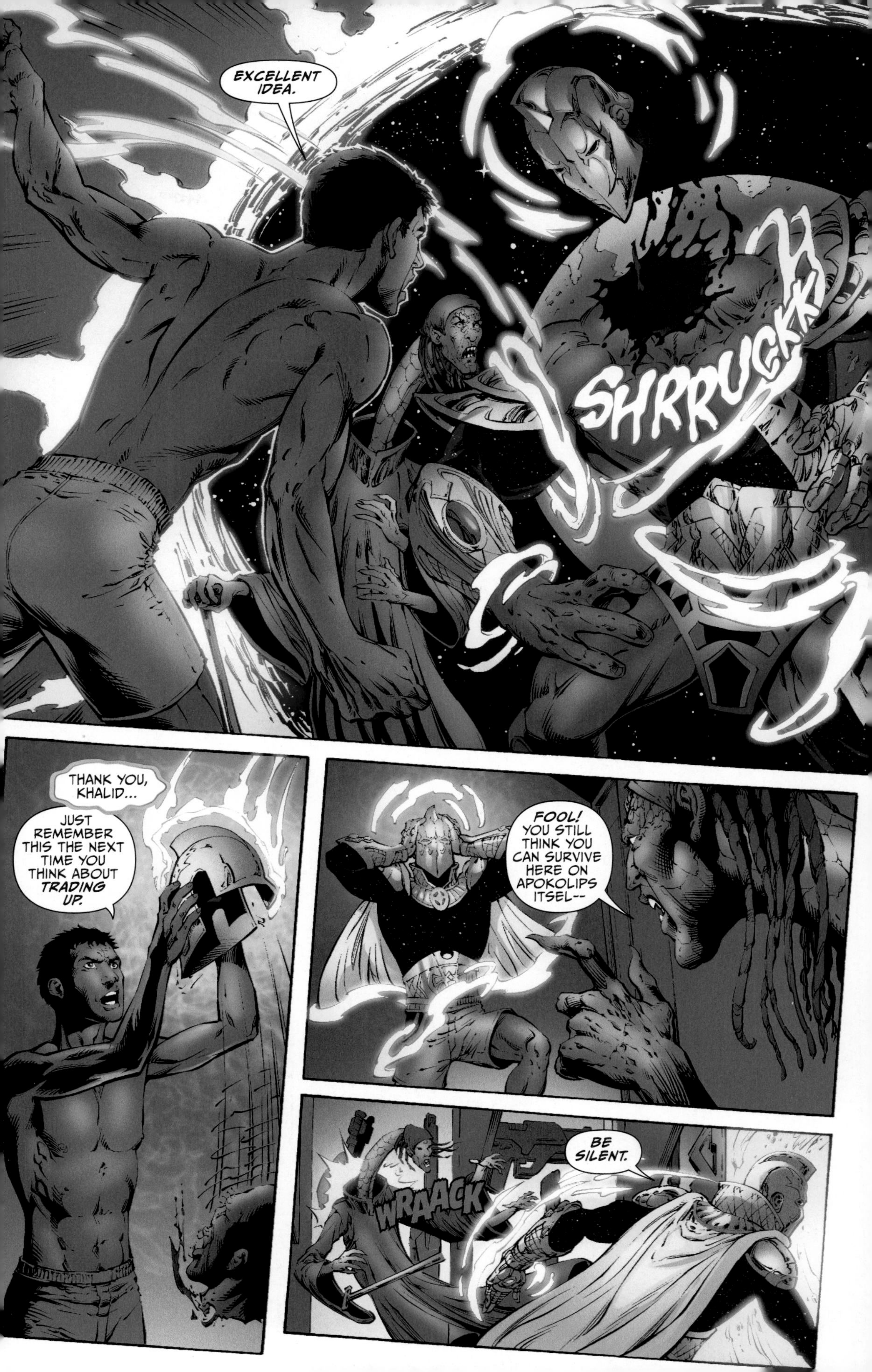
EXCELLENT IDEA.
SHRRUCKK
THANK YOU, KHALID...
JUST REMEMBER THIS THE NEXT TIME YOU THINK ABOUT TRADING UP.
FOOL! YOU STILL THINK YOU CAN SURVIVE HERE ON APOKOLIPS ITSEL--
BE SILENT.
WRAACK

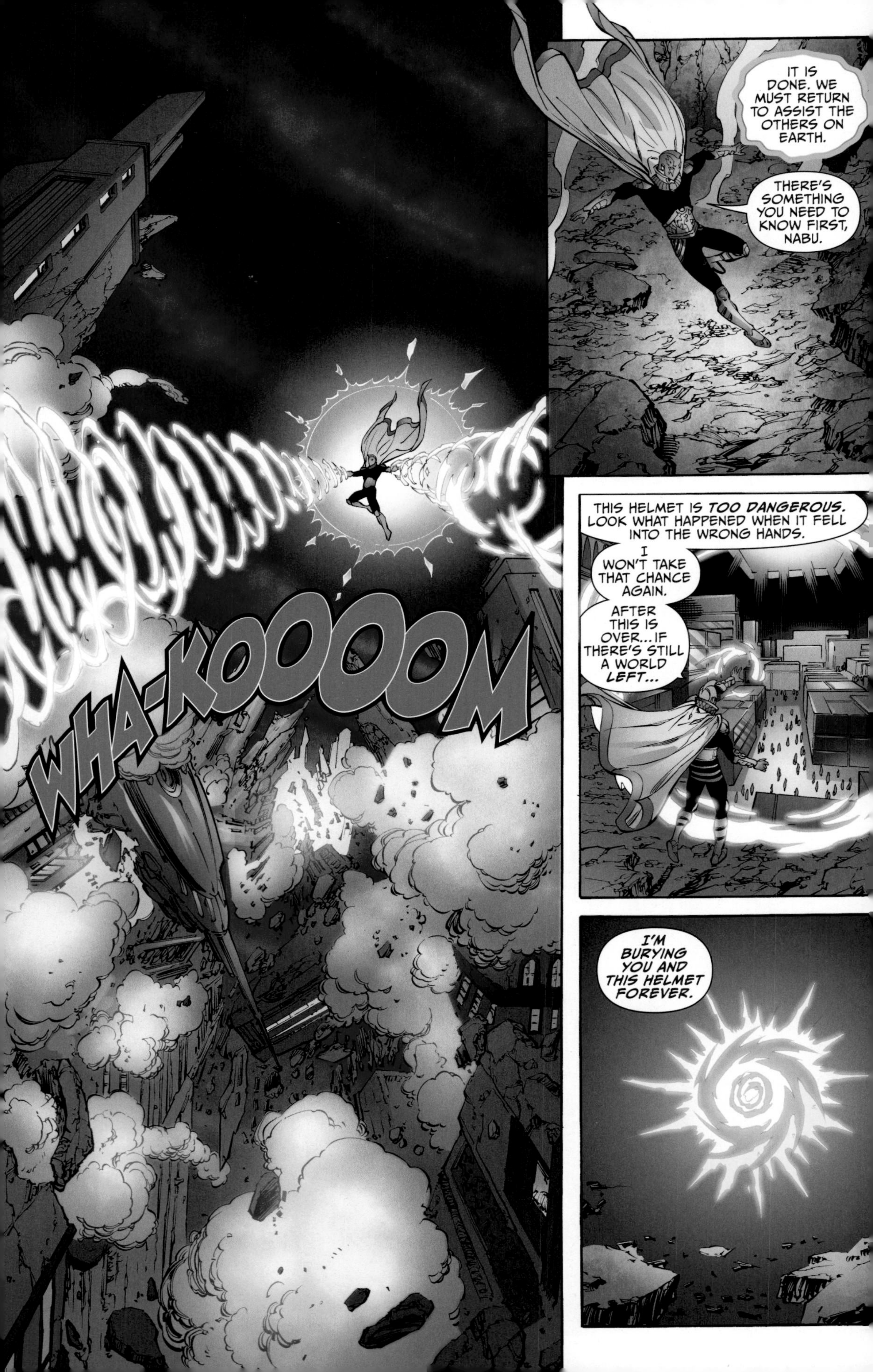
WHA-KOOOOM
IT IS DONE. WE MUST RETURN TO ASSIST THE OTHERS ON EARTH.
THERE'S SOMETHING YOU NEED TO KNOW FIRST, NABU.
THIS HELMET IS *TOO DANGEROUS.* LOOK WHAT HAPPENED WHEN IT FELL INTO THE WRONG HANDS.
I WON'T TAKE THAT CHANCE AGAIN.
AFTER THIS IS OVER... IF THERE'S STILL A WORLD *LEFT*...
I'M BURYING YOU AND THIS HELMET FOREVER.

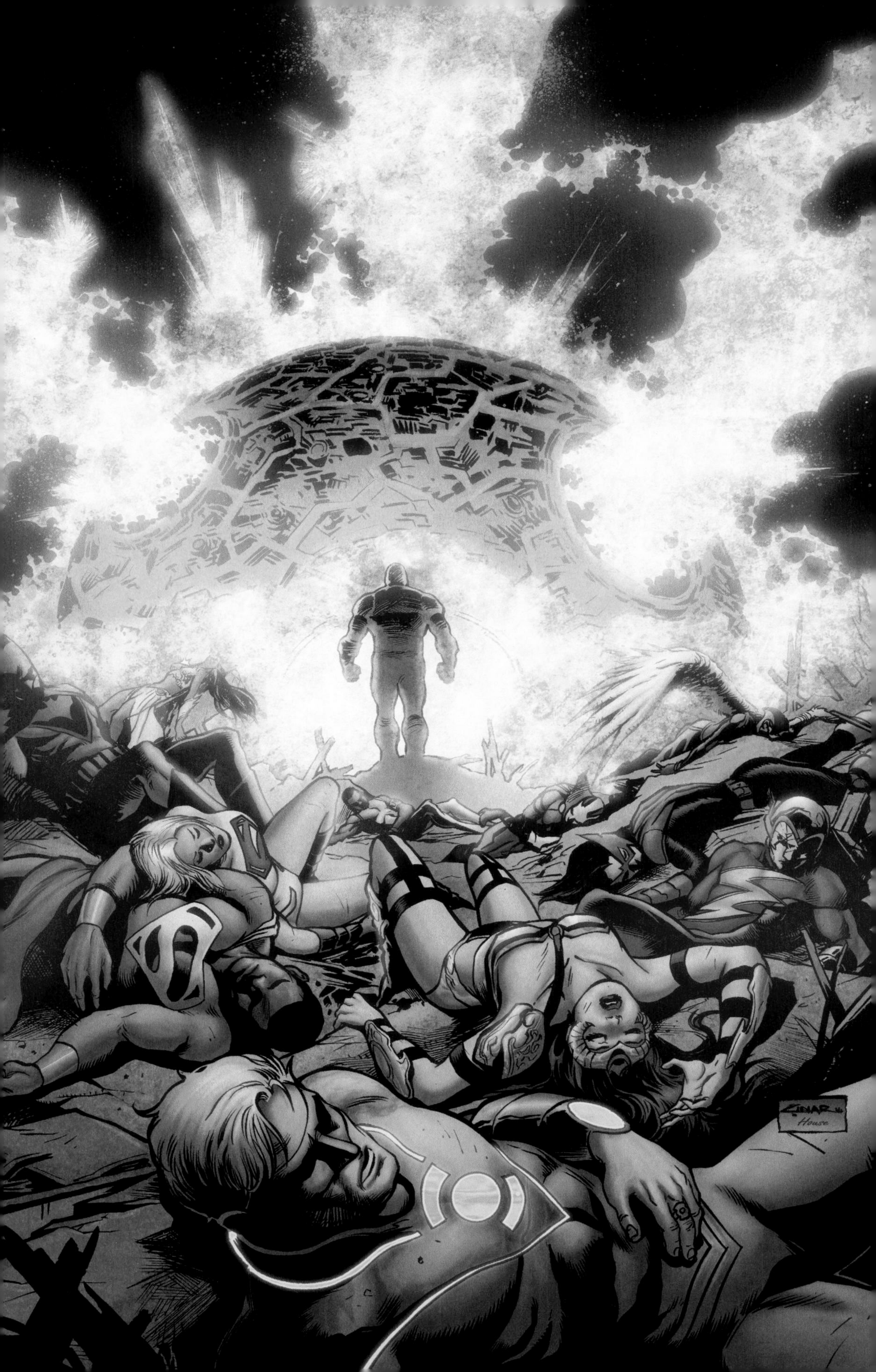

GROUNDED

DANIEL H. WILSON, MARGUERITE BENNETT, MIKE JOHNSON writers **ANDY SMITH, AIRI KAMIYAMA** pencillers **TREVOR SCOTT, AIRI KAMIYAMA** inkers **PETER PANTAZIS** colorist **TRAVIS LANHAM** letterer cover by **YILDIRAY CINAR** and **ANDREW DALHOUSE**

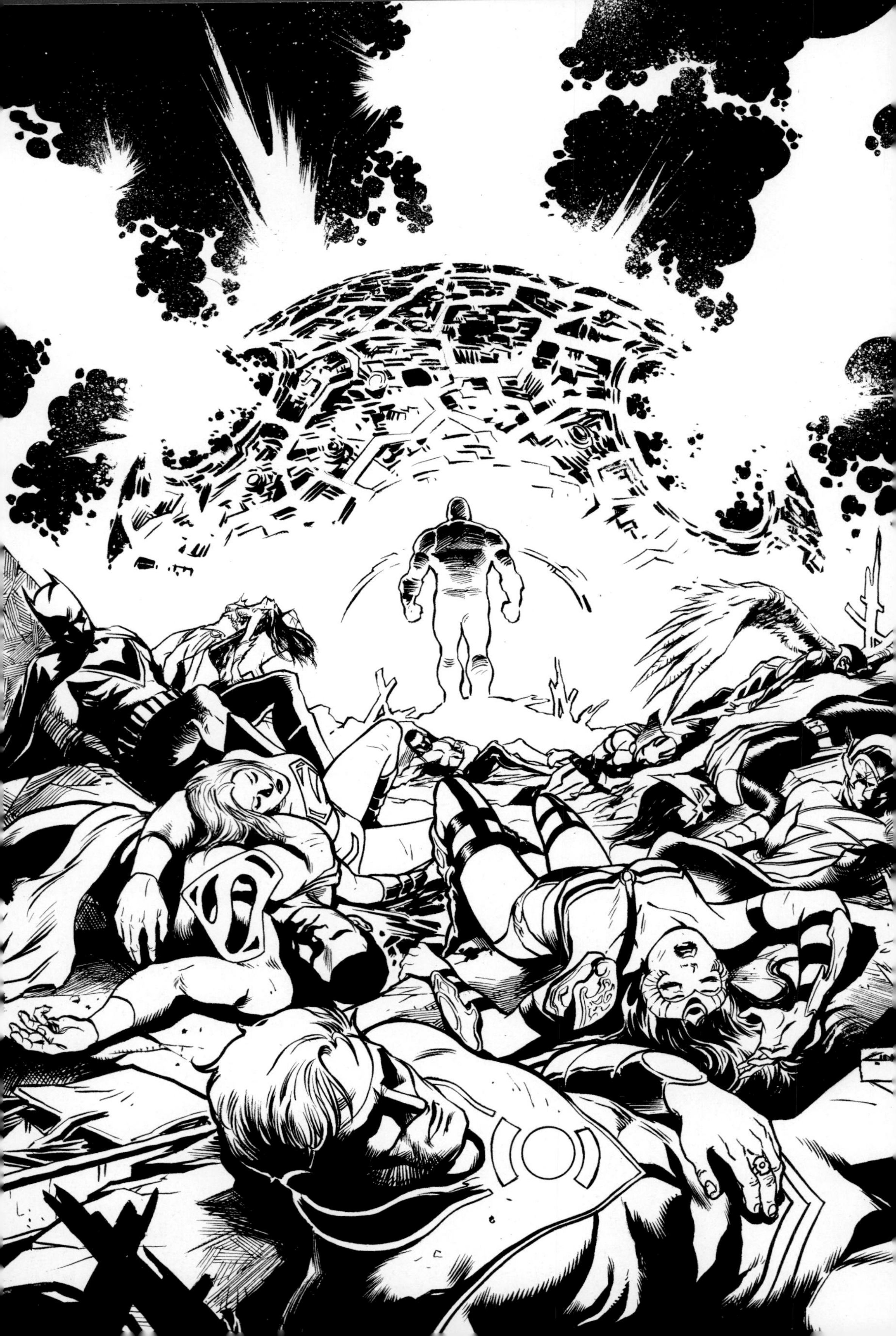

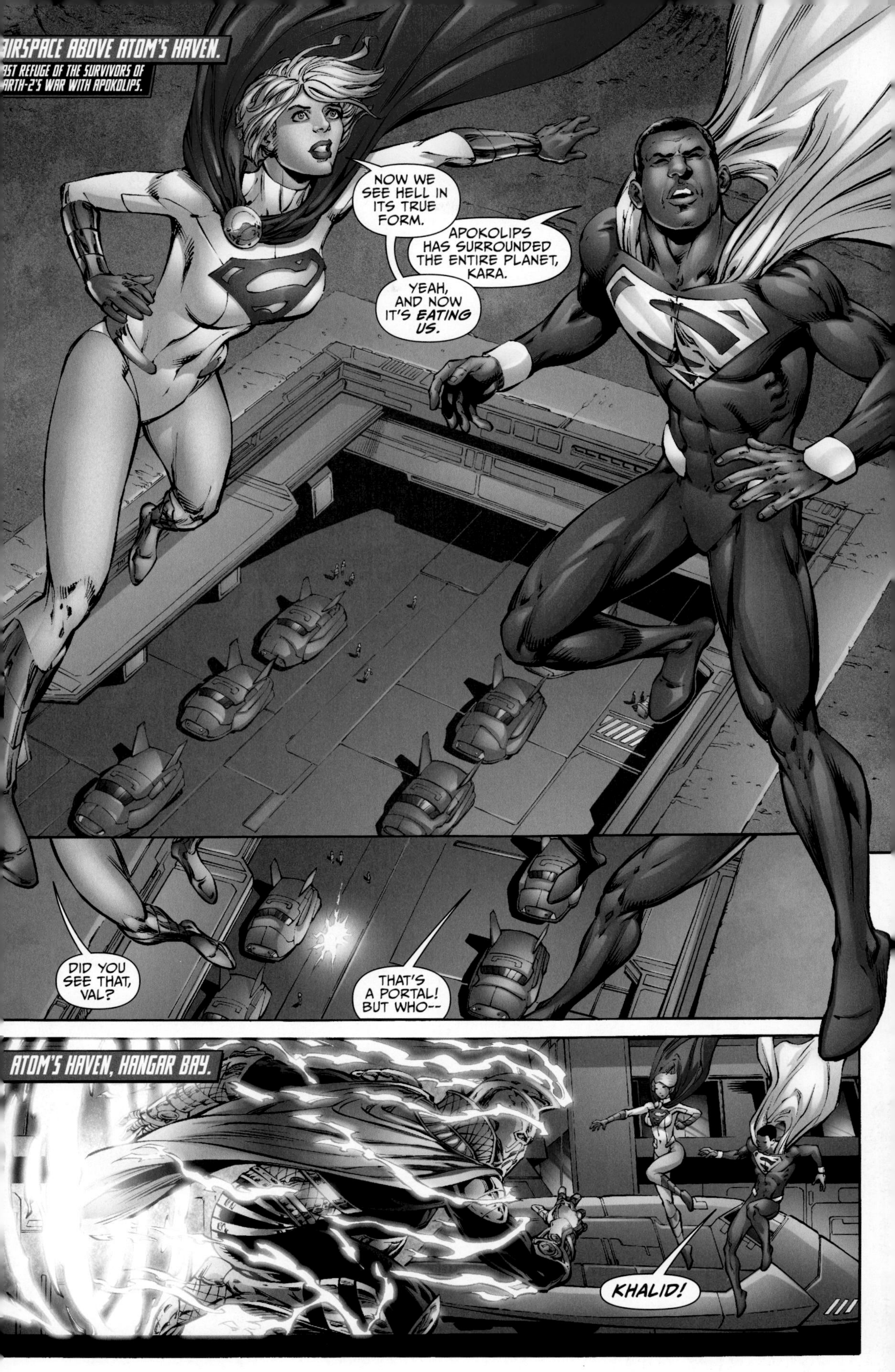
AIRSPACE ABOVE ATOM'S HAVEN.
LAST REFUGE OF THE SURVIVORS OF EARTH-2'S WAR WITH APOKOLIPS.
NOW WE SEE HELL IN ITS TRUE FORM.
APOKOLIPS HAS SURROUNDED THE ENTIRE PLANET, KARA.
YEAH, AND NOW IT'S EATING US.
DID YOU SEE THAT, VAL?
THAT'S A PORTAL! BUT WHO--
ATOM'S HAVEN, HANGAR BAY.
KHALID!

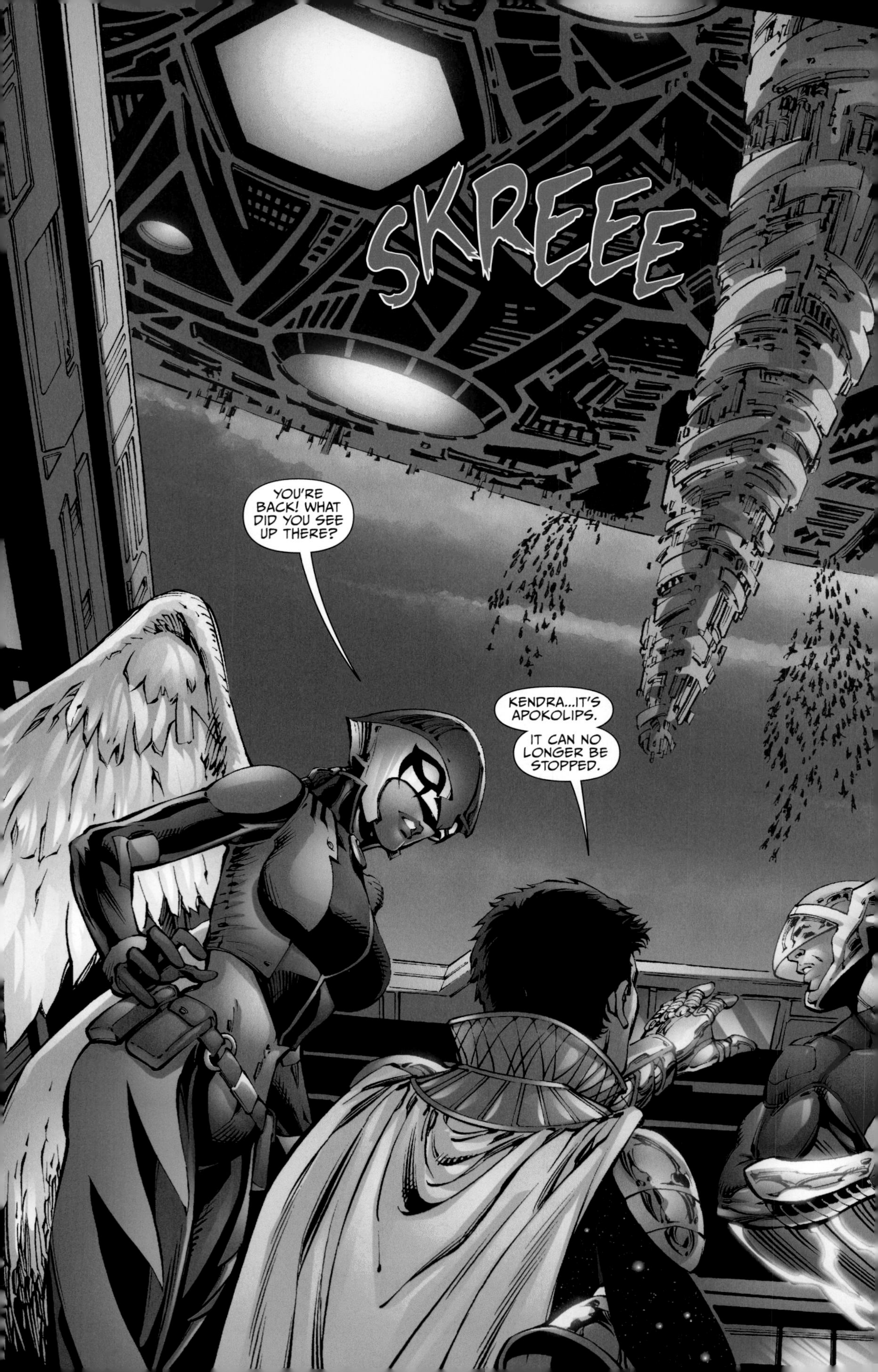
SKREEE
YOU'RE BACK! WHAT DID YOU SEE UP THERE?
KENDRA...IT'S APOKOLIPS.
IT CAN NO LONGER BE STOPPED.

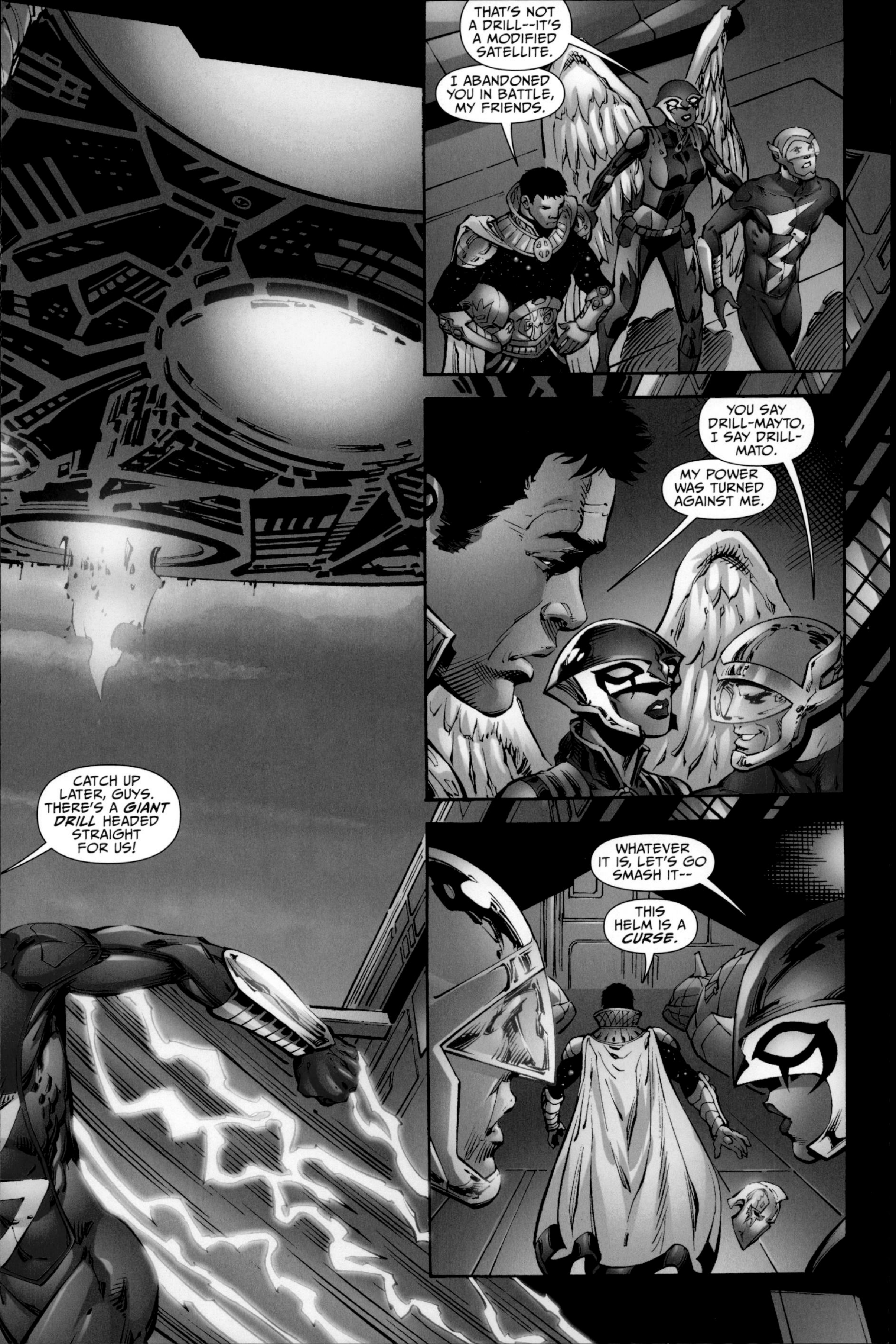
THAT'S NOT A DRILL--IT'S A MODIFIED SATELLITE.
I ABANDONED YOU IN BATTLE, MY FRIENDS.
YOU SAY DRILL-MAYTO, I SAY DRILL-MATO.
MY POWER WAS TURNED AGAINST ME.
CATCH UP LATER, GUYS. THERE'S A GIANT DRILL HEADED STRAIGHT FOR US!
WHATEVER IT IS, LET'S GO SMASH IT--
THIS HELM IS A CURSE.

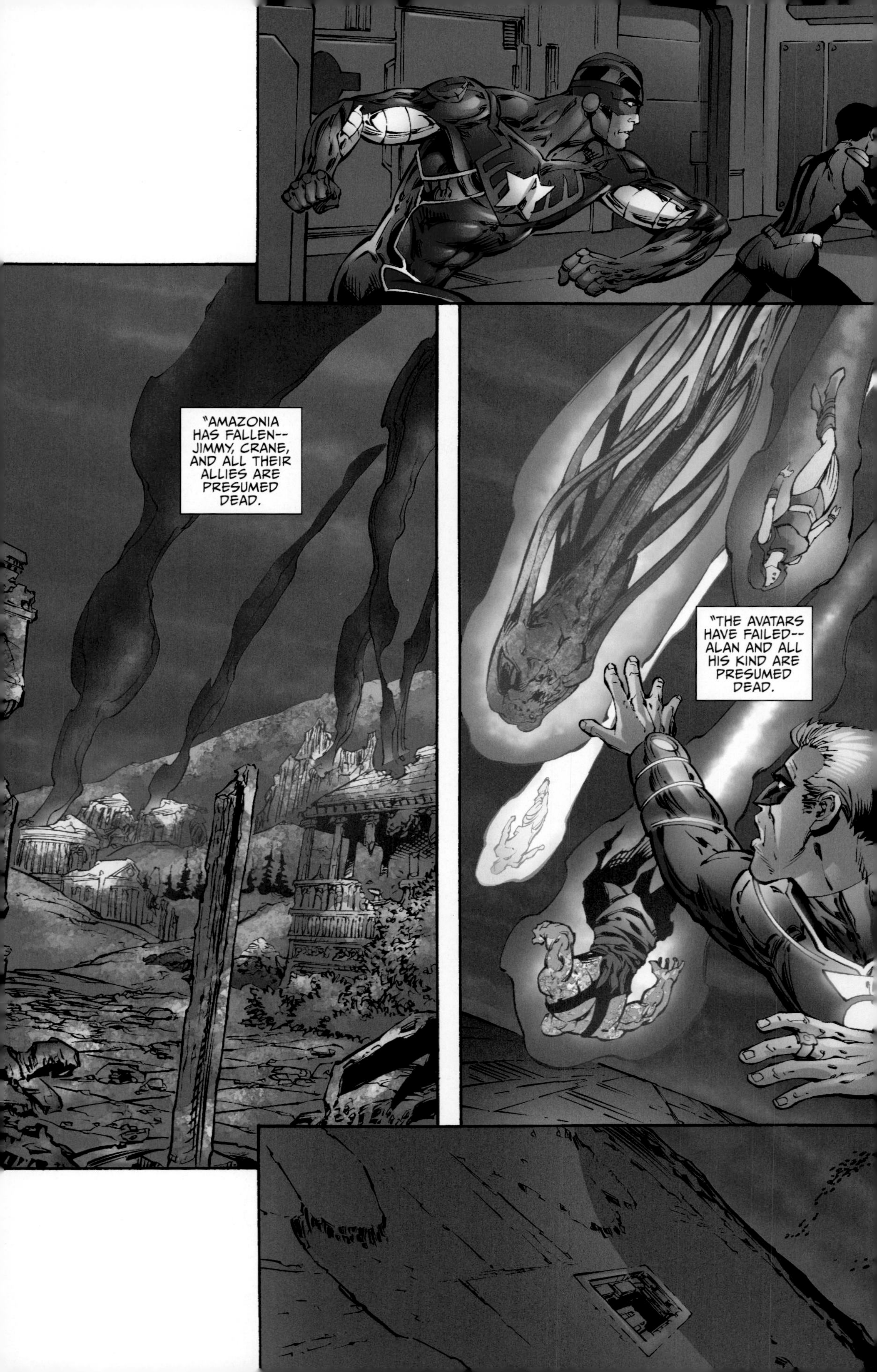
"AMAZONIA HAS FALLEN-- JIMMY, CRANE, AND ALL THEIR ALLIES ARE PRESUMED DEAD.
"THE AVATARS HAVE FAILED-- ALAN AND ALL HIS KIND ARE PRESUMED DEAD.

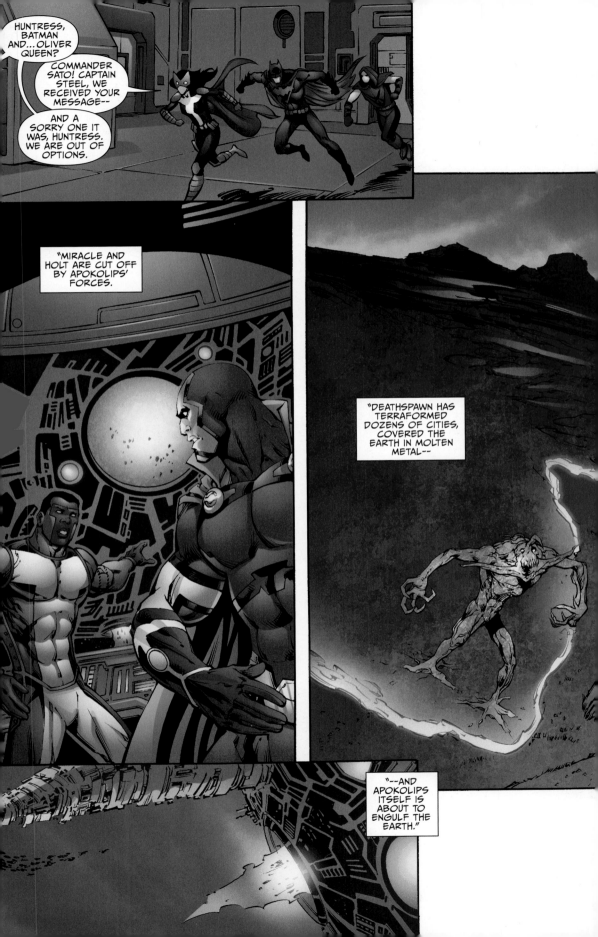

HUNTRESS, BATMAN AND... OLIVER QUEEN?

COMMANDER SATO! CAPTAIN STEEL, WE RECEIVED YOUR MESSAGE--

AND A SORRY ONE IT WAS, HUNTRESS. WE ARE OUT OF OPTIONS.

"MIRACLE AND HOLT ARE CUT OFF BY APOKOLIPS' FORCES.

"DEATHSPAWN HAS TERRAFORMED DOZENS OF CITIES, COVERED THE EARTH IN MOLTEN METAL--

"--AND APOKOLIPS ITSELF IS ABOUT TO ENGULF THE EARTH."

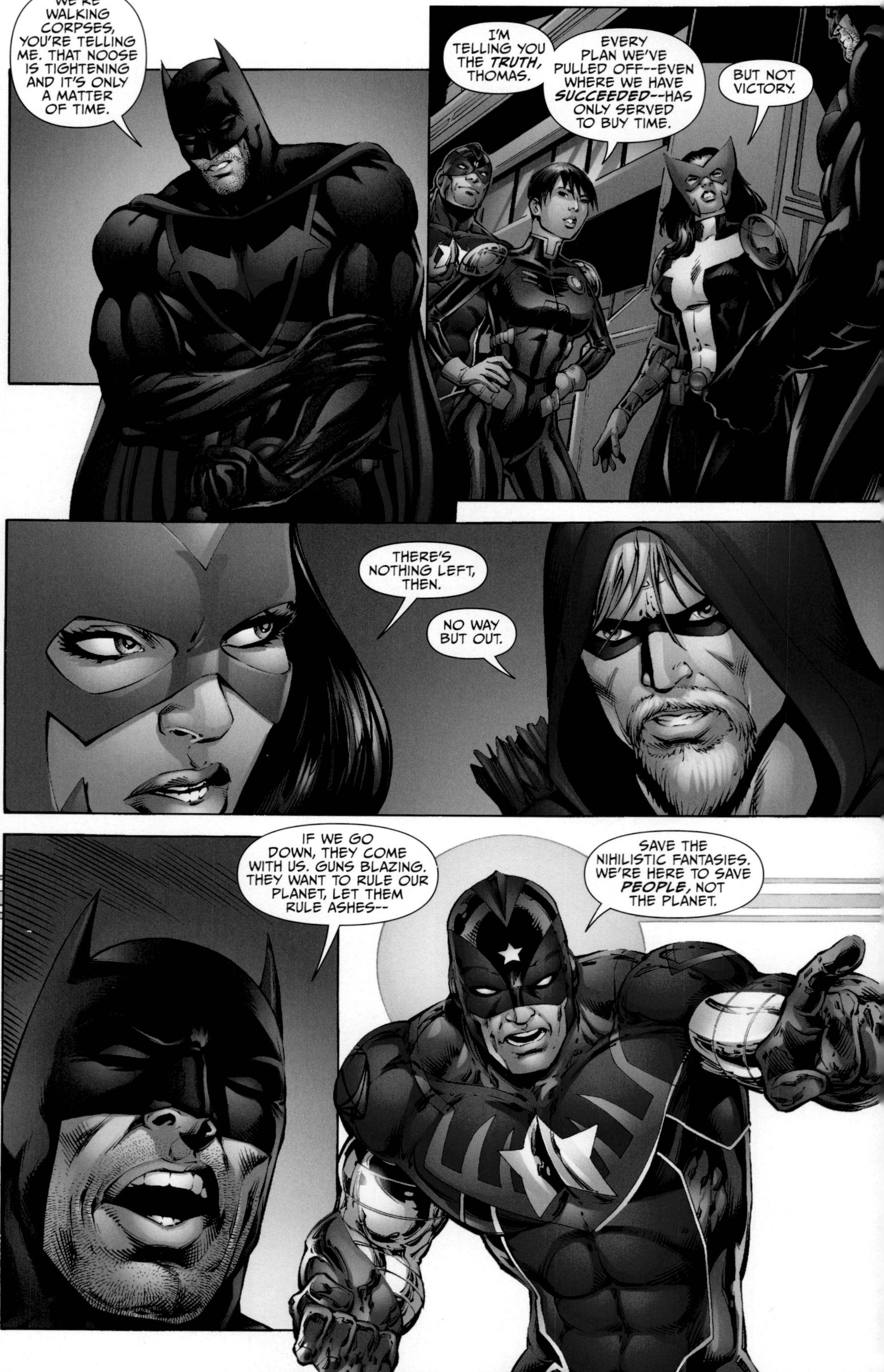
WE'RE WALKING CORPSES, YOU'RE TELLING ME. THAT NOOSE IS TIGHTENING AND IT'S ONLY A MATTER OF TIME.
I'M TELLING YOU THE *TRUTH*, THOMAS.
EVERY PLAN WE'VE PULLED OFF--EVEN WHERE WE HAVE *SUCCEEDED*--HAS ONLY SERVED TO BUY TIME.
BUT NOT VICTORY.
THERE'S NOTHING LEFT, THEN.
NO WAY BUT OUT.
IF WE GO DOWN, THEY COME WITH US. GUNS BLAZING. THEY WANT TO RULE OUR PLANET, LET THEM RULE ASHES--
SAVE THE NIHILISTIC FANTASIES. WE'RE HERE TO SAVE *PEOPLE*, NOT THE PLANET.

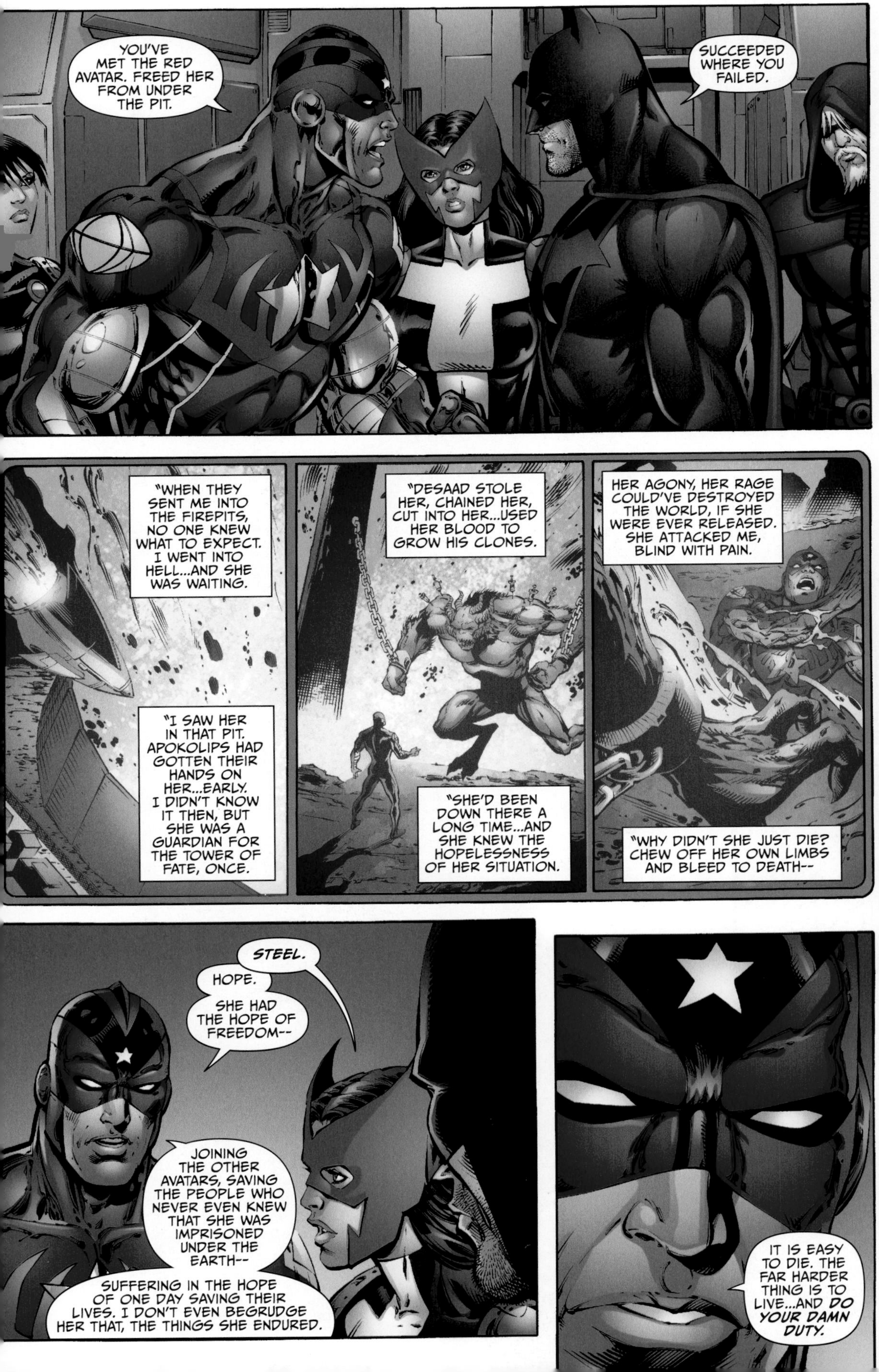
YOU'VE MET THE RED AVATAR. FREED HER FROM UNDER THE PIT.
SUCCEEDED WHERE YOU FAILED.
"WHEN THEY SENT ME INTO THE FIREPITS, NO ONE KNEW WHAT TO EXPECT. I WENT INTO HELL...AND SHE WAS WAITING.
"I SAW HER IN THAT PIT. APOKOLIPS HAD GOTTEN THEIR HANDS ON HER...EARLY. I DIDN'T KNOW IT THEN, BUT SHE WAS A GUARDIAN FOR THE TOWER OF FATE, ONCE.
"DESAAD STOLE HER, CHAINED HER, CUT INTO HER...USED HER BLOOD TO GROW HIS CLONES.
"SHE'D BEEN DOWN THERE A LONG TIME...AND SHE KNEW THE HOPELESSNESS OF HER SITUATION.
HER AGONY, HER RAGE COULD'VE DESTROYED THE WORLD, IF SHE WERE EVER RELEASED. SHE ATTACKED ME, BLIND WITH PAIN.
"WHY DIDN'T SHE JUST DIE? CHEW OFF HER OWN LIMBS AND BLEED TO DEATH--
STEEL.
HOPE.
SHE HAD THE HOPE OF FREEDOM--
JOINING THE OTHER AVATARS, SAVING THE PEOPLE WHO NEVER EVEN KNEW THAT SHE WAS IMPRISONED UNDER THE EARTH--
SUFFERING IN THE HOPE OF ONE DAY SAVING THEIR LIVES. I DON'T EVEN BEGRUDGE HER THAT, THE THINGS SHE ENDURED.
IT IS EASY TO DIE. THE FAR HARDER THING IS TO LIVE...AND DO YOUR DAMN DUTY.

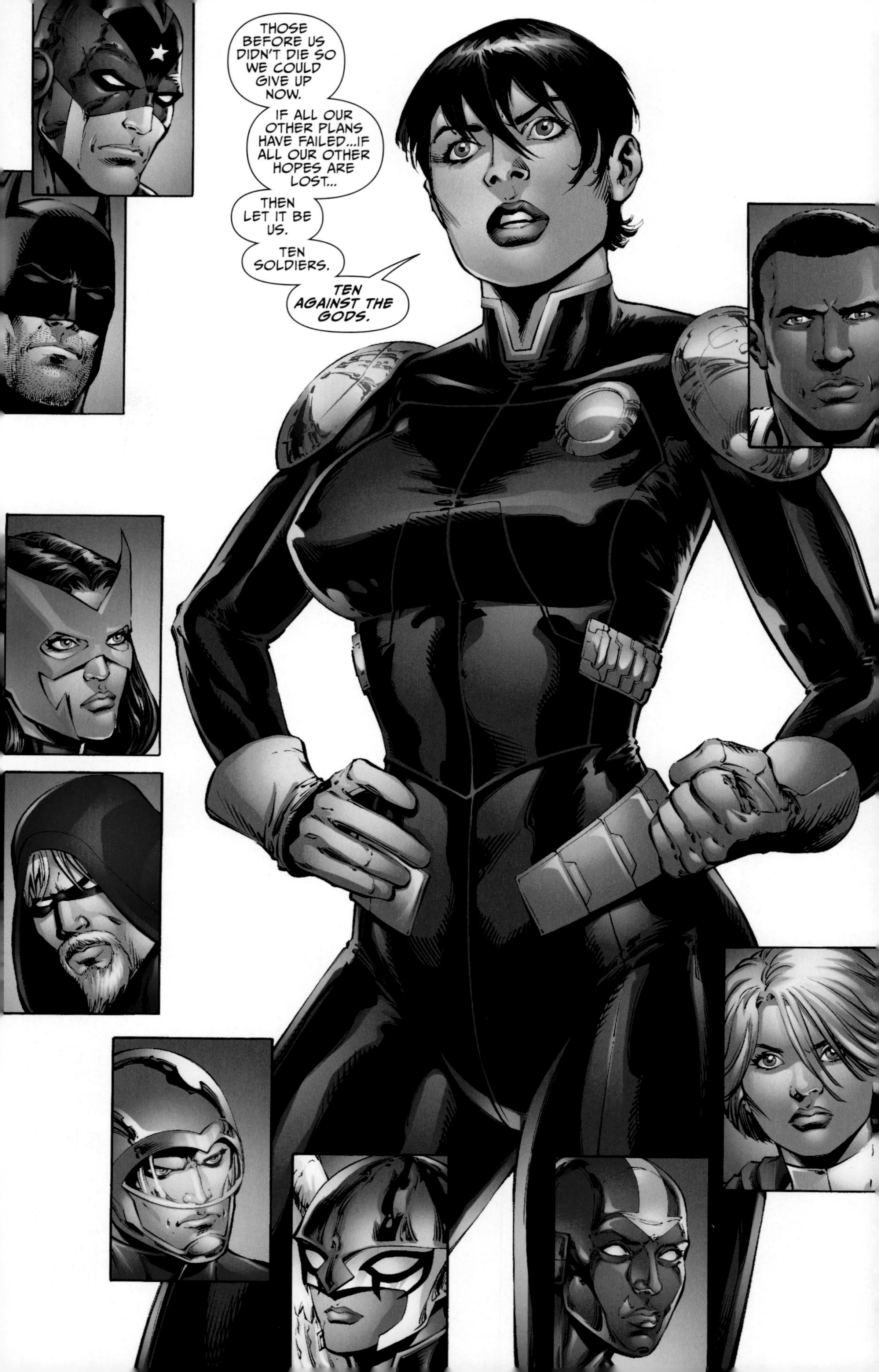
THOSE BEFORE US DIDN'T DIE SO WE COULD GIVE UP NOW.
IF ALL OUR OTHER PLANS HAVE FAILED...IF ALL OUR OTHER HOPES ARE LOST...
THEN LET IT BE US.
TEN SOLDIERS.
TEN AGAINST THE GODS.

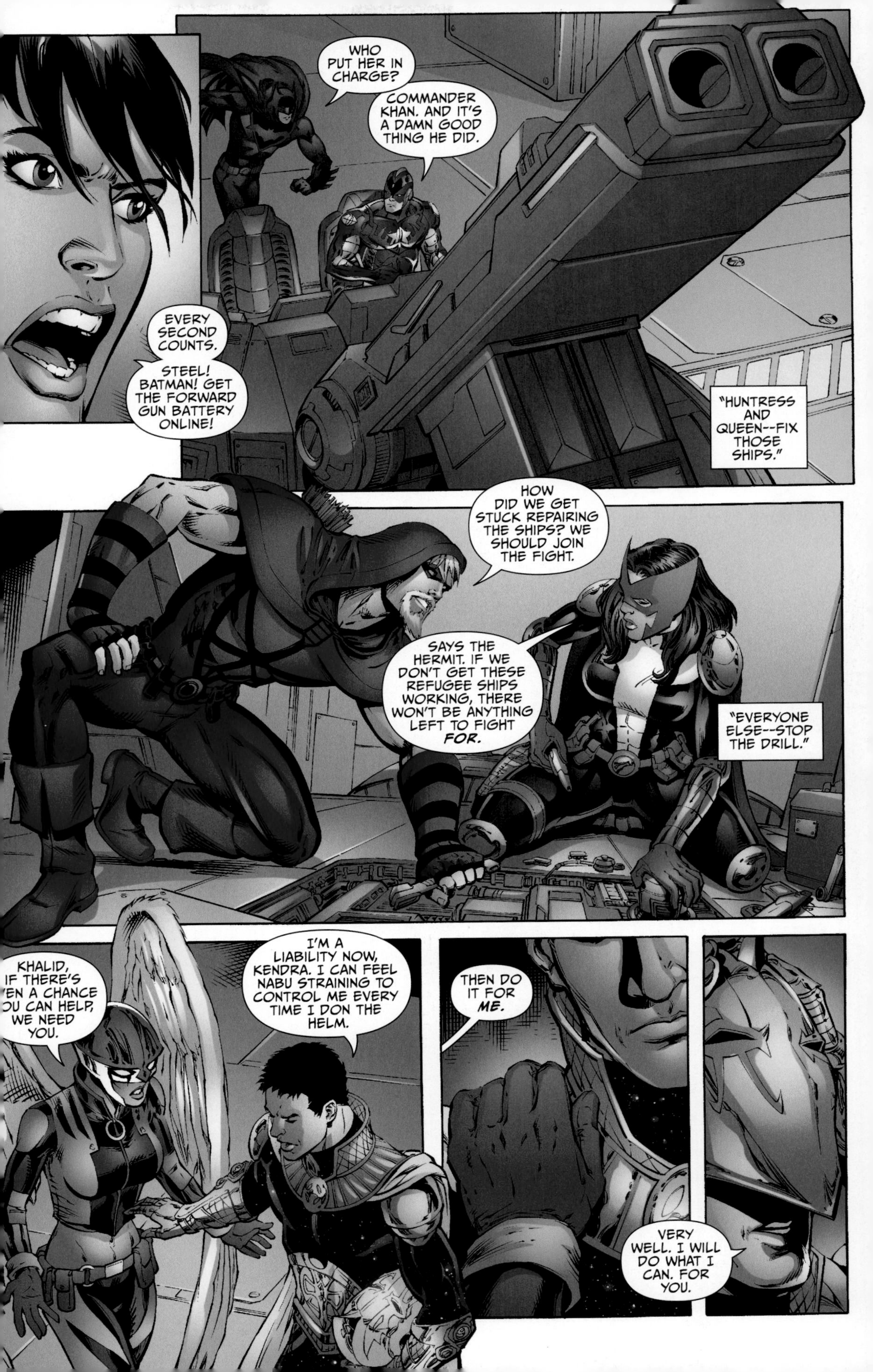
WHO PUT HER IN CHARGE?
COMMANDER KHAN. AND IT'S A DAMN GOOD THING HE DID.
EVERY SECOND COUNTS.
STEEL! BATMAN! GET THE FORWARD GUN BATTERY ONLINE!
"HUNTRESS AND QUEEN--FIX THOSE SHIPS."
HOW DID WE GET STUCK REPAIRING THE SHIPS? WE SHOULD JOIN THE FIGHT.
SAYS THE HERMIT. IF WE DON'T GET THESE REFUGEE SHIPS WORKING, THERE WON'T BE ANYTHING LEFT TO FIGHT *FOR.*
"EVERYONE ELSE--STOP THE DRILL."
I'M A LIABILITY NOW, KENDRA. I CAN FEEL NABU STRAINING TO CONTROL ME EVERY TIME I DON THE HELM.
THEN DO IT FOR *ME.*
VERY WELL. I WILL DO WHAT I CAN. FOR YOU.

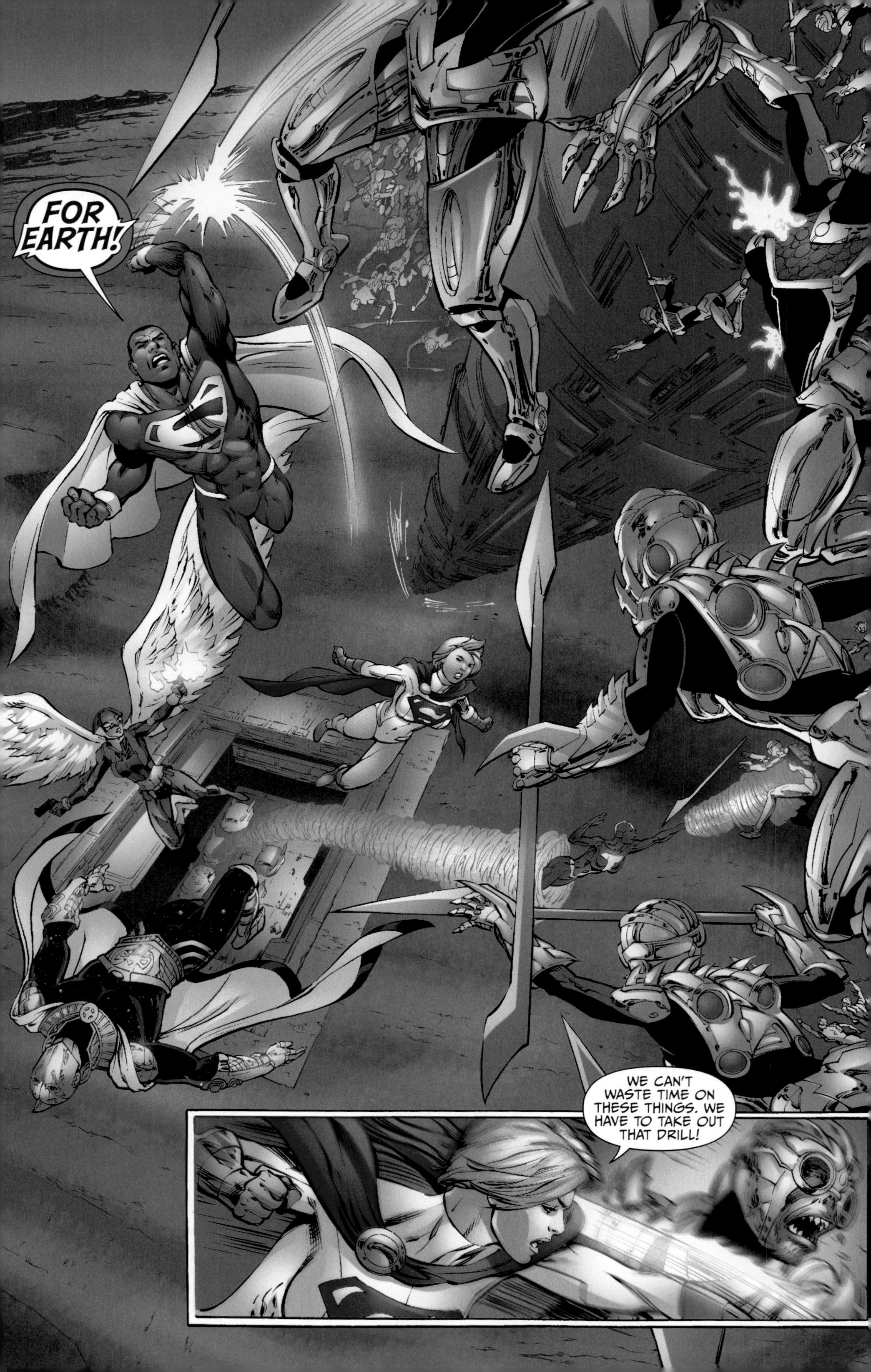
FOR EARTH!
WE CAN'T WASTE TIME ON THESE THINGS. WE HAVE TO TAKE OUT THAT DRILL!

WHAT'S THIS THING MADE OF? I'M BARELY MAKING A DENT.

WHAM
WHAM
WHAM

BRUTE FORCE WON'T DO IT. WE HAVE TO SHUT DOWN ITS POWER SOURCE.

IF WE KNEW WHERE IT WAS.

DID YOU FORGET WHAT I USED TO DO FOR A LIVING, KHALID?

FINDING SECRET ENTRANCES PAID MY BILLS. COMBINE THAT WITH A HAWK'S EYESIGHT AND...

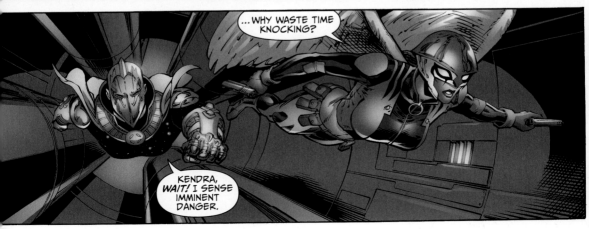

...WHY WASTE TIME KNOCKING?

KENDRA, WAIT! I SENSE IMMINENT DANGER.

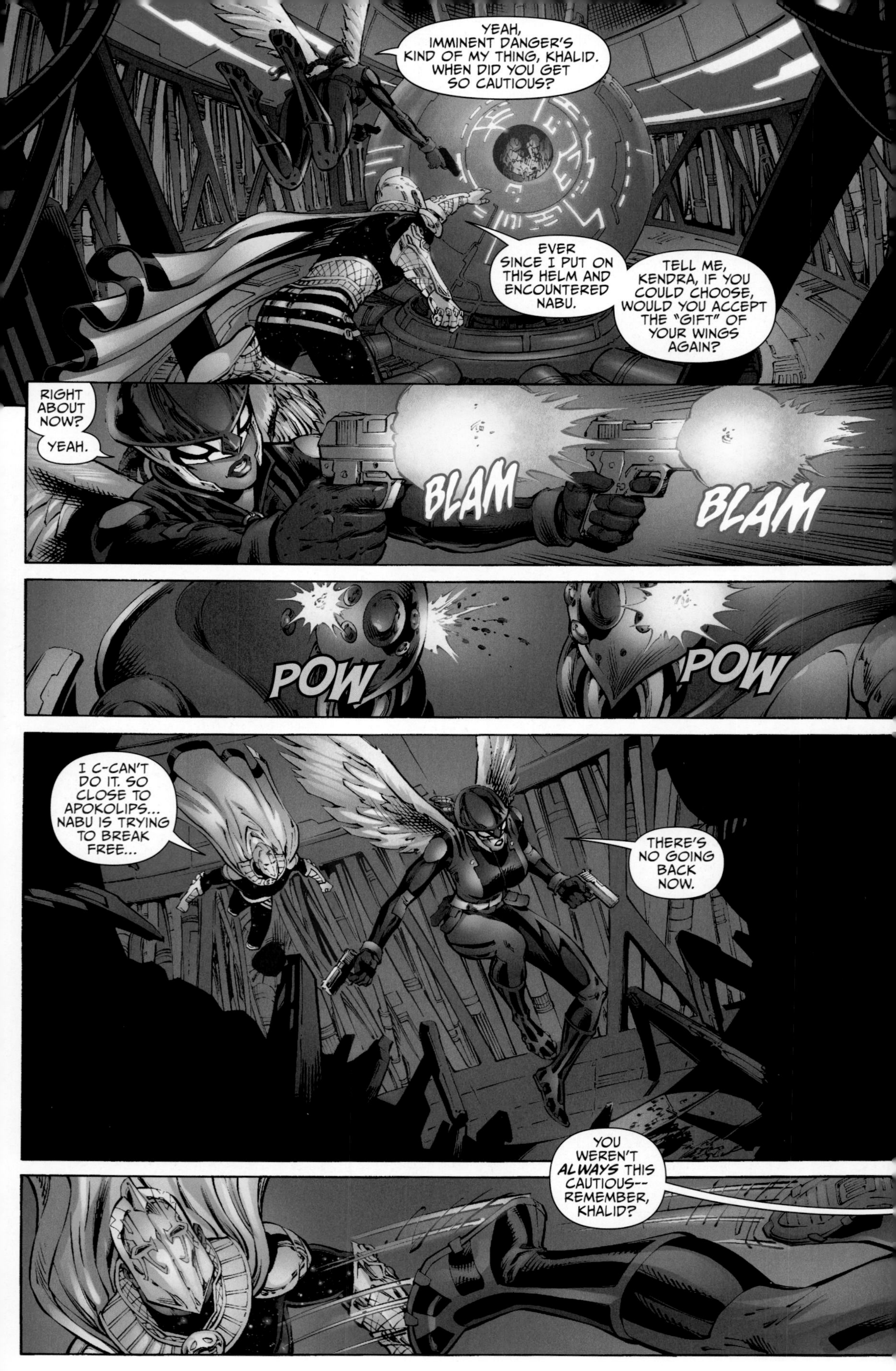

YEAH, IMMINENT DANGER'S KIND OF MY THING, KHALID. WHEN DID YOU GET SO CAUTIOUS?
EVER SINCE I PUT ON THIS HELM AND ENCOUNTERED NABU.
TELL ME, KENDRA, IF YOU COULD CHOOSE, WOULD YOU ACCEPT THE "GIFT" OF YOUR WINGS AGAIN?
RIGHT ABOUT NOW?
YEAH.
BLAM
BLAM
POW
POW
I C-CAN'T DO IT. SO CLOSE TO APOKOLIPS... NABU IS TRYING TO BREAK FREE...
THERE'S NO GOING BACK NOW.
YOU WEREN'T ALWAYS THIS CAUTIOUS-- REMEMBER, KHALID?

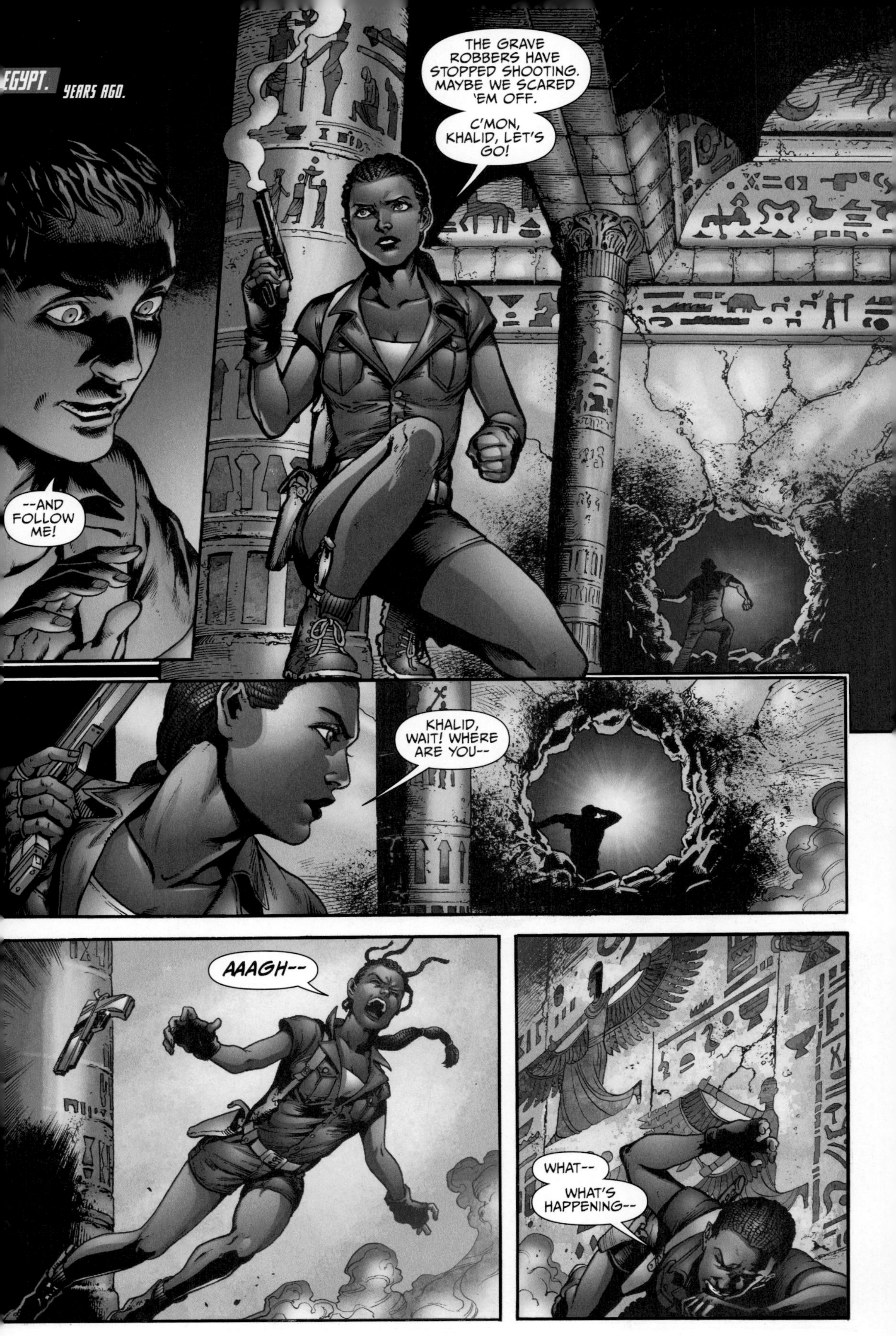
EGYPT. YEARS AGO.
THE GRAVE ROBBERS HAVE STOPPED SHOOTING. MAYBE WE SCARED 'EM OFF.
C'MON, KHALID, LET'S GO!
--AND FOLLOW ME!
KHALID, WAIT! WHERE ARE YOU--
AAAGH--
WHAT--
WHAT'S HAPPENING--

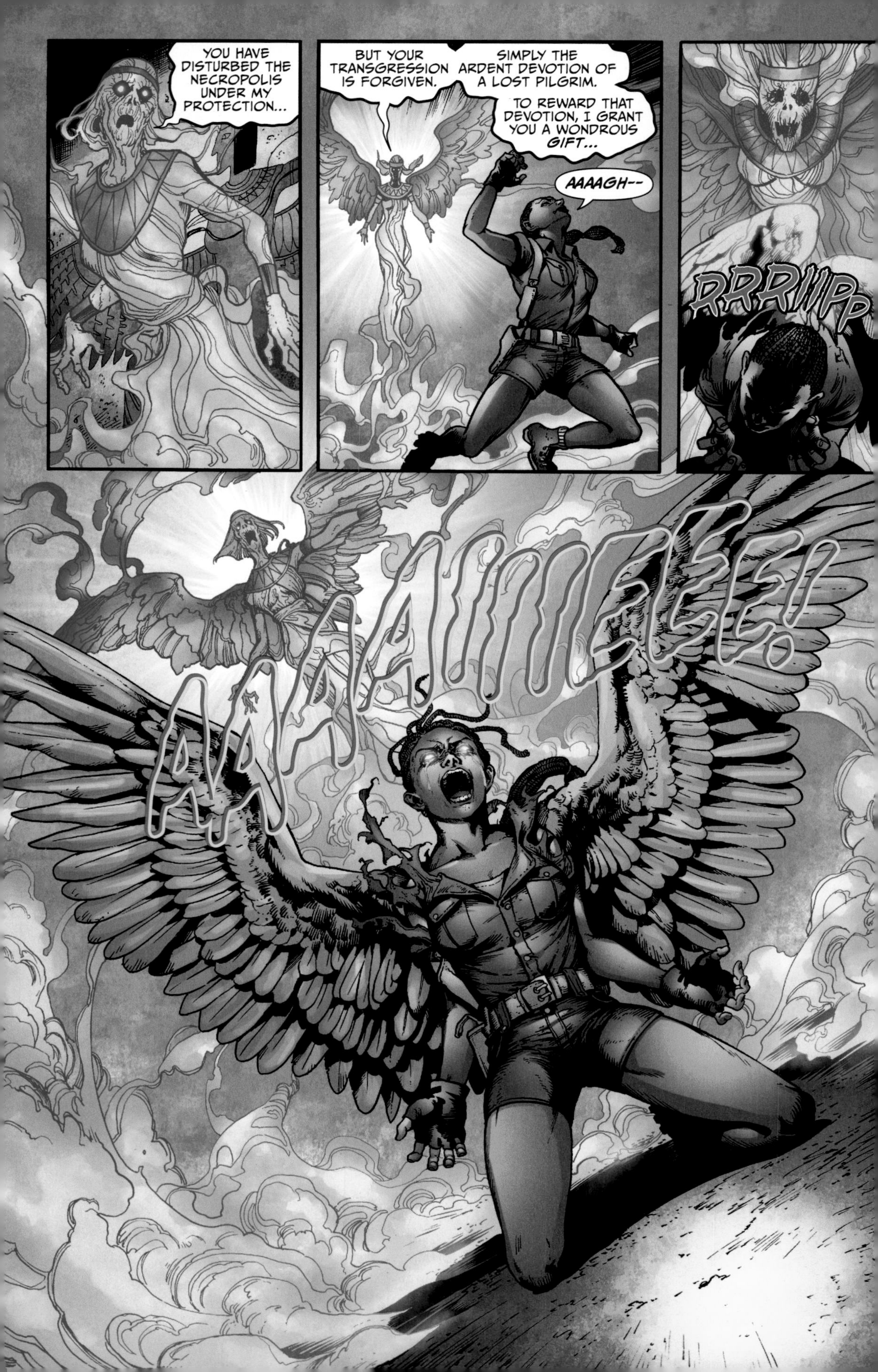
YOU HAVE DISTURBED THE NECROPOLIS UNDER MY PROTECTION...
BUT YOUR TRANSGRESSION IS FORGIVEN.
SIMPLY THE ARDENT DEVOTION OF A LOST PILGRIM.
TO REWARD THAT DEVOTION, I GRANT YOU A WONDROUS GIFT...
AAAAGH--
DRRIIPP
AAAAIIIEEE!

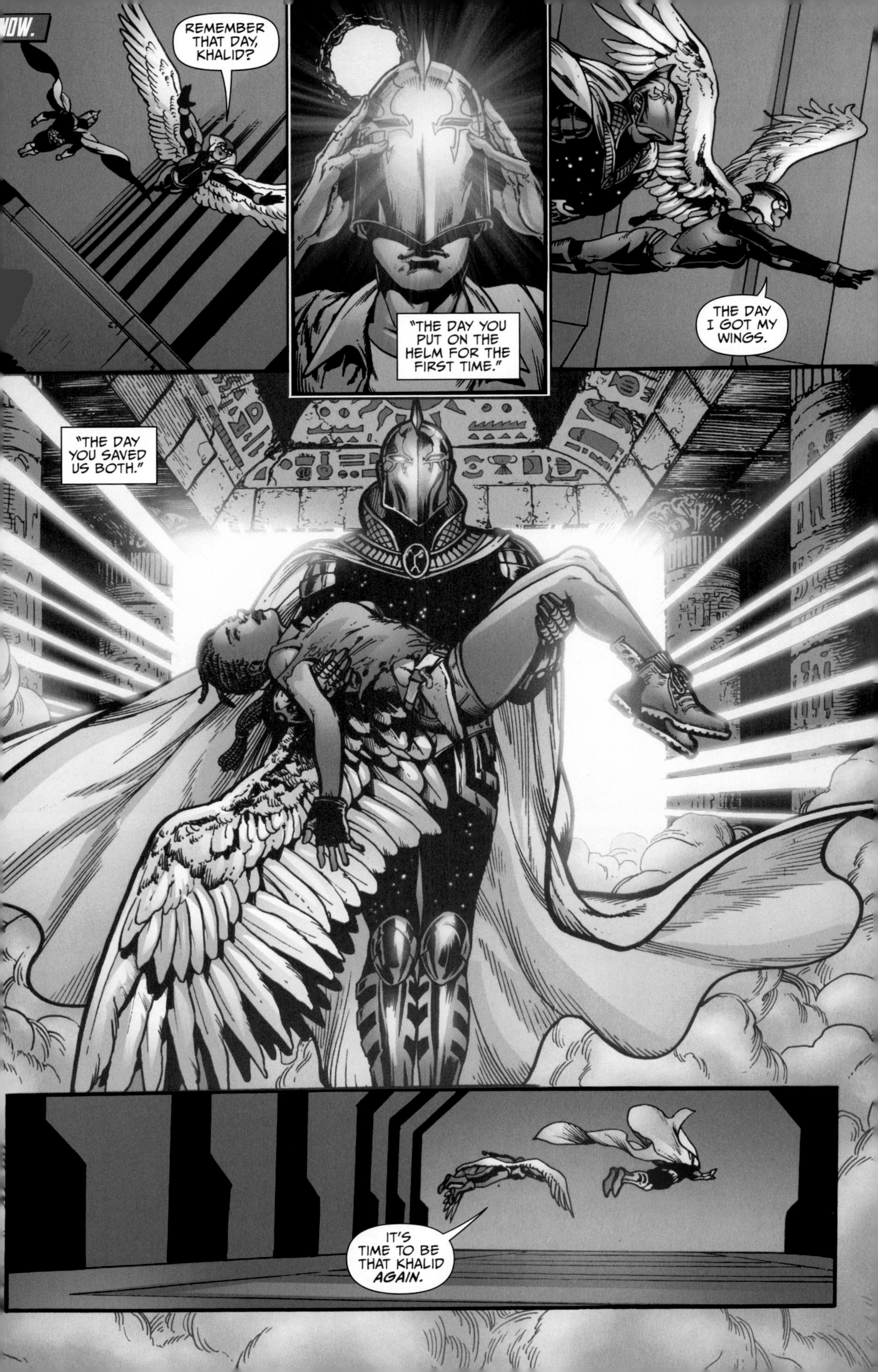
NOW.
REMEMBER THAT DAY, KHALID?
"THE DAY YOU PUT ON THE HELM FOR THE FIRST TIME."
THE DAY I GOT MY WINGS.
"THE DAY YOU SAVED US BOTH."
IT'S TIME TO BE THAT KHALID *AGAIN.*

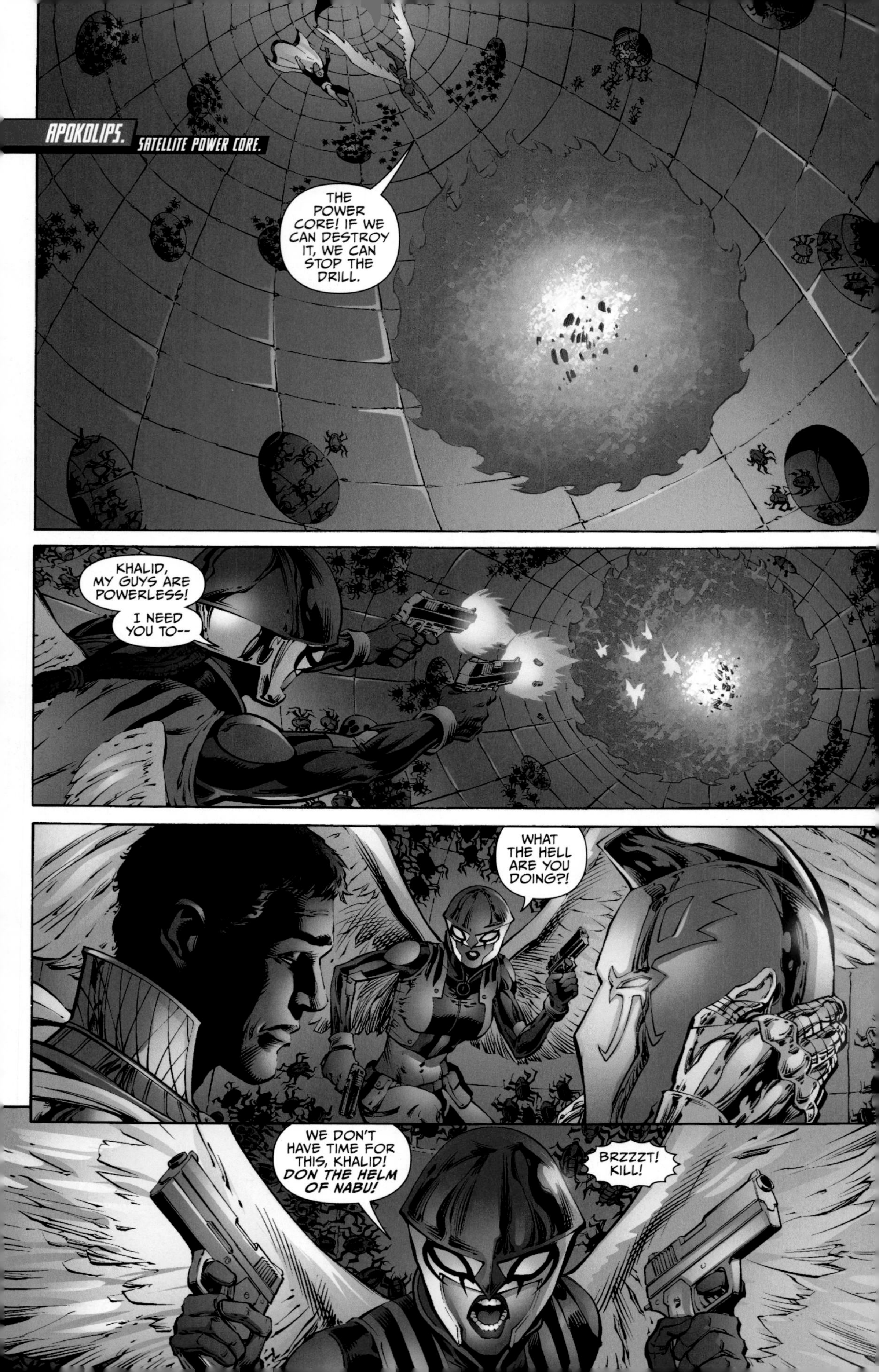
APOKOLIPS.
SATELLITE POWER CORE.
THE POWER CORE! IF WE CAN DESTROY IT, WE CAN STOP THE DRILL.
KHALID, MY GUYS ARE POWERLESS!
I NEED YOU TO--
WHAT THE HELL ARE YOU DOING?!
WE DON'T HAVE TIME FOR THIS, KHALID! DON THE HELM OF NABU!
BRZZZT! KILL!

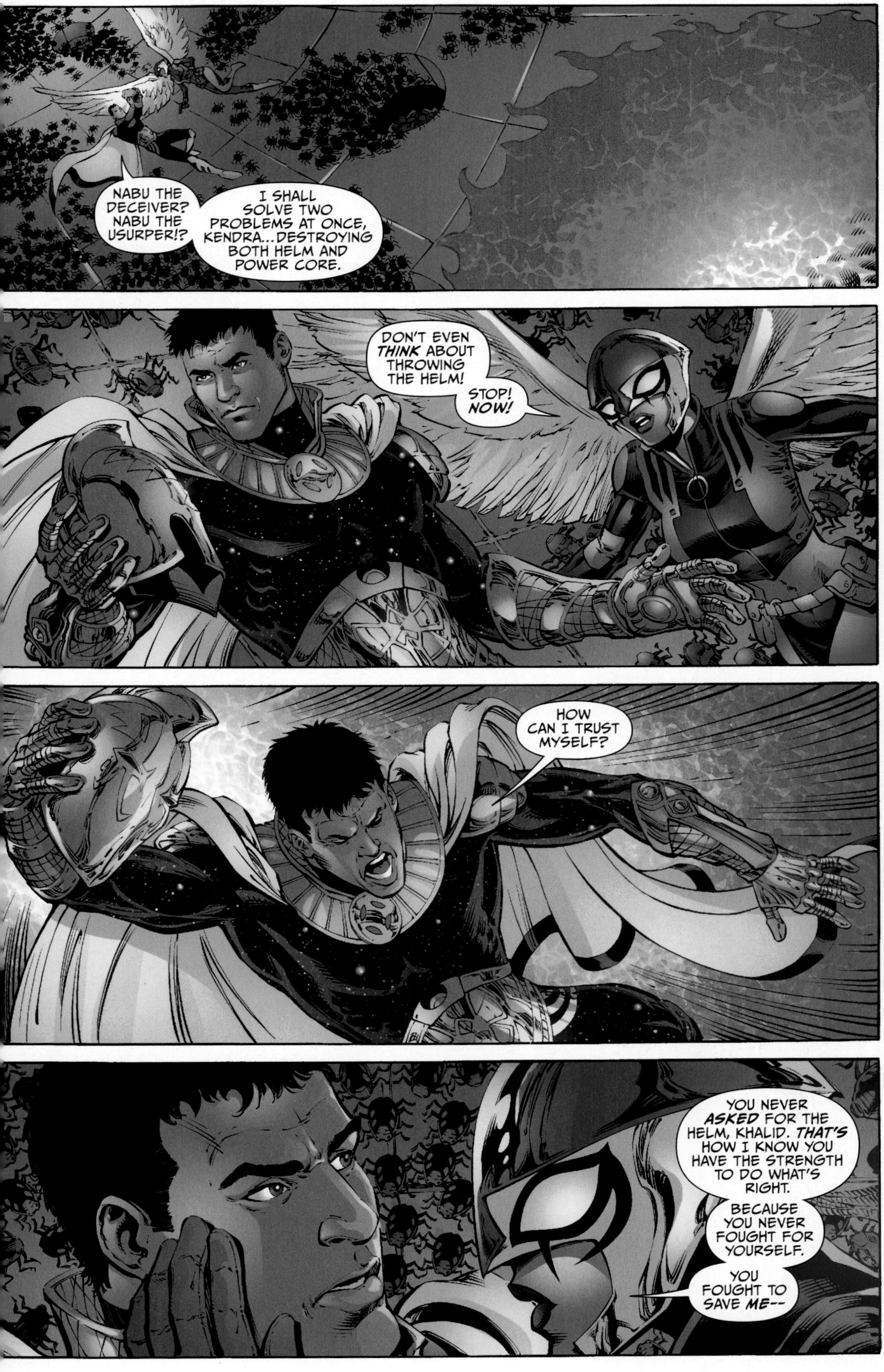
NABU THE DECEIVER? NABU THE USURPER!?
I SHALL SOLVE TWO PROBLEMS AT ONCE, KENDRA...DESTROYING BOTH HELM AND POWER CORE.
DON'T EVEN *THINK* ABOUT THROWING THE HELM!
STOP! *NOW!*
HOW CAN I TRUST MYSELF?
YOU NEVER *ASKED* FOR THE HELM, KHALID. *THAT'S* HOW I KNOW YOU HAVE THE STRENGTH TO DO WHAT'S RIGHT.
BECAUSE YOU NEVER FOUGHT FOR YOURSELF.
YOU FOUGHT TO SAVE *ME*--

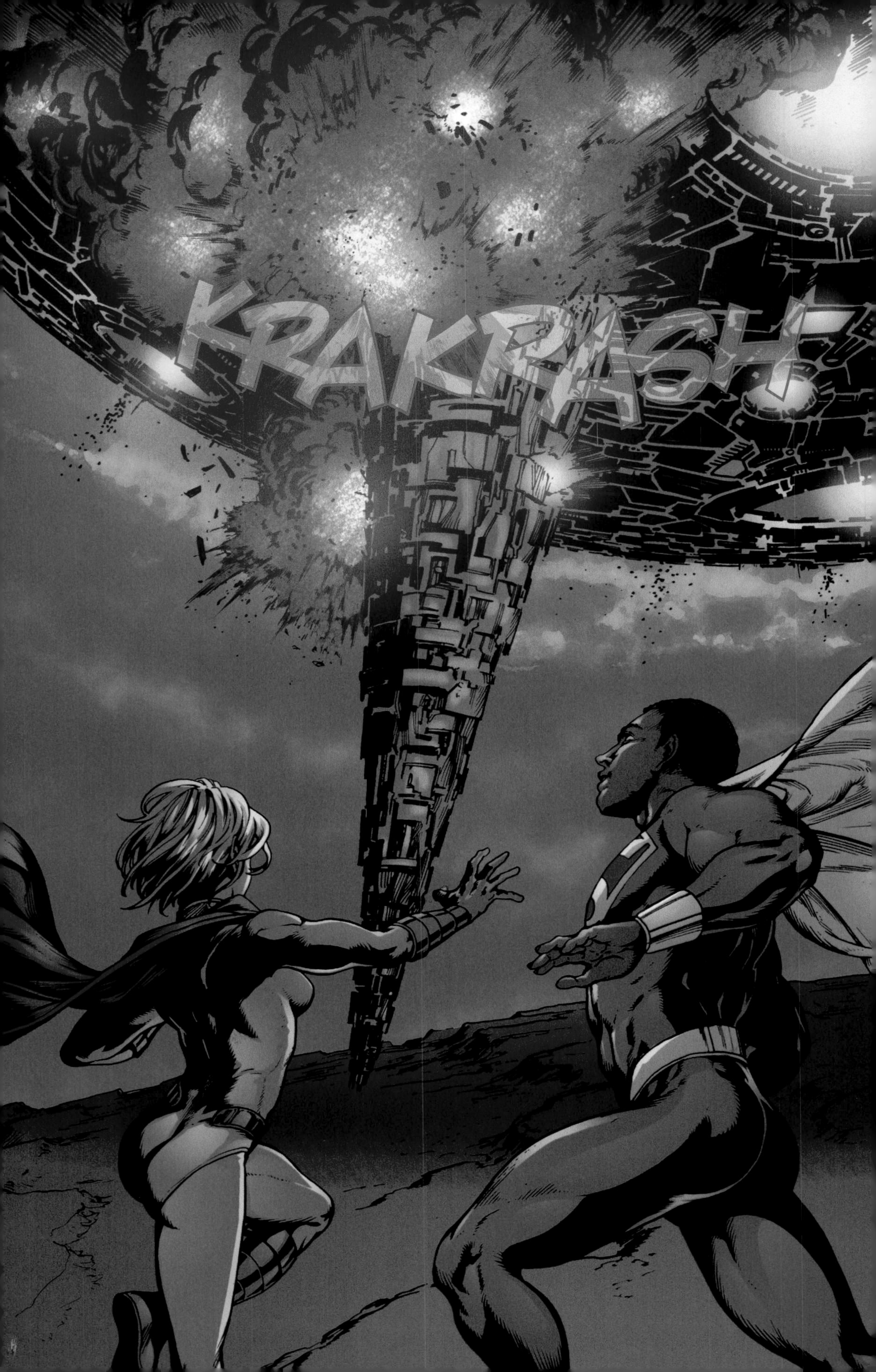
KRAKRASH!

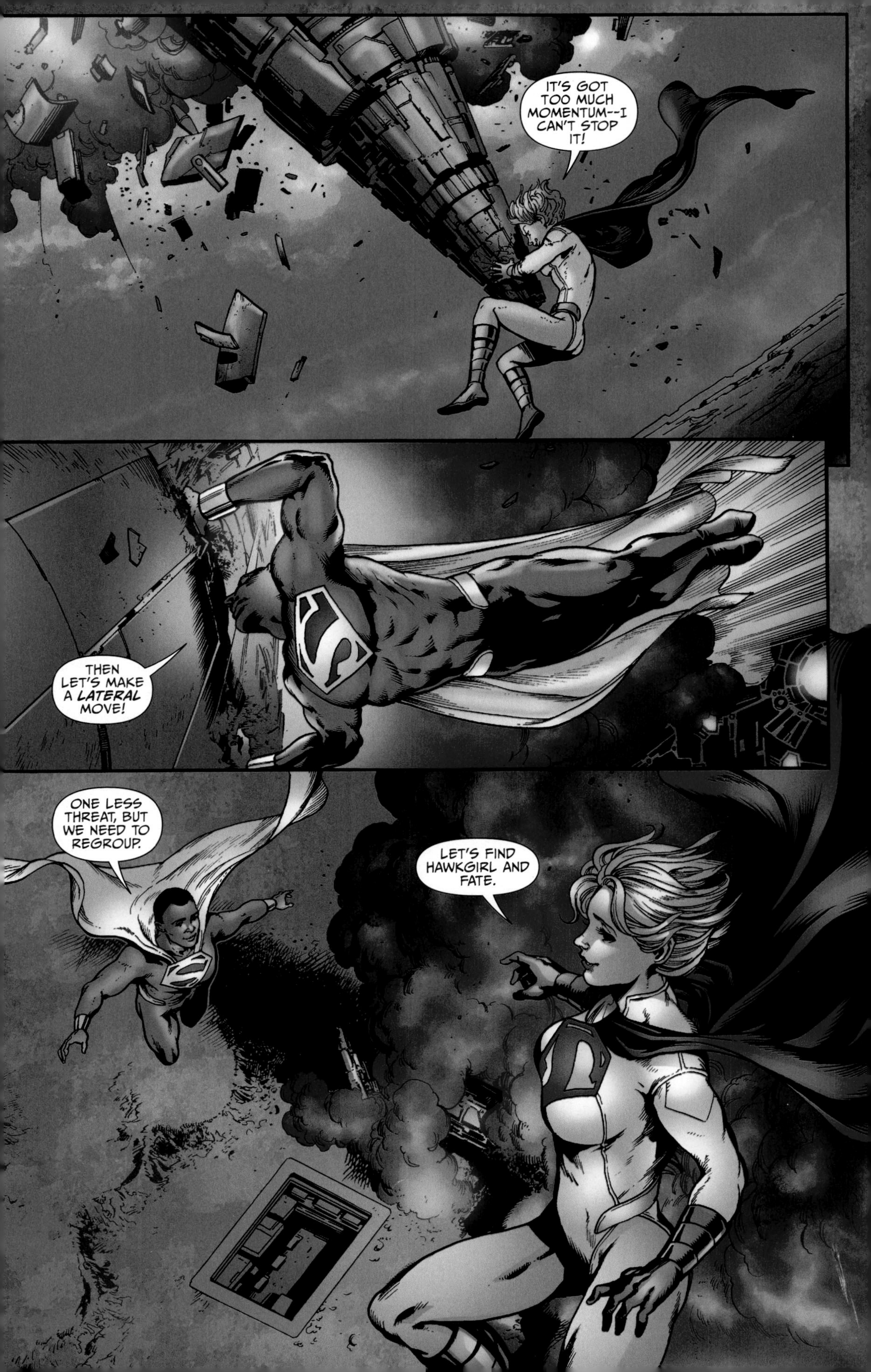
IT'S GOT TOO MUCH MOMENTUM--I CAN'T STOP IT!
THEN LET'S MAKE A *LATERAL* MOVE!
ONE LESS THREAT, BUT WE NEED TO REGROUP.
LET'S FIND HAWKGIRL AND FATE.

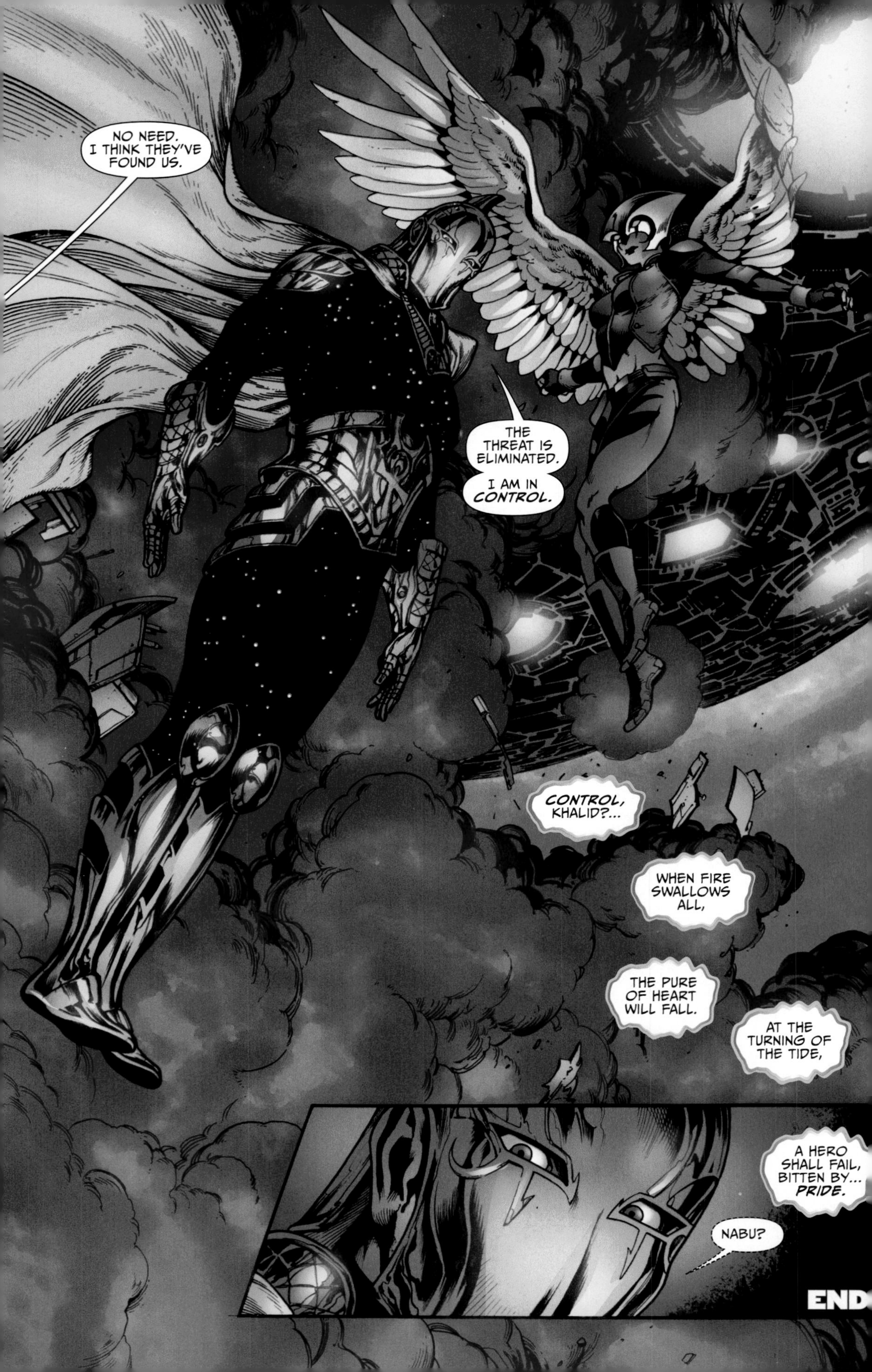
NO NEED. I THINK THEY'VE FOUND US.
THE THREAT IS ELIMINATED.
I AM IN *CONTROL*.
CONTROL, KHALID?...
WHEN FIRE SWALLOWS ALL,
THE PURE OF HEART WILL FALL.
AT THE TURNING OF THE TIDE,
A HERO SHALL FAIL, BITTEN BY... *PRIDE*.
NABU?
END

EARTH 2 #27
monster variant cover by
Timothy Green with Dave McCaig

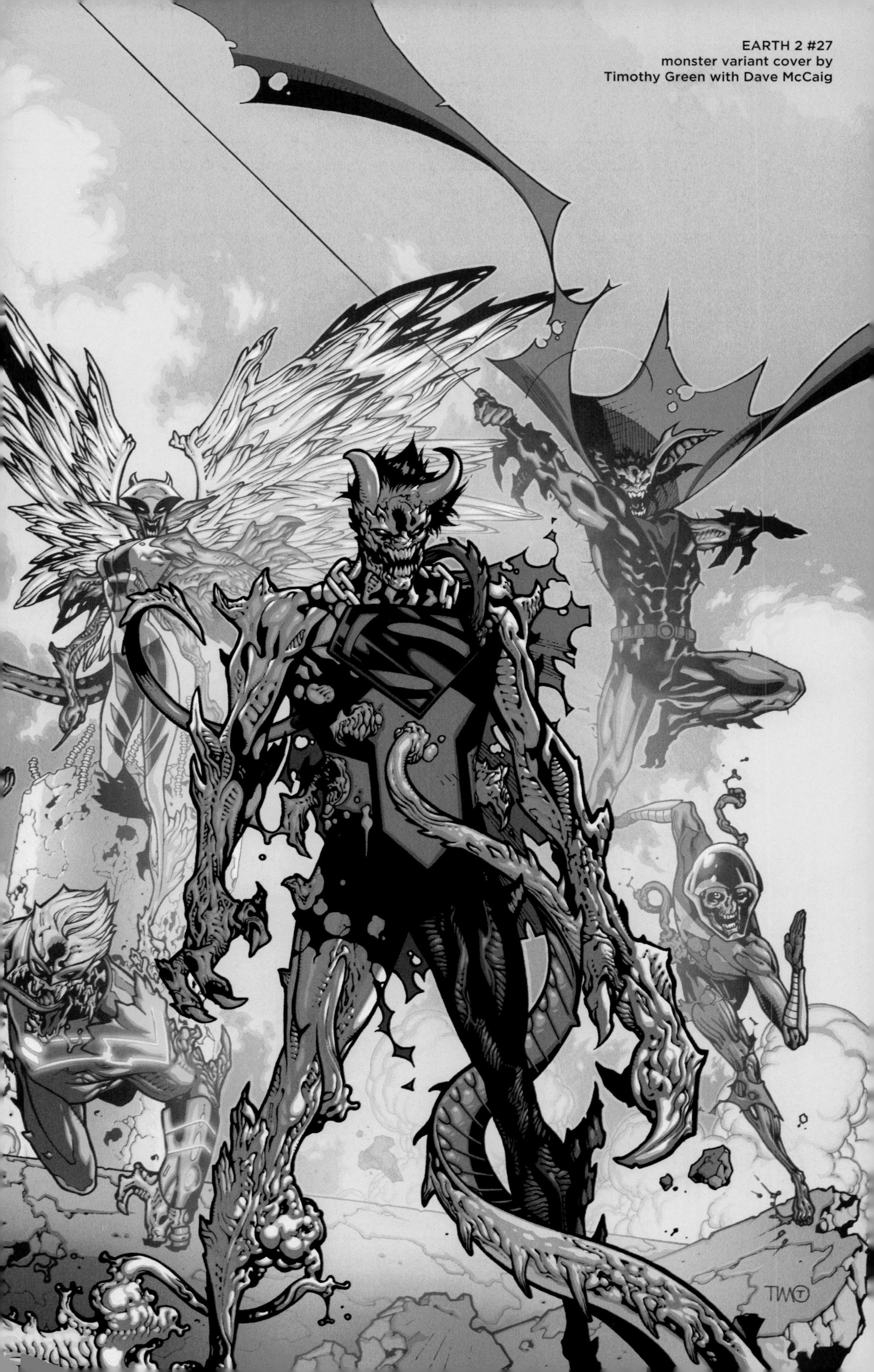
TWG

A

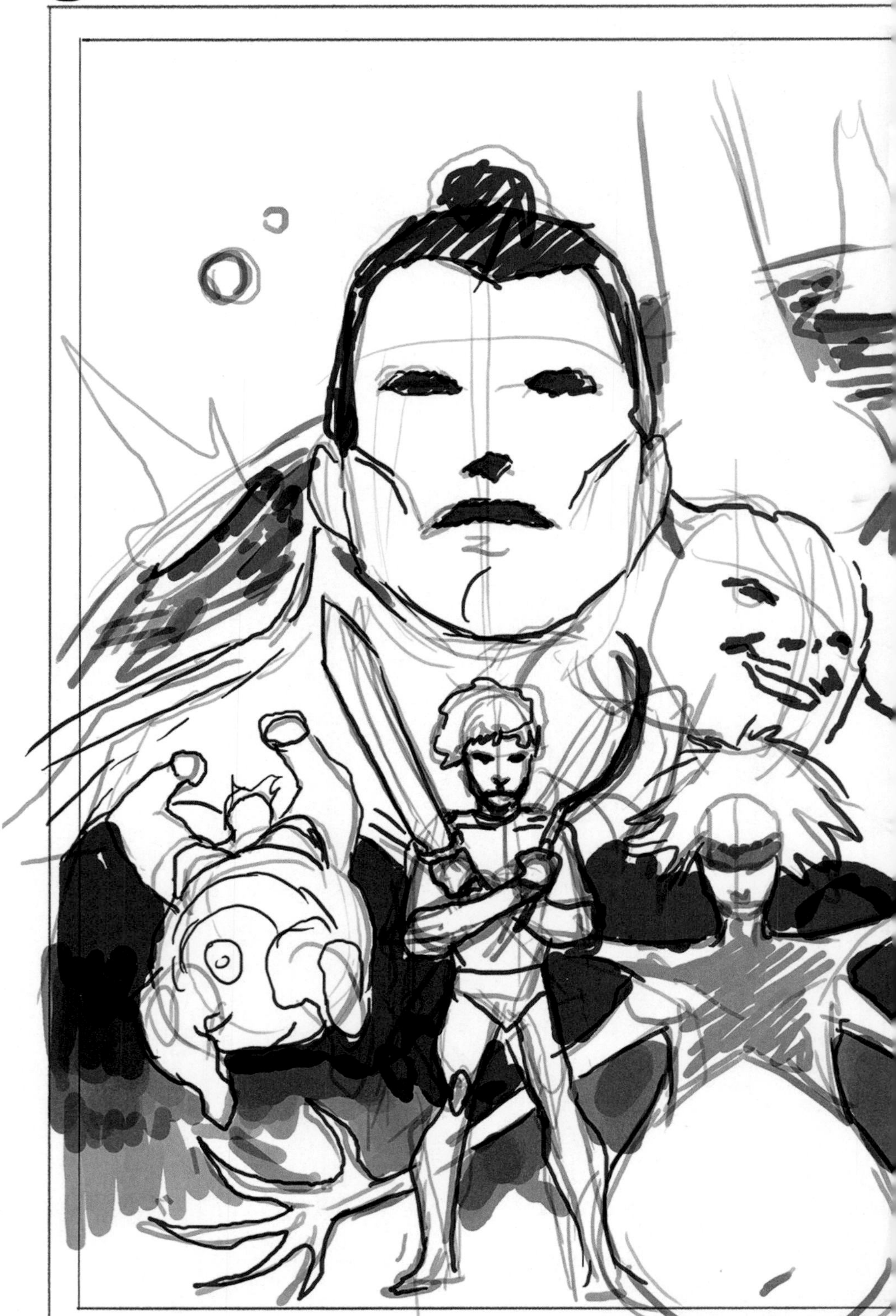

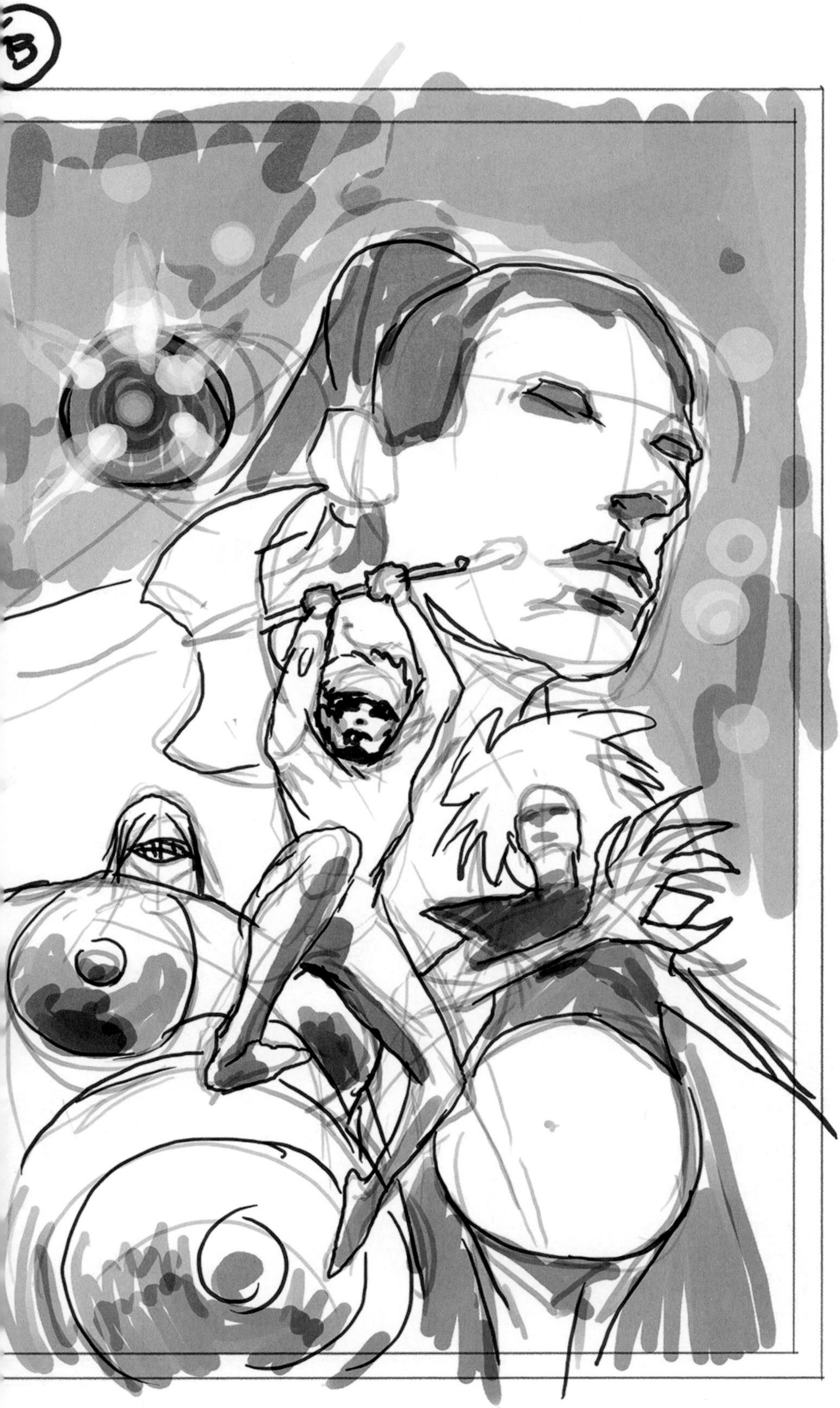

EARTH 2 #28 cover sketches
by Stephen Segovia

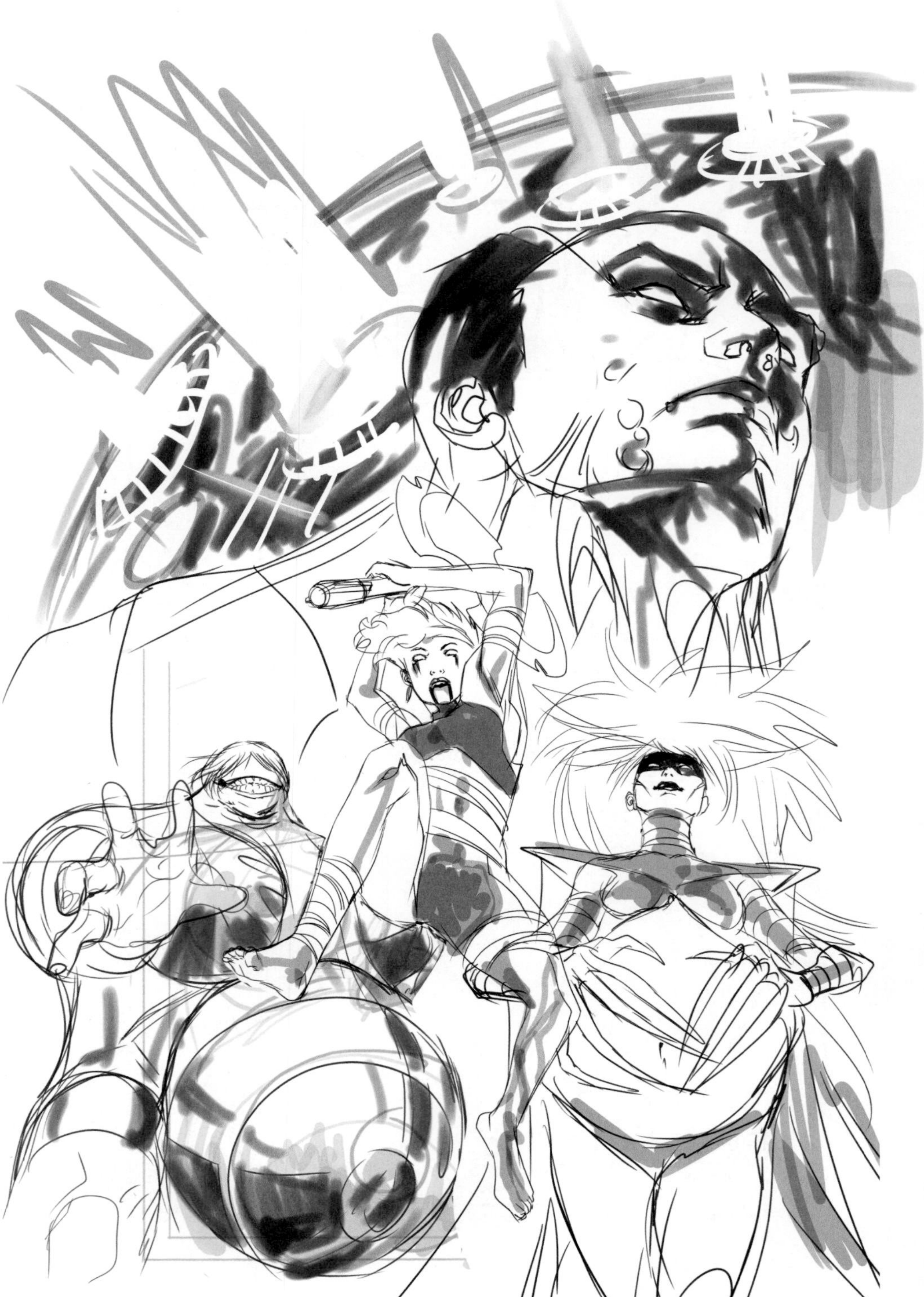

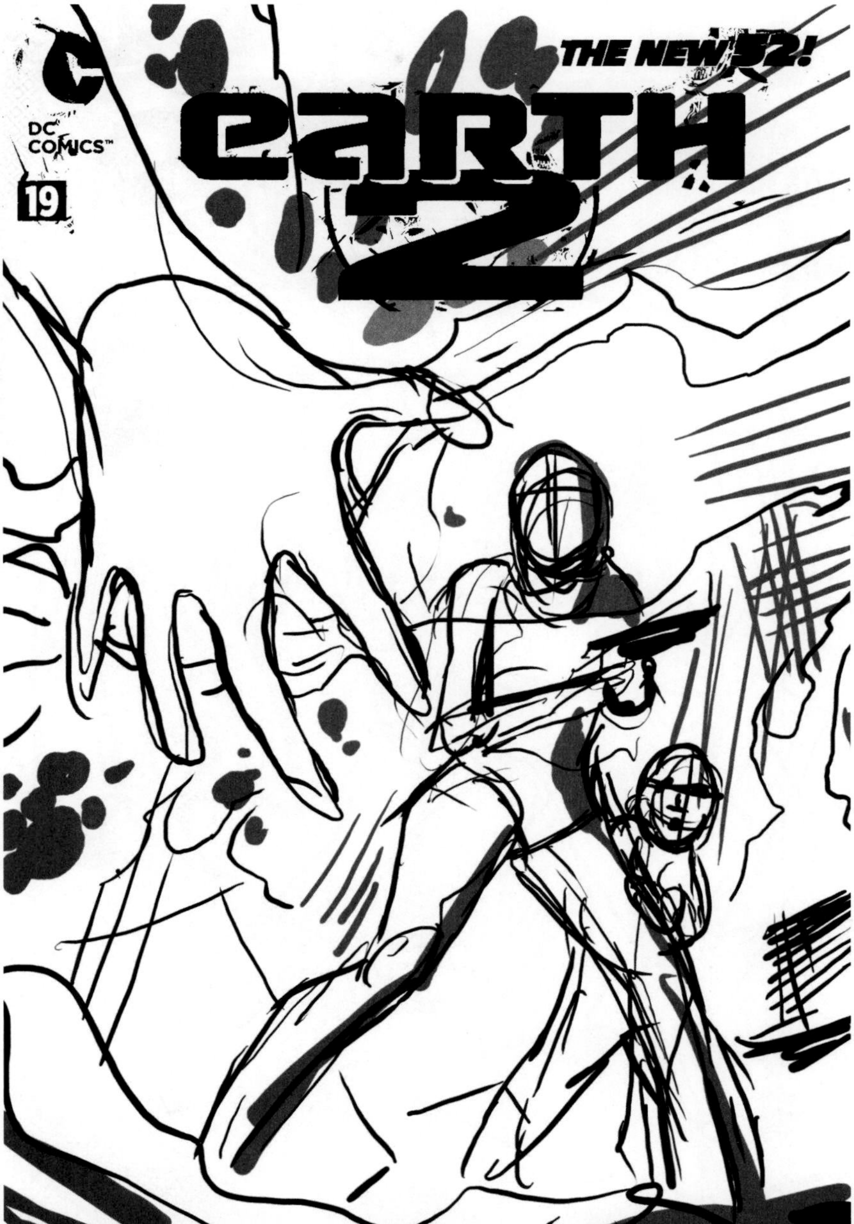
THE NEW 52!
DC COMICS
19
EARTH 2

EARTH 2 #29 cover sketches
by Yildiray Cinar

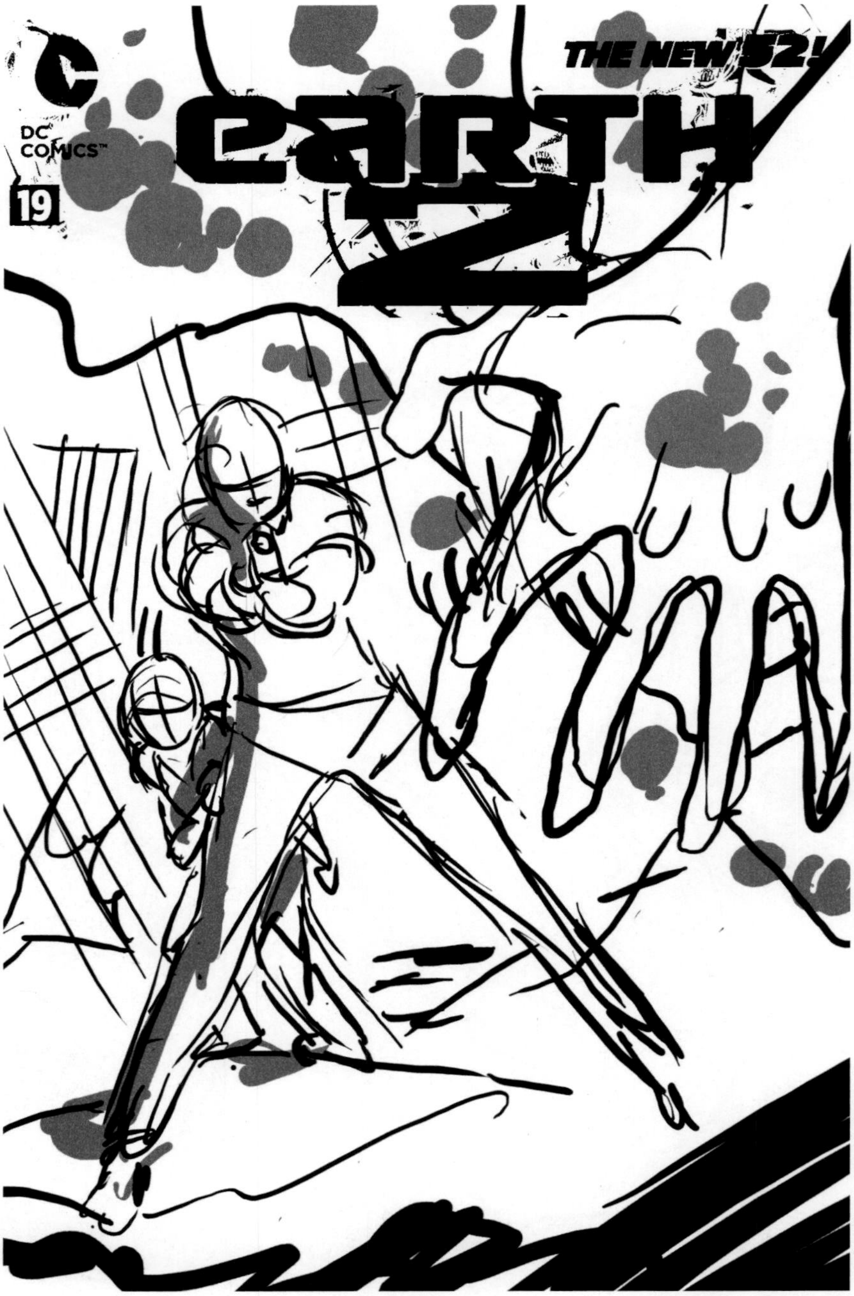
DC COMICS™
19
THE NEW 52!
EARTH 2

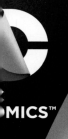

“Great characterization and exciting action sequences continue to be the hallmarks of this series, along with someinteresting meta commentary as well.”—IGN

“EARTH 2 is an incredibly entertaining ride. The freedom to create a world from the ground up has allowed it to be one of the most exciting, diverse, and entertaining titles DC puts out.” –CRAVEONLINE

START AT THE BEGINNING!
EARTH 2
VOLUME 1: THE GATHERING

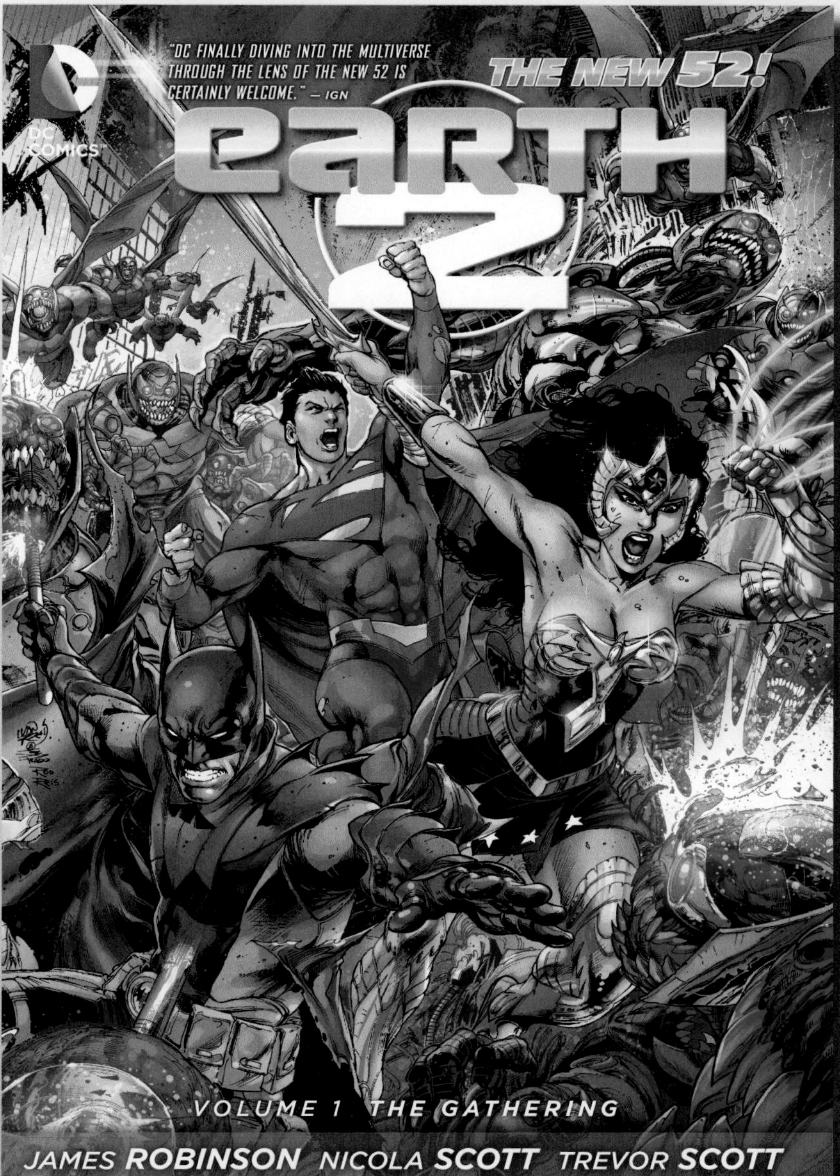

"DC FINALLY DIVING INTO THE MULTIVERSE THROUGH THE LENS OF THE NEW 52 IS CERTAINLY WELCOME." — IGN
DC COMICS
THE NEW 52!
EARTH 2
VOLUME 1 THE GATHERING
JAMES ROBINSON NICOLA SCOTT TREVOR SCOTT

EARTH 2 VOL. 2: THE TOWER OF FATE

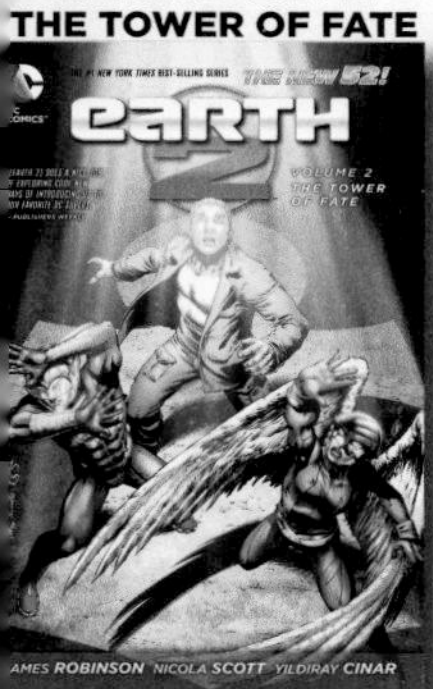

EARTH 2
JAMES ROBINSON NICOLA SCOTT YILDIRAY CINAR

with JAMES ROBINSON, NICOLA SCOTT and YILDIRAY CINAR

EARTH 2 VOL. 3: BATTLE CRY

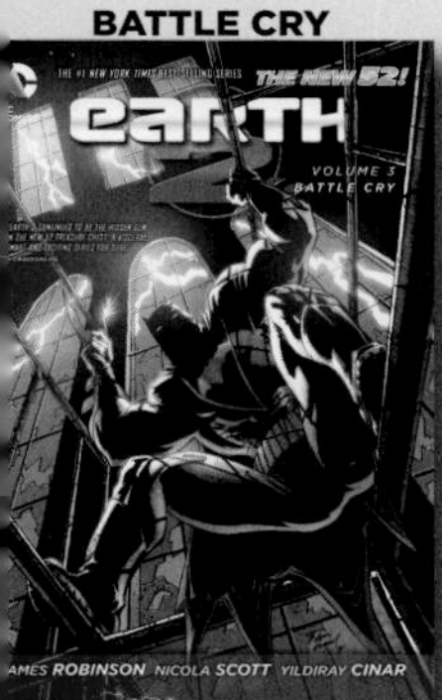

THE NEW 52!
EARTH 2
JAMES ROBINSON NICOLA SCOTT YILDIRAY CINAR

with JAMES ROBINSON, NICOLA SCOTT and YILDARAY CINAR

EARTH 2 VOL. 4: THE DARK AGE

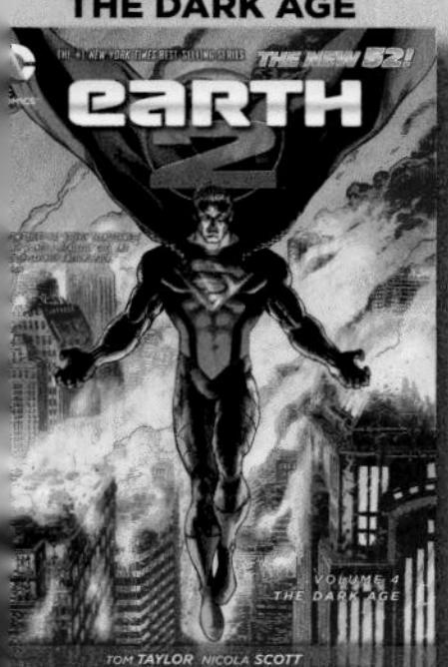

THE NEW 52!
EARTH 2
TOM TAYLOR NICOLA SCOTT

with TOM TAYLOR and NICOLA SCOTT

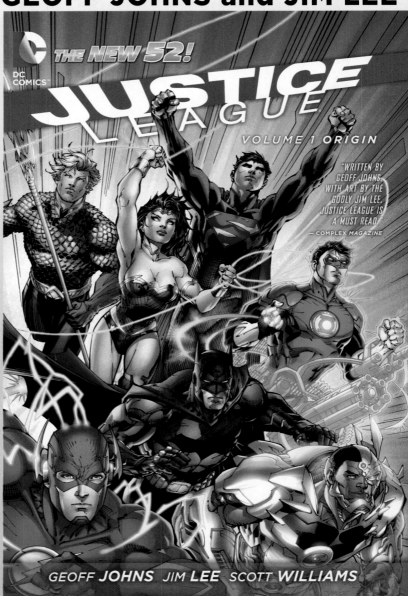